Sport Funding and Finance

Sport Funding and Finance provides a complete introduction to the macro-level and micro-level aspects of sport finance. It describes the evolution of sport from a kitchen-table operation into the sophisticated, boardroom-driven global financial industry that it is today. It uses the professional sport leagues of the US and Europe as an international benchmark, and explains why the financial context is so important for all managers working in sport. The book also provides a step-by-step introduction to the principles and practice of effective financial management, providing the reader with a complete set of professional tools and skills for use in the sport industry.

Now in a fully revised and updated new edition, the book develops the reader's understanding by first explaining basic concepts in finance and accounting before progressing to more complex issues and ideas. It covers every key topic in financial management, including:

- planning and strategy;
- budgeting;
- financial projections;
- fundraising;
- pricing;
- costing;
- feasibility studies;
- economic impact analysis;
- ratio analysis.

Every chapter includes a blend of theory, contextual material and real-world data and case studies from around the world, clearly linking principles to practice, as well as review questions and problem-solving exercises to test the reader's understanding. *Sport Funding and Finance* is the perfect foundation text for any degree-level course in sport finance, and an invaluable reference for any sport management professional looking to deepen their understanding of funding and finance.

Bob Stewart is Associate Professor in Sport Management and Policy at Victoria University, Melbourne, Australia. He is also an affiliate of the University's Institute of Sport, Exercise and Active Living (ISEAL). Bob has taught both undergraduate and postgraduate sport management programmes for fifteen years, and is one of Australia's leading sport management educators. His primary responsibilities have been sport finance, the management of drugs and supplements in sport settings, and sport regulation.

Sport Management Series

Series Editor: Russell Hoye, La Trobe University, Australia

This **Sport Management Series** has been providing a range of texts for core subjects in undergraduate sport business and management courses around the world for more than ten years. These textbooks are considered essential resources for academics, students and managers seeking an international perspective on the management of the complex world of sport.

Many millions of people around the globe are employed in sport organizations in areas as diverse as event management, broadcasting, venue management, marketing, professional sport, community and collegiate sport, and coaching, as well as in allied industries such as sporting equipment manufacturing, sporting footwear and apparel, and retail.

At the elite level, sport has moved from being an amateur pastime to one of the world's most significant industries. The growth and professionalization of sport has driven changes in the consumption and production of sport and in the management of sporting organizations at all levels.

Managing sport organizations at the start of the twenty-first century involves the application of techniques and strategies evident in leading business, government and non-profit organizations. This series explains these concepts and applies them to the diverse global sport industry.

To support their use by academics, each text is supported by current case studies, targeted study questions, further reading lists, links to relevant web-based resources, and supplementary online materials such as case study questions and classroom presentation aids.

Also available in this series:

Sport Management
Principles and applications (3rd edition)
Russell Hoye, Matthew Nicholson, Aaron Smith, Bob Stewart, Hans Westerbeek

Sport and Policy
Barrie Houlihan, Chris Auld, Matthew Nicholson, Russell Hoye

Sports Economics
Paul Downward, Alistair Dawson, Trudo Dejonghe

Sport and the Media
Matthew Nicholson

Sport Governance
Russell Hoye, Graham Cuskelly

Sport Funding and Finance

SECOND EDITION

Bob Stewart

Routledge
Taylor & Francis Group

LONDON AND NEW YORK

First published 2015
by Routledge
2 Park Square, Milton Park, Abingdon, Oxon OX14 4RN

and by Routledge
711 Third Avenue, New York, NY 10017

Routledge is an imprint of the Taylor & Francis Group, an informa business

British Library Cataloguing-in-Publication Data
A catalogue record for this book is available from the British Library

Library of Congress Cataloging-in-Publication Data
Stewart, Bob, 1946–
Sport funding and finance/by Bob Stewart.—Second edition.
    pages cm
    1. Sports—Finance. 2. Sports administration. I. Title.
    GV716.S725 2014
    796.06'9—dc23   2014005205

ISBN: 978-0-415-83983-9 (hbk)
ISBN: 978-0-415-83984-6 (pbk)
ISBN: 978-0-203-79497-5 (ebk)

Typeset in Berling and Futura
by Florence Production Ltd, Stoodleigh, Devon, UK

Contents

Figures and tables

FIGURES

TABLES

Simulation exercises and case studies

SIMULATION EXERCISES

CASE STUDIES

Preface

As noted in the first edition of this book – which was released in 2006 – sport has come a long way over the last fifty or so years. It does not matter where you look, because at every turn there are sport enterprises that employ scores of people to manage facilities, organize events, monitor member conduct, service corporate partners and keep players at peak performance levels.

This book is about the financial management of sport enterprises, be they highly corporatized and profit-seeking on the one hand, or community-based and member-serving on the other. It is built on a foundation of managerial rationality, professional practice and social responsibility, and therefore frames its skill development and capacity building within a context of the commercial, cultural and social forces operating on sport. It gives special attention to the 'integrity' issue, and how this worthy concept can be used to operationalize financial management systems so that they ensure accountable management policies, financial transparency, full public disclosure and public trust.

By adopting this approach this book aims to give readers a deep understanding of the commercial and financial structure of sport in its various contexts, and explain how these contexts shape the expectations communities may have about how sport enterprises can be best managed, especially with respect to their finances. It also aims to give readers the opportunity to build a diverse range of skills and capabilities for doing not only operational things such as budget construction, cost controls and pricing, but also more strategic things such as financial planning, capital investment, feasibility analysis, ratio analysis and performance evaluation. To this end, this book provides readers with a three-phase learning experience.

The first phase, which covers Chapters 1–5, provides the 'backdrop' by examining sport's *cultural and commercial context*. It thus gives readers a broad appreciation of the evolution of sport, and how it has moved from the kitchen-table model to the corporate-boardroom model, and along the way has become a sophisticated industry from a financial viewpoint. So, in the first phase of the book, attention will be given to the meaning people give to sport, and the intimate connections they develop as officials, players and spectators. This is followed by a discussion of the commercial development of sport using US and European pro-sport leagues as a benchmark. This will be followed by a close look at the different legal structures for sport enterprises, and the financial management implications for each structural type. This section will include an analysis of the changes in the funding arrangements of sport, where different funding sources will be examined in detail. A special focus will be given to 'big time' sport and the ways in which it has not only built its brand profile and value, but has also created clubs and associations with marked financial inequalities.

The second phase, which covers Chapters 6–10, discusses the 'basics' by focusing on *foundation competencies* for sport club managers. It thus promotes a more operational approach – or micro-analysis, if you will – of sport funding and finance by giving readers a grounding in the principles and practice of financial management. Readers will be introduced to key accounting principles and practice using accrual accounting principles as the conceptual starting point. Readers are then led into the more complex areas of account construction, the preparation of financial statements, pricing, costing and budgeting. Each of these topic areas will provide considerable skill development by giving readers the core concepts and principles, and then applying them to both fictitious and real-world case studies.

The third phase, which covers Chapters 11–15, provides the analytical 'clout' by building the reader's *critical capabilities*. It looks at financial management functions from a strategic perspective. It does this by visiting the notions of mission statements, statements of purpose, vision statements and statements of strategic intent, to set the operational parameters for making decisions about the things to do with money and finance. It also provides readers with a financial analysis 'toolkit' that can be used not only to better manage day-to-day operations, and diagnose the enterprise's financial health, but also to design financial plans for taking the enterprise forward in a sustainable and viable manner. To assist the learning experience it takes a detailed look at incidents and cases where, on the one hand, effective financial management was used to grow and develop a sport enterprise, and, on the other hand, where slack financial management led to escalating debt, ongoing losses, occasional insolvency and the winding up of the business.

Within this three-phased framework, the book will provide readers with multi-layered learning outcomes. In the first instance, context, strategy and knowledge will be fused in order to deliver a broad-based understanding of the financial operation of sport enterprises, and how it all fits together as we approach the 2020s. The book includes:

- a grounded appreciation of the commercial evolution of sport from the 1970s to the present;
- a clear understanding of the different commercial phases sport goes through to reach commercial maturity;
- a sound knowledge of the major global sport events and leagues, and their financial arrangements;
- a sharp insight into the financial strengths and weaknesses of contemporary sport at both the commercial and community levels.

The next learning outcome is more skill-based, and by absorbing the theory, completing exercises and reading cases, and critically assessing the processes and outcomes – and thus looking at both good and bad practice – readers will be able to:

- identify the different legal structures of sport organizations and the financial implications of each structure;
- explain the main accounting conventions and how they impact on the financial management of sport organizations;

- identify the foundations of double-entry bookkeeping;
- construct a simple set of accounts for a sport organization;
- explain how sport organizations can create profits, value and wealth;
- understand different methods of constructing budgets, and use them to control the financial operation of a sport organization;
- set up models for identifying and managing costs;
- identify different methods for setting prices for sport goods and services, and apply them to specific settings and events.

The final learning outcome is more about using financial data either to initiate strong remedial action for achieving a positive turnaround, or to undertake new strategic initiatives. With this strategic approach in mind, readers will be able to drive the following activities:

- construct a commercial, social and cultural context for undertaking a financial analysis initiative for a sport enterprise;
- assemble a broad range of financial data for subsequent analysis;
- use financial ratio analysis to evaluate the data and recommend on remedial or opportunistic action;
- undertake financial planning exercises and feasibility studies for a sport organization or facility;
- complete a cost–benefit analysis for a sport organization event;
- and do it all in such a way that it meets three operational guidelines: first, key financial decisions are taken in a transparent manner where public disclosure is front and centre; second, clear lines of accountability are identified; and, finally, the subsequent strategic initiatives are not only commercially sound, but also deliver positive social outcomes.

The book will be relevant to readers from English-speaking countries such as Australia, the USA, New Zealand, Great Britain and Canada. Each of these countries has a mature university sector that offers a broad range of programmes in sport management and sport studies. It will also be attractive to readers from the Asia-Pacific region (which includes China, India, Indonesia, Japan, Korea, Malaysia, Singapore and Thailand). There is a rapidly growing interest in sport management training in these countries, with sport funding and finance being integral to any programme.

So, to summarize, this book is based on the premise that large segments of sports are akin to businesses, and therefore have to be managed in business-like ways. It is now expected that sport enterprises at all levels will be run in a professional and strategic manner. Also, at the heart of any professionally run sport enterprise is a rational and transparent system for managing its finances. This is the focus of this book. At the same time, it is not enough to be trained in the basic skills and operations of accounting and financial management to ensure a properly managed enterprise that looks after its stakeholders and provides for its sustainability into the future. It is also crucial that managers of sport enterprises properly understand the context in which they operate, and how this context shapes the actions of managers and impacts on their operations.

This book therefore not only examines specific financial management functions in detail, but also situates the study of financial management in sport in a 'field' bounded by its contextual forces. They are its history and heritage, its commercial evolution, its cultural value, its special features, its social responsibilities and its purpose and strategic intent. As such, this book is more than just a student text covering the accounting essentials. It goes beyond being just a run-of-the-mill instruction manual. It also offers its readers an overview of the structure and conduct of sport, and explains how the financial management function fits into this unique organizational 'setting'. It thus places readers in a management role, and invites them to engage in a variety of experiential activities. These experiential activities will build their skills, knowledge and financial-management vocabulary by delivering a set of learning activities and exercises. They will also allow readers to examine critically the ways in which clubs, associations, agencies and leagues go about their financial management operations by undertaking a number of case analyses. They will additionally give readers the ability to create guidelines, principles and policies by which sport enterprises can not only manage their finances in a professional manner, but also do it with transparency and accountability front and centre. As a result, readers, in their future roles as managers, will be able to engage constructively with their stakeholders, and thus ensure a sustainable financial future where their sporting products and leisure experiences deliver a regular supply of social utility and community goodwill.

Notes on the second edition

The second edition of *Sport Funding and Finance* has been completely reconfigured and updated. This reconfigured edition has been broken down into three thematic sections, or phases as they were labelled in the preface. The first phase, which covers Chapters 1–5, provides the 'backdrop' to the chapters that follow. It delivers the *cultural and commercial context*. It sets the scene for what is to come, and gives the context for the analysis of the cases. The second phase, which covers Chapters 6–10, discusses the 'basics'. It delivers the *foundation competencies* and provides the essential accounting knowledge, develops the base-level financial management skills, and builds readers' 'financial literacy'. The third phase, which covers Chapters 11–15, provides the 'analysis'. It delivers the *critical capabilities*, beginning with the use of financial ratios to evaluate performance. This is then followed by detailed exposure to the forensic diagnosis of financial reports, the building of performance standards, the setting of minimum levels of public disclosure, the valuation of social outputs and outcomes, the completion of feasibility studies, the use of economic impact statements and the undertaking of cost–benefit analysis. This is framed with the goal of optimizing the benefits not only to the sport enterprise, but also to the community it serves.

This second edition also includes a number of new case studies. These new case studies address a diverse range of financial problems, and include the following clubs, associations, agencies and leagues:

- Borussia Dortmund Football Club;
- Coventry City Football Club;
- International Olympic Committee;
- Glasgow Rangers Football Club;
- Pittsburgh Pirates Baseball Club;
- Women's National Basketball Association.

As a result of the book's reconfiguration, it now contains ten simulation exercises and thirty-two case studies. The second edition of *Sport Funding and Finance* has thus become far more than an instruction manual, and goes beyond being just another standard accounting text for students doing a sports, events, facilities or recreation management programme. It is a study into the financial management of sport enterprises, and the ways in which managers can best handle financial issues so as to achieve their strategic goals, ensure their long-term sustainability and properly meet the interests of the communities they serve.

About the author

Bob Stewart is Associate Professor in Sport Management and Policy at Victoria University, Melbourne, Australia. Bob is an affiliate of the University's Institute of Sport, Exercise and Active Living (ISEAL). He has taught undergraduate and postgraduate sport management programmes for fifteen years, and is one of Australia's leading sport management educators. His primary responsibilities have been sport finance, the management of drugs and supplements in sport settings, and sport regulation.

Bob is the joint-author of *Drugs in Sport: Why the War will Never be Won* (Routledge 2014), joint editor of *Drugs and Sport: Writing from the Edge* (2014) and co-author of *Sport Management: Principles and Practice*, 3rd edition (Routledge 2012), *Organisation Culture and Identity: Sport, Symbols & Success* (2012) and *The National Game: The Penguin History of Australian Football* (2008). He is also editor of *The Games Are Not the Same: The Political Economy of Football in Australia* (2007), author of *Sport Funding and Finance* (2006) and co-author of *Australian Sport: Better by Design? The Evolution of Sport Policy in Australia* (Routledge 2004).

Bob is currently researching the regulation of sport with an emphasis on financial transparency, and drug and supplement use disclosure. He also has a special research interest in the political economy of football and the impact of neo-liberal ideologies on the practice of sport.

A note on currencies and exchange rates

Many cases are provided throughout this book. In some instances the cases are taken from the real world, and in other instances the cases are fictitious. While the data in the real-world cases are expressed in specific national currencies (e.g. GBP, EUR, AUD, USD and YEN), the fictional exercise data are expressed through the traditional dollar sign ($).

In order to make relevant comparisons between the different data in the real-world cases, it is important to be clear about currency conversion rates. The following approximate exchange rates applied in January 2014:

Australian dollar to British pound
1 AUD = 0.58 GBP
1 GBP = 1.86 AUD

Japanese yen to British pound
1 YEN = 0.006 GBP
1 GBP = 173.20 YEN

Australian dollar to US dollar
1 AUD = 0.89 USD
1 USD = 1.3 AUD

Japanese yen to US dollar
1 YEN = 0.011 USD
1 USD = 100.51 YEN

Australian dollar to euro
1 AUD = 0.65 EUR
1 EUR = 1.55 AUD

Japanese yen to Australian dollar
1 YEN = 0.01 AUD
1 AUD = 93.20 YEN

British pound to US dollar
1 GBP = 1.845 USD
1 USD = 0.61 GBP

British pound to euro
1 GBP = 1.19 EUR
1 EUR = 0.83 GBP

(Sourced from www.OANDA.com/currency/converter.)

Cultural and commercial context

CHAPTER 1

Financial literacy and the culture of sport

LEARNING OUTCOMES

At the end of this chapter readers will be able to:

- articulate the passion people have for sport, and why it gives so many people so much meaning
- list the main structures and systems that comprise the world of contemporary sport, identify its key stakeholders, and describe those things that make it so diverse
- explain the role of government in assisting and controlling sport practices
- understand the increasing financial complexity of sport, and explain why high levels of financial literacy are now a taken-for-granted feature of good sport enterprise management.

CHAPTER SUMMARY

This chapter sets the scene for what is to follow. It does this by, first, noting sport's cultural and social significance and, second, charting its commercial progress over the last fifty years. It looks at old models of amateurism and volunteerism, and traces through their trans-formation into a sport system centred on fans, professional athletes, governing boards, new generation stadia, large-scale multifunction venues, the electronic media, and a bevy of paid managers and support staff. The effect of this commercial and ideological shift in the sporting landscape on the finance skill requirements of sport managers is investigated, together with the call for greater financial literacy among the sporting community. The role of corporate partnerships and government initiatives in shaping sport's commercial development and financial arrangements will also be noted. The chapter concludes by reiterating the argument that despite the growth of the professional sport sector, there is, additionally, a diverse community-sport sector that also demands effective financial management for its ongoing sustainability. In short, financial literacy is a prerequisite for sound sport management at all levels of its operation.

SPORT DIVERSITY

Sport is an enigmatic institution, and comes in many forms and shapes. For instance, the mainstay of sport in many countries is the community club, which relies on the support of its members to sustain its activities. These clubs can be single-sport organizations, such as tennis clubs and swimming clubs, but they can also be multifunctional, and provide a range of sport programmes under the same roof. This happens in many Western European nations, with Germany being an exemplar. Small, member-based clubs are nearly always managed by volunteers who also pay fees for the privilege of playing. There are also sporting associations whose primary role is to provide administrative support – and often through the employment of professional staff – to clubs, to organize competitions and generally develop the sport they represent, whether it is netball, table tennis or volleyball. While these organizations have many paid employees, they also rely on volunteer staff to deliver their programmes. Then there are commercial leisure centres that provide sport-related services – and especially fitness programmes – on a fee-for-service or user-pay principle. Gymnasia and swim centres often fall into this category, and can be either privately owned or owned by local councils. There is also a raft of professional sport clubs and leagues that play in large stadia, attract thousands of spectators and generate mass media coverage. In addition, these structures have been recently stretched to accommodate the explosive growth of lifestyle sports such as windsurfing and snowboarding, and extreme sports such as base-jumping and big-wave surfing (Robinson 2013). These sport organizations are book-ended by, first, government and its agencies and, second, the sponsors, the media and sport merchandisers who promote sport and use its star players to endorse products, and thus attract customers.

The different types of sport organizations that comprise the sport system are listed in Table 1.1. The structural features of sport will vary from nation to nation, depending on their levels of industrialization, urbanization, per-capita incomes and systems of governance.

THE ROLE OF THE STATE, THE MARKET AND CIVIL SOCIETY

While Table 1.1 confirms the contribution that government – whether national or local – makes to sport, it also needs to be recognized that it is just one of a number of contributors to sport's ongoing development. In some societies government, or the state as it is broadly identified, may play a dominant role, but in other societies its role may be far more circumspect (Houlihan 2011). A useful way of understanding the relationship between the state and society is to distinguish between three distinct but interdependent structures, or 'social orders' as they are sometimes called (Ibsen and Jorgensen 2002).

The first social order is the state and its apparatus. The role of the state is to govern members of society by establishing a bureaucracy that enforces an array of rules and regulations, and manages the delivery of its services. It also mobilizes resources through its taxing powers, and uses them to establish an economic and cultural infrastructure that allows both commerce and the arts to flourish. It also aims to give people a better quality of life by building education and health systems that can be accessed by all, and

TABLE 1.1 Main organizational players in sport

	Government	Non-profit organizations	Commercial organizations
National spread	Minister for Sport	National Olympic Committee	TV and radio stations
	Government departments	International games associations	The internet and social media
	Sports commissions and agencies	National sport leagues	National newspapers
	Anti-doping authorities	National sport associations	National brand name sponsors
	Integrity and anti-corruption authorities	University sport associations	National sport goods suppliers
State and province spread	State Minister for Sport	State sporting associations	State-based media
	State sport academies	State sport leagues	Local brand name sponsors
	Health promotion agencies	Sport stadiums (outdoor)	
	Major event corporations	Sport arenas (enclosed)	
Local spread	Municipal councils	Universities and schools	Sport goods retailers
		Sport clubs	Sport and leisure centres
		Sport grounds and venues	Gym and fitness centres
		Sport and leisure centres	

Source: adapted from Oakley (1999: 62–3).

redistributing income in order to protect the vulnerable and disadvantaged members of society. The state can be interventionist, which means it directs the flow of resources into those fields of activity that it wants to see developed. This can involve anything from civil defence, the military, roads and railway lines. The state can also adopt an arms-length approach, which means it leaves it to the market – comprising thousands, and sometimes millions, of sellers and buyers – to decide what gets supplied, what gets consumed, and at what price.

The second social order is the market, which is the focal point for business activity. This is the home of the private sector, which is driven primarily by the desire for market expansion and profits, while also serving many essential needs such as food and housing. It includes heavy industries such as steel making, and complex consumer goods such as motor vehicles and television sets. In most nations around the world agricultural production is also dominated by the private sector operating through a multitude of markets. In advanced economies the largest share of the market system is taken up by the supply and use of services. Services are enormously diverse, and include things as disparate as legal work, teaching, retail, theatre, music and psychological therapy.

The third social order is civil society, which comprises a complex web of informal, non-market relationships that are mainly situated around households, neighbourhoods and local communities. Religious organizations, political parties, book-reading groups, disability support agencies and self-help groups all fall into this category. Civil society is clearly visible in the unstructured networks that characterize the dynamics of social clubs and friendship groups. Over the last thirty to forty years civil society has been bolstered by the establishment of what are commonly called non-government organizations, or NGOs for short. NGOs take on many forms. They may include health promotion agencies such as anti-cancer councils, heart foundations and drug awareness agencies. They can also take the form of international aid agencies such as Oxfam and World Vision.

The intersections of these three social orders create four different sectors and organiza-tional forms. They are (1) the non-profit public sector, which is driven by the state, (2) the profit-based commercial sector, which is driven by the market, (3) the informal com-munity aid sector, which is driven by civil society and, finally, (4) the voluntary sector, which is driven by aspects of all three social orders. The organization of society between the state, the market and civil society is illustrated in Figure 1.1.

Sport can fit into any of the four sectors depending on, first, the traditions and values that underpin the sport experience and, second, the scale of resources that each sector can command. In Australia, Great Britain and New Zealand, for example, sport has traditionally taken place in the voluntary and informal sectors, where clubs and associa-tions take in members, run events and organize competitions in and around local communities and regional districts. In the USA, high schools and colleges have been the mainstay of non-elite sport. This grass-roots structure, if you like, is still crucially important to sports' sustainability, but over recent times there has also been an exponen-tial growth in the commercial sector, which has led to an explosive increase in the number of professional sport leagues operating around the world, and a concomitant growth in the number of players who make a living out of their sport practices. Thus, whereas the idea of amateurism was crucially important to many sports in the 1960s, it now means very little to most sports players and watchers. In the 1960s only amateurs were allowed to play at the Wimbledon tennis championships, while professionals were banned from partici-pating in the Olympic Games. Today it is taken for granted that, in whatever sport league you care to examine, some players will be paid, while others will not. This is the market at work, and as a result players with extraordinary talents are paid extraordinary salaries. On the other hand, the ordinary weekend player usually has to pay for the experience. Again, this is the market at work, where the relationship between supply and demand sets the price for both products (which includes sport equipment and venue hire) and labour (which includes managers and players).

The other significant trend in recent times has been the growing involvement of government in sport (Downard 2011). Government sees itself as having two key roles to play. The first is to assist ordinary people to participate in sport. This assistance can be directed to players, but it can also be directed to managers and officials. Additionally, in community sport, many players forget that the activity they engage in so passionately

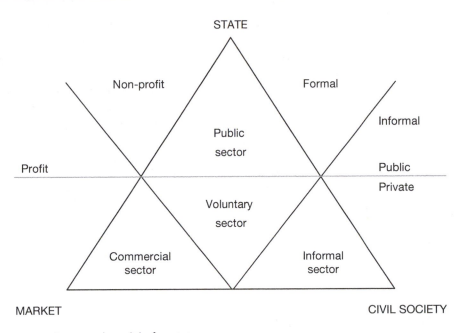

FIGURE 1.1 A sectoral model of society

Source: adapted from Ibsen and Jorgensen (2002).

is only there because of the time spent by volunteer officials organizing it with the aid of a government grant. The second role is to assist players to achieve their potential and attain their desire for athletic excellence. This is done by establishing training, coaching and sport science facilities that enable talented young athletes to be spotted, trained up and transformed into the very best players they can be. This role is not altogether a selfless one, since government also gets a lot of kudos when a team it helped to resource achieves international acclaim. The Australian government understood this in the lead-up to the Sydney 2000 Games, and so too did the United Kingdom government in the countdown to the London 2012 Games. This is also why the Brazilian government was so joyous when it was awarded the 2016 Olympic Games. It can use the Games to not only confirm its international sporting excellence, but also to claim its position as a sophisticated and cosmopolitan nation with both economic and cultural clout around the planet.

It would thus be fair to say that sport has never been so flush with funds (Fried *et al.* 2013). With such a massive inflow of private sector funds, together with greater direct involvement by the state and public sector, there has been continuous growth in the allocation of sport resources into these areas of society. However, it has not delivered anything approaching a sporting nirvana for two reasons. First, the flow of funds to sport is often very erratic. For example, sponsors may decide to reallocate their corporate partnership budget elsewhere, while government may decide that the arts are more deserving of their support than sports. Second, the flow of funds is unequal. At first glance it seems to follow the 80–20 rule, which in this case means that 20 per cent of the sports claim 80 per cent of the funds. This is highly inequitable, but what can be done about it? Governments try to get some balance by giving funds to all sports, no matter how marginal some may be, but this is never enough to bridge the disadvantage gap.

Figure 1.1 provides a context within which to discuss the sport funding roles of the state, the market and the volunteer sector. It indicates that, while the state may have enormous influence over the structure and practice of sport in one set of political conditions, it can just as easily have minimal influence over sport in some other situation. The model also suggests that even where the state is passive in respect of sport development, there may be a flourishing sport system in one or more of the other sectors, depending on how highly sport is valued in each sector. The model also implies that there is no single or best way for society to organize its sport systems and practices. It all depends upon which sector is seen to be the appropriate provider of sport facilities and activities, and what types of sport outcomes are intended. For example, the state may be seen as the most effective provider of elite athlete training facilities and large stadia, while the voluntary sector may be used to provide community sport and sport-for-all activities. Apart from the USA, where the private sector dominates sport funding, there has been a significant expansion of national government funding of sport. In Western Europe and the Asia-Pacific region most international standard venues are funded by government, as are elite training facilities (Stewart *et al.* 2004; Green and Houlihan 2005; Collins 2011).

THE PRACTICE OF SPORT

As the previous discussion suggests, the practice of sport can also be viewed from different perspectives. For some it is all about participation, playing the game for its own sake, and using the game to develop character and leadership. In other words, sport can be a vehicle for making better people and better communities. In these instances commercialism is often viewed as a problem because of its tendency to overemphasize winning, encourage gambling and undermine the values of amateurism. On the other hand, some people believe that sport can only achieve its potential if it is well supported and funded. In other words, commercialized sport will increase standards of play by sustaining professional sport leagues and meet the ever increasing demands of sport fans. At the same time the benefits of commercial sport are not always shared equally, since some sports are inherently more popular than others, and thus attract more funding. As a result, sports such as canoeing, water polo and rowing will always be disadvantaged so long as they are played in the shadows of such popular spectator sports as the various codes of football (American football, Australian football, Gaelic football, rugby league, rugby union and world football), tennis, basketball and cricket.

Essentially then, sport practice comprises two distinctive but connected strands. The first strand is community sport, which comprises participant-based sport geared around the local club, the volunteer administrator, a simple organizational structure and the recreational player (Keech 2011). While a few talented young players will use the local club as the springboard for entry into the world of elite sport development, most club members will focus their energies on interclub competition, having fun and building their social networks. The second strand is professional sport, which is centred on the elite performer and geared around spectators who provide the catalyst for sport's commercial development (Ibsen *et al.* 2011). It attracts media coverage, which in turn provides a promotional impetus for further spectator interest. Broadcasting of events emerges, rights fees are negotiated, corporate sponsors see the benefits of linking their brands to a sport league or club, and all of a sudden professional sport leagues and mega-sport events begin to occupy large slabs of the sports landscape. When sport becomes commercial, rather than recreational, officials, players and fans begin to take it very seriously. It becomes 'more than a game'.

THE MEANING OF SPORT

Whatever the commercial scale of sport, and whatever its level of government support, sport is important to people in many ways. It provides a perfect forum for expressing one's physicality, it improves fitness and it builds social networks, particularly when played in a club setting. In professional sport, team games are particularly popular because they meet a deep-seated need for tribal identity, and provide an archetypal ritual where fans can relive ancient ceremonies, and connect with others through ritualistic social practices.

According to some sport theorists spectator sports have become modern counter-parts of ancient hunting patterns where different tribes compete for power, status and recognition (Morris 1981). Team sports provide strong tribal connections that allow members to play out a variety of traditional roles and practices. In the clubs, for example, the tribal elders comprise the club president or chairperson, senior officials, coaches, fitness advisers and medical support staff. The elders and players enact tribal rituals that both reinforce the sport's values and regulate the behaviours of its participants. Rituals include mid-week commentary, pre-game preparation, the display of signs and slogans that emphasize discipline and endeavour, and pre-match addresses that urge players to selflessly contribute to the greater good. The players are the tribal heroes, and are cheered and lauded, and perform on the field of play until their time is up, in which case they are replaced by new personalities. There are also many tribal trappings that provide colour, noise and public exposure. They include player outfits, club photos, club colours, insignia, badges, emblems and trophies. Central to the tribal practices are the fans, or tribal followers. They provide the passion and commitment by proudly displaying their loyalty and affiliation. The fans and tribal followers accentuate inter-tribal rivalries through the purchase of memorabilia, dressing in club colours and inciting the followers of other teams and rival tribes. They also compose tribal chants and team songs, which are used not only to assert their identity, but also to intimidate rival tribes.

However, these strong tribal connections to sport have been often threatened by the growing financial sophistication of leagues and events and the consequent changes to sport's cultural practices (Schirato 2007). This is because old traditions are jettisoned and replaced by modern practices, which can include a change in club colours, a change in the home ground, a change in game schedules and fixtures, and even a change in the viewing arrangements. In British football, for example, the introduction of all-seat stadia met strong resistance from some fans because it took away the 'standing in the terraces' experience (Buford 1992). But for other fans, the removal of the standing room spaces could not come quickly enough, since it partitioned off the angry male fans and provided safer spaces for family attendance.

THE CHANGING FAN–CLUB RELATIONSHIP

The close relationship between sport fans and their clubs is pivotal to the ongoing sustainability of professional sport competitions and leagues (Crawford 2004; Rein *et al.* 2006). In the various codes of football, for example, there has been a steady growth in the fan-base, particularly when television viewers of sport are added to the fans who attend the venues. The audience for major global events is no longer measured in millions of supporters, but billions of watchers. However, as noted above, the relationship between clubs and fans has also been problematic in response to the many changes that have taken place in the structure and practice of many sports. Over the last five decades the sport–fan relationship has gone through three developmental phases, with each phase corresponding to an increase in sport's commercialization and financial expansion.

Phase 1

As noted above, in many countries sporting organizations have traditionally been community-centred and member-based, and as a result fans have always had a formal way of influencing the clubs' direction. This member-based structure meant that, for the price of a membership fee, fans could vote for committee members, or alternatively seek election themselves. Clubs also depended for their survival on the contribution of volunteers. This constituted the first phase of the fans' relationship with their club, team or event. It was engaged and local, and can be called the *integration phase*.

Phase 2

As sport organizations become more commercial there is pressure to develop a business dimension to the clubs' operations. Professional staff are hired to secure the clubs' future through increasing funding and membership. Decisions are made about a sport club's traditional practices in response to the claims of sponsors, conflict occurs over the distribution of revenues, and vested interests emerge. While disputes are frequent, fans still believe they can play a part in the club's progress. This can be called the *negotiation phase*.

Phase 3

The final phase coincides with sport's commercial entrenchment and professionalization. As sport tightens its connections with the sponsor, the merchandiser and the television networks, a number of things happen. Players' earnings increase rapidly, volunteer officials are replaced by paid staff, and many fans see sport as just another leisure experience for sale in a competitive market place. It becomes just another form of entertainment, although one where customers have high expectations. They want a quality show. As a result, venues are upgraded and replaced with large-scale all-seat stadiums that have customized corporate suites, and a range of catering and hospitality services are provided. All of this improves the fan experience, but it also escalates the costs of running leagues and clubs, and in turn memberships and admission charges rise dramatically. The whole fan profile changes in this phase. Traditional fans are marginalized, and their space is occupied by supporters whose focus is entertainment as well as tribal identities. This is called the *commodification phase*.

Consequently, by the end of phase 3 fans have been transformed into customers (King 1998; Foster *et al.* 2006; Rein *et al.* 2006). The fans-as-customers model has influence insofar as they have purchasing power, and provide market research data from their participation in surveys and focus groups. While fans are now consulted on all manner of things, they are generally excluded from their club's decision-making processes, whether it is a not-for-profit or a commercial enterprise. While some fans are critical of this state of affairs, others are happy to leave it all to the clubs so long as they achieve success. When this fragmentation is combined with escalating costs, low-income fans are pushed to the margin and the privileged fans are those who are prepared to pay for an entertaining experience. The growing emphasis on entertainment and the increasing costs of attending major sport events are most clearly evident in major sport leagues around the world.

In the USA and Western Europe in particular, the continual increase in player salaries and improvement in venue amenities has produced a general improvement in the quality of the contest and the fan experience. However, these changes have also led to an increase in player salaries and stadium rentals, which in turn has increased the cost of staging games (Howard and Crompton 2004; Foster *et al.* 2006; Winfree and Rosentraub 2012). As a result admission and ticket prices have increased dramatically (in Chapter 10 a more detailed analysis of sport event pricing is undertaken). Despite this shift to the fan-as-customer, and the escalating costs of consuming sport, the tribal nature of professional sport is still strong (Crawford 2004). This neo-tribalism not only differentiates sports consumption for other types of buyer behaviour, but also explains sport's importance in a world where traditional identities and loyalties are increasingly under threat.

MONEY AND SPORT

This commodification and professionalization of sport has produced many strains and tensions, and has led to the creation of the 'elusive fan' who has to deal with a vast array of experiential options (Rein *et al.* 2006: 50). But, overall, it has strengthened its hold over the public consciousness (Wann *et al.* 2001; Foster *et al.* 2006; Schirato 2007). Sport has established its position as a vehicle for creating personal meaning and cultural identity, and has provided a lucrative career path for many people. In Western Europe and North America in particular, professional sport clubs are multimillion-dollar enterprises, where players frequently earn more than corporate CEOs and senior politicians. A recent survey of European world-football clubs found that ten clubs earned more than 300 million EUR a year. The rankings for 2005 and 2011 are listed in Table 1.2.

With an increase in revenue comes an increase in club wage costs. In 2013 Barcelona FC had the highest salary scale of any professional sporting club in the world, with players on average annual salaries of more than USD 8 million. To some people these pay rates are an obscenity, but to others they are just another example of the market at work. That is, it is nothing more than a reflection of the fact that some players have scarce and special skills that are in very high demand in an industry that has a very high capacity to pay.

In addition, recent studies of professional sport in the USA have revealed that many players earn more than USD 4 million a year. In the National Basketball Association

(NBA), for example, the average annual player salary in 2012 was just over USD 5 million. The sharp upward trend in player salaries in the other major USA professional sport leagues – the National Football League (NFL), the National Hockey League (NHL) and Major League Baseball (MLB) – from 1991 to 2003 is summarized in Table 1.3.

TABLE 1.2 Europe's most profitable sport clubs, 2005 and 2011

Club name			Annual revenue (EUR millions)
Real Madrid	was	. . .	276
	now	. . .	496
Manchester United	was	. . .	245
	now	. . .	367
AC Milan	was	. . .	234
	now	. . .	211
Juventus	was	. . .	229
	now	. . .	195
Chelsea	was	. . .	221
	now	. . .	254
Barcelona	was	. . .	208
	now	. . .	451
Bayern Munich	was	. . .	190
	now	. . .	321
Liverpool	was	. . .	181
	now	. . .	203
Inter Milan	was	. . .	177
	now	. . .	170
Arsenal	was	. . .	171
	now	. . .	251

Source: Deloitte Sports Business Group (2006, 2013).

TABLE 1.3 USA professional sport league average player salaries, 1991 to 2003 (USD millions)

Year	MLB	NFL	NBA	NHL
2003	2.6	1.3	4.5	1.6
1991	0.6	0.35	0.99	0.32

Source: Howard and Crompton (2004: 40).

CASE STUDY 1.1

Sport finance hubs

The above discussion shows that sport around the world has become increasingly commercialized since the 1970s. While the USA was the home of professional sports for most of the twentieth century, Western Europe has also built up many professional sport competitions over the last thirty years. It now supports professional sport leagues and circuits in car rallying, Formula 1, motorcycling, athletics, basketball and handball, with world football being dominant.

At the same time, a third significant sports hub has been formed in East Asia and the Pacific, with a build-up of sport resources in Japan, China, South Korea, Australia and New Zealand, and to a lesser extent in India. It therefore came as no surprise to see Beijing host the summer Olympics in 2008, and Delhi host the Commonwealth Games in 2010. In 2013 Tokyo was awarded the 2020 Olympic Games. Tokyo, which had previously hosted the Games in 1964, received spirited opposition from Istanbul and Madrid, but in the end secured sixty votes, while Istanbul only obtained thirty-six. Despite International Olympic Committee (IOC) concerns about the 2011 Fukushima nuclear power plant meltdown and concomitant earthquake and tsunami, which killed more than 18,000 people, Prime Minister Abe allayed fears of a repeat incident by promising a safe and financially secure 2020 Games in 'uncertain times'. The decision meant that Japan will host the Olympic Games for the fourth time, having also delivered the winter Games in Nagano (1998) and Sapporo (1972). Additionally, the South Korean resort of Pyeongchang will be hosting the 2018 winter Games. The South Korean city of Seoul also hosted the 1988 Olympic Games, which was especially memorable in the light of, first, the Ben Johnson drug-use scandal and, second, the match-fixing fiasco at the boxing tournament.

CASE STUDY 1.2

The Olympic Games – its commercial evolution

It is now invincibly clear that sport organizations, whether they are structured as public enterprises, private companies or non-profit entities, must have sound financial management systems embedded in the operations. Sport is now a multimillion-dollar enterprise with a sophisticated funding base. At the last count it was estimated that the American sports industry generated just under USD 82 billion (Brown *et al.* 2010: 14). These figures – in pro rata terms – are replicated around the world, and the sport industry therefore demands professional management to sustain its viability and extend its global footprint. The following case shows how sport has evolved over the last fifty years, and also makes it clear why good financial management is essential for sport's effective development and longevity.

Despite the social problems arising out of sport's cultural and structural changes – with corruption, fan violence and drug-use being current examples – it has strengthened its organizational and commercial foundations enormously. Things were done more slowly and more simply in the 1950s. Take, for example, the Olympic Games. In 1956 the summer Games were held in Melbourne, Australia. While the Games were rated a success, they were nearly cancelled in 1954 when it was found that the Organizing Committee could not agree on which venue was to be the main stadium (there was heated debate as to whether it was to be an inner suburban sports ground at Carlton, or the better known and more centrally located Melbourne Cricket Ground (MCG). The IOC, the world governing body for the Olympics, was concerned that the Organizing Committee was poorly managed and could not make effective decisions. This organizational inertia was compounded by a tight budget, although the budget deficit was ultimately filled by the generous support of the Victorian State Government and the Commonwealth (Federal) Government. It should also be remembered that there was virtually no sponsorship income at this time, and the income from broadcasting rights was negligible. In fact there was a dispute over the extent to which radio and television stations should be charged for the right to cover the Games.

Coincidentally, the staging of the Melbourne Olympic Games occurred at the same time that television was introduced into Australia. The Games were immediately seized upon by the television industry as a vehicle for stimulating the purchase of television sets, while the Games Organizing Committee reflected on how television could be used as a means of raising extra revenue. In 1955 the Organizing Committee considered the possibility of selling the exclusive television and news-reel rights to an English company. The Committee confirmed that such an arrangement was being considered and, if successful, would provide much needed funds for amateur sport in Australia. However, in response to claims that such a decision would deny other television stations access to the Games, and diminish the Games' international promotion, the plan was abandoned. As a result, there was no income to be sourced from this area. In short, the Melbourne Olympic Games Organizing Committee relied exclusively on income from government and ticket sales to fund this major sporting festival.

The 1956 Melbourne Olympics provide an exemplar of how major sport events were funded and managed during the early post-Second World War period. They were the last of the so-called 'amateur Games'. Most of the athletes were not paid and participated for the glory of winning a medal on the international sporting stage. Competition was intense and serious but the athletes received little material benefit. In addition, the Organizing Committee for the Melbourne Games comprised a few paid officials, but many more volunteers who were involved in both games management and operational activities.

However this all changed. The Sydney 2000 Games and Athens 2004 Games were mega-sport events that cost around USD 3,500 million and USD 5,000 million to mount respectively. By contrast the average costs of running the Games in the 1970s and 1980s was around USD 600 million, the lowest being Montreal in 1976, which ran a tight budget of USD 476 million, although a larger proportion of its funds were borrowed (Preuss 2000).

Over this period there was also a concomitant increase in revenue. The most explosive increase came through the sale of the broadcast rights to television stations. As noted previously, the fee for the Melbourne Games was negligible. However, with the development of a global satellite network in the late 1960s and a consequent expansion in the global audience, the fees increased substantially over the next twenty years. For instance, the rights fee for the 1968 Mexico Games was USD 46 million. A subsequent increase in competition between the US television networks led to spirited bidding for the rights, which was reflected in a USD 106 million fee for Montreal in 1976 and a fee of USD 594 million for Seoul in 1988. The broadcasting fee continued to rise during the early part of the twenty-first century. The Sydney and Athens Olympics attracted over USD 1,000 million and the fee for Beijing gave the Organizing Committee USD 1,700 million. It should also be noted that nearly 90 per cent of the total broadcast fee income came from two sources. NBC, the major American network, contributed USD 1,000 million to the Organizing Committee for Beijing, while the European Broadcast Union (EBU), a consortium of mainly government stations in Western Europe, contributed another USD 500 million (Preuss 2000, 2004). For the London 2012 Olympics the numbers are bigger again.

The same explosive increase is evident in the area of sponsorship. Between 1956 (the Melbourne Games) and 1972 (the Munich Games) sponsorship did not register at all on the Organizing Committee budget scale. The only commercial support came from a few billboards around the main facilities and a number of advertisements in the Games' programmes and publicity documents. However, as the global television audience for the games expanded it became increasingly attractive for globally marketed products (e.g. Coca Cola, American Express and Ford) to promote their products through Olympic Games' sponsorship. Sponsorship made its mark at the 1984 Los Angeles Games when the Organizing Committee secured USD 250 million from the corporate sector. For the 1996 Atlanta Games, sponsorship increased to USD 658 million, and at the Athens Games the Organizing Committee obtained USD 690 million of sponsorship (Preuss 2000). For the 2012 London Olympics sponsorship revenues increased to more than USD 1 billion.

The third significant expansion in Olympic revenue came through income from merchandising. At both the Munich and Montreal games, merchandising income averaged out at USD 6 million, but by Seoul in 1988 it had increased to USD 26 million. During this period it became clear that the Olympic emblems and symbols (in particular the Olympic Rings) had become a highly marketable brand. In order to protect the brand and preserve its monopoly ownership the IOC registered it as an official trademark and sought legislative support for its exclusive use of the symbols from the host nations to the Games. This monopoly control, combined with an increase in global recognition, enabled the IOC to expand its merchandising income to more than USD 80 million for the Atlanta and Athens Games (Preuss 2004). It is now more than USD 150 million.

The other interesting change in Olympic Games financing relates to the balance between government funding and private commercial funding. During the 1970s, 80 per cent of Games funding was sourced from government, but this figure progressively fell during the 1980s and 1990s. For the Seoul Games of 1988 only 53 per cent of its costs were sourced from government, while for Sydney the percentage of government funding was around 40 per cent. The two most privately financed games were Los Angeles in 1984 and Atlanta in 1996. In fact, in the case of the Los Angeles Games, a referendum resulted in a vote not to provide significant public finance for the Games since it was feared that a drain of resources from other state programmes would lead to a deterioration of the quality of life for Californians. Nearly all the facilities were privately funded, some of the venues were named after global businesses and this led to an operating surplus of USD 381 million (Preuss 2000). The experiences of Los Angeles and Atlanta can be contrasted with the funding arrangements for the 1980 Moscow Games. Given its economic structure at the time (it was the archetypal command economy) it was axiomatic that all funding was from government. The balance between government and private/market-based funding will vary from nation to nation, depending upon the relative size of each sector.

The 2004 Athens Games, the 2008 Beijing Games and the 2012 London Games have all required massive expenditures, and as a result the minimum amount to stage and operate the Games is now more than USD 8 billion. For both London and Rio de Janeiro billions of dollars have also been used to undertake major urban renewal projects (Hoye *et al.* 2010: 144). To make the London Games happen, just under GBP 1 billion was spent on security, be it civilian or military. GBP 1.8 billion was spent on preparing the Olympic Park site, while another GBP 1 billion was spent on creating a user-friendly park once the Games had been completed, and the Games experience was a distant memory. And this does not even include the facility construction costs or the operating costs. The escalating costs of running the Olympic Games were starkly revealed soon after Tokyo was awarded the right to host the 2020 Games. Hakubun Shimomura, the Minister for Education, Sports and Finance, proudly announced that the showpiece of the Games would be an 80,000-seat stadium that would double as a major public artwork. But when it was stated that the stadium would cost YEN 130 billion, or around USD 1.2 billion, enormous criticism erupted, with local architects claiming the project was indefensible, even if the stadium became an international design masterpiece. Even when the Olympics are involved, there are financial limits to be observed.

FINANCIAL LITERACY AND SPORT MANAGEMENT

Despite sport's rapid commercialization there are many gaps in the financial knowledge and skills of sport organization managers. One of the most common features of contemporary sport management is the growing demand for staff with extensive training and experience in finance and funding. As previously noted, money is now the basis of most sport, and sport managers can no longer get away with being financially irresponsible or, even worse, financially illiterate. This is a problem around the world. Even in Australia's most professionalized sport leagues there are many examples of ineffective financial management. In the highly profitable Australian Football League (AFL), for example, at least three clubs are technically insolvent, with liabilities nearly double their assets, which does not reflect well on the competencies of club administrators. And, what is more, these enterprises continue to operate.

Similar situations are being faced in the newly formed A-League, which is Australia's premier soccer competition. The Central Coast Mariners, who play out of Gosford, a prosperous seaside city 50 kilometres north of Sydney, have been plagued by financial instability throughout their existence. Despite winning the 2012 premiership, the club has rarely run a profit, and has for the most part been propped up by Football Federation Australia (FFA), the sport's national governing body. This situation is replicated many times over around the world, as the case studies to follow demonstrate. Moreover, there are many examples of sports clubs operating in elite competitions that have made large losses despite building up massive revenue streams. This seems like highly irresponsible conduct, but more about this later.

All of the above discussion points to the need for the training of managers who are good at not only setting strategic directions, keeping stakeholders happy and handling a diverse group of employers, but also handling money. The finance function in sport is a crucially important management task, and given the growing complexity of so much sport there is now an incontrovertible need to employ sport club staff with a range of financial management competencies that can be proactively used to 'protect valuable revenue sources' (Brown *et al.* 2010: 28). These competencies are multi-fold and include the ability to:

- keep accurate financial records;
- construct realistic budgets and financial plans;
- monitor expenses and revenue;
- ensure adequate cash flows and ongoing liquidity;
- create income-generating assets;
- control debt levels;
- and, most crucially, balance financial constraints against strategic aspirations.

These are base-level competencies, and it is therefore important that they become taken-for-granted expectations of sport club management. At the moment many sport enterprises do not give financial prudence the weight it deserves and, as many of the cases discussed in this book demonstrate, the costs of poor financial management are significant. They include:

- loss of management control;
- inability to accurately measure performance;
- falling asset values;
- increasing levels of debt;
- escalating costs;
- lack of cash;
- operating losses;
- liquidation.

CASE STUDY 1.3

The Japan J.League

The financial evolution of the Olympic Games suggests that – at the surface level at least – its management is underpinned by a high level of financial expertise. That is to say, the professionals who bid for it, plan for it and run it are, from a financial management perspective, highly literate. It also appears to be the case in East Asia, which, as noted above, has become a major sporting hub. Sport has not only undergone a commercial transformation in Europe and the USA, it has also been similarly affected in Asia. A good illustration of this trend is Japan's professional world-football J.League (www.j-league.or.jp), which was established in 1992, and has since gone on to establish a strong presence in the highly competitive Japanese sports market. However, recent incidents suggest the level of financial literacy and financial discipline in Japanese football may have been overrated.

The first thing to note is that the J.League was a risky development since world football was, at the time, far less popular than baseball and sumo wrestling. The Nippon Professional Baseball (NPB) League had come to dominate Japan's sports scene during the 1980s, and it was not clear as to the J.League's ability to secure a viable market share. But, as it transpired, it carved out a strong niche in the nation's commercial sport sector.

The J.League had three primary goals when it first got under way. They were to, first, diffuse and improve Japanese football, second, develop a sporting culture that focused on both fandom and participation and, third, use the league to build international exchanges and recognition. Each club based its activities in a 'home town' area, and worked in close cooperation with local residents, administrators and corporations. The home town was viewed not so much as a franchise, but rather as the place where stakeholders worked to improve community life through sport. The J.League was also a deliberate move away from company-based sports teams, which previously dominated the sporting landscape. Clubs were encouraged to diversify their ownership base so that the business fortunes of a single organization did not endanger club management. Team names were thus changed from those of private businesses such as Hitachi, to home-city names such as Kawisha.

The J.League competition commenced in 1993 with a single division of ten clubs. The first game was played at the Tokyo National Stadium in front of 60,000 expectant fans. It marked not only the long-awaited start of a professional world-football league in Japan, but also a new sporting culture based on city-based markets and community identification with clubs and teams. The emphasis on tribal identity worked well, and stadiums were packed with fans wearing their team colours. The recruitment of internationally recognized players improved the skills of local players, and volunteers provided match-day support for their local teams. Words such as 'supporter' and 'fan' were added to the Japanese vocabulary, and many Japanese children began to now dream of playing in the J.League.

Aggregate season attendances briefly fell after hitting a peak of 5.6 million in 1994, but increased strongly again after 2000 with the addition of a Division 2 competition (J2). In the 2003 season the aggregate attendance was just over 7 million, while average attendances were 17,000 in Division 1 (J1) and 8,000 in J2. This compared favourably with equivalent world-football leagues in the USA and South Korea, where average game attendances were just over 15,000 and 10,000 respectively. Albirex Niigata had the League's highest average attendance of just over 30,000. In fact, nearly every financial indicator improved over the first ten years of the League's operation. Ticket sales revenue increased by 50 per cent between 1999 and 2003, League sponsorship was YEN 2,310 million in 1993, but had increased to YEN 4,020 million in 2003, while broadcasting rights increased from YEN 1,093 million in 1993 to YEN 4,820 million in 2003. By 2004 the number of clubs has grown to twenty-eight playing in two divisions, and the quality of play has risen steadily. Japan qualified for the FIFA 1998 World Cup, and reached the last sixteen at the 2002 event, which was co-hosted by Japan and South Korea.

In 2012 there were thirty-eight teams in the two leagues, club revenues were growing at more than 5 per cent and in some cases – the Urawa Reds, for instance – individual club annual incomes had reached YEN 5,000 million (USD 65 million) a year. The average club income was around YEN 2,000 million a year. Things looked so buoyant that the League's governing body announced that a J3 competition would be in place for 2014. However, behind this rapid League expansion lurked a pack of undisciplined club managers. In 2013 it was found that twenty clubs, including eight from J1, had not been able to generate enough revenue to cover their spending. A number of clubs were forced to take out loans of up to YEN 50 million to pay their debts when they fell due. As a result of these developments J-League administrators introduced a number of regulations to limit club spending (Watanabe 2012). First, clubs who incurred three consecutive annual operating losses would be demoted to lower-level competitions and, second, clubs that had more liabilities than assets would not be allowed to start the new 2014 season. Like many professional leagues around the world, Japan's J.League is, from a financial perspective, quite brittle, despite its access to substantial streams of revenue. What is more, these incidents do not reflect well on the financial discipline exerted by many club managers.

WHERE TO FROM HERE FOR SMALL-SCALE SPORT?

Despite the hype and glamour that surrounds the highly cashed-up sport enterprises and the mega-sport leagues, community sport clubs are not disappearing. In the UK, Australia, Germany, New Zealand and many parts of Western Europe they continue to be the pivotal spaces for participation. And, what is more, they confirm the need to have well-trained, competent volunteer officials who can not only deliver good experiences to members, but also do it in a sustainable way. It also needs to be noted, even at this early stage of the book, that one of the key contributors to sustainability is effective financial management. Big or small, excessively professional or nominally amateur, self-consciously earnest or brazenly chaotic, no sport enterprise – even if it has a benefactor with a bottomless pit of cash – can survive in the long run without a proper and professional system of financial management that balances the enterprise's resource base against its strategic aspirations. In other words, financial strategies need to be viewed as not only an opportunity for action, but also, in many instances, a constraint to unrestrained spending. This is a theme that threads its way through the remainder of this book.

RECAP

To repeat an earlier claim, sport has changed dramatically over the last fifty years. The transition has been gradual, but the overall outcome has been significant. There was a time when sport was viewed as a leisurely pasttime, and something you did to escape the mechanized world of work and business, using this spare time to rebuild your strength in order to repeat the work processes all over again (Mussell 2013: 104–5). Today there is no such escape because so much sport is a means of employment and, thus, is in fact a form of business. And, what is more, community sport has also adopted many business models and practices. Additionally, government has decided that it needs to involve itself in sport's progress and fund it where appropriate. So, with these points in mind, it is prudent to, first, revisit a few crucial issues around sport's importance to society, second, look at what has driven its commercial transformation and, finally, assess its impact on the capabilities needed to properly manage its finances.

REVIEW QUESTIONS

There are no longer any excuses for sport managers to be financially illiterate. Its scale of operations, its level of fan passion, the amount of public support it has and the amount of funding it gets from government are all well and good, but the key to long-term viability is proper financial management. Good financial management matters in every sporting space. Moreover, the idea that sport does not have to worry about financial discipline, since it is fundamentally about heroic exploits, the emotional attachment to clubs and teams, and the quest for sporting immortality, is no longer a sensible excuse. A memorable sport experience may give us a warm inner glow and make us feel part of a tightly integrated tribal family that transcends the banal experiences of everyday life, but it becomes fanciful and irresponsible when it means that the disciplined use of money is pushed to the side and, in extreme cases, kicked out of sight. It is in this context that the following questions come to mind.

1 Why is sport so important to so many people?

2 Do you agree with the statement that without fans there would be no commercialized sport? And, if so, why?

3 What are the main differences between sport organizations of yesteryear and those of today?

4 What were the strengths and weaknesses of traditional sport, and how do they compare with the strengths and weaknesses of contemporary sport?

5 Discuss the relative importance of the state, the market and civil society in driving sport in your region or nation.

6 Why should government want to finance sport, and would it not be better for everyone if sport could be self-sustaining from a financial perspective?

7 Describe the main features of professional sport, and identify the main beneficiaries.

8 What has led to the explosive increase in club revenues at the top flight of European football?

9 Italian clubs have been left behind, though. What might be the cause of this relative decline in the profitability of Italian football over recent times?

10 Explain how the Olympic Games transformed itself financially over the last fifty years.

11 Does this mean that the Games now deliver superior experiences to those of yesteryear?

12 What are the two already dominant financial hubs, and the one emerging, financial hub of world sport? And how do you explain the emergence of this third hub?

13 Why is good financial management so important to the viability of sport?

14 What are the main items that impact on the operating costs of sport organizations?

15 Why does it appear to be so difficult to curb cost increases in professional sport leagues?

16 What factors may have caused some J.League clubs to exhibit so much financial instability?

17 What does it take to be financially literate?

18 Is financial literacy really necessary for the management of community sport enterprises?

FURTHER READING

For a detailed analysis of the consumer culture surrounding sport, why sport is so important to people and how the fan has become the cornerstone of commercial sport, see Crawford, G. (2004) *Consuming Sport: Fans, Sport and Culture*, Routledge. To get a more nuanced analysis of sports fandom as a form of neo-tribalism, see Morris, D. (1981) *The Soccer Tribe*, Jonathon Cape. An excellent follow-up reading is Wann, D., Melnick, M., Russell, G. and Pease, D. (2001) *Sport Fans: The Psychology and Social Impact of Spectators*, Routledge. Additional references include Bognon, P. (2008) *The Anatomy of Sports Fans*, Booksurge; and Quinn, K. (2009) *Sports and Their Fans: The History, Economics and Culture of the Relationship Between Spectator and Sport*, McFarland and Co.

A broad analysis of trends in commercialized sport throughout the world is provided in Westerbeek, H. and Smith, A.C.T. (2003) *Sport Business in the Global Marketplace*, Palgrave Macmillan. For a more critical stance on global sport see Miller, T., Lawrence, C., McKay, J. and Rowe, D. (2001) *Globalization and Sport*, Sage. See also Schirato, T. (2007) *Understanding Sports Culture*, Sage.

And, for a much earlier critique of modern sport, it is worth reading Whannel, G. (1983) *Blowing the Whistle: The Politics of Sport*, Pluto Press. Whannel, for instance, reckoned contemporary, commercialized sport is 'dominated by elaborate spectacles, which serves to mask the ruthless exploitation of the existing social order', and additionally acts as a diversion which keeps 'the working class. . . from engaging in class struggle'. It is, in the ancient Roman tradition, all about 'bread and circuses' for the masses (Whannel 1983: 20–1).

For a succinct review of the evolution of sport stadia design and construction, and the associated escalation of costs, see Thompson, P., Toolczko, J. and Clarke, J. (eds) (1998) *Stadia, Arenas and Grandstands: Design, Construction and Operation*, E. and F.N. Spon. See, in particular, Chapter 3 for an analysis of stadia costing. A recent update of trends in sport stadia design and construction is contained in Sheard, R. and Bingham-Hall, P. (2005) *The Stadium Architecture for the New Global Culture*, Pesaro Publishing.

An expansive account of the financial transformation of motor sports is contained in Beck-Burridge, M. and Walton, J. (2001) *Sport Sponsorship and Brand Development: The Subaru and Jaguar Stories*, Palgrave Macmillan (Chapter 2: Marketing). The transformation of English world football during the 1990s is thoroughly documented by King, A. (1998) *The End of the Terraces*, Leicester University Press.

For a good summary of how the USA has set the commercial and cultural parameters of sport around the world, see Allison, L. (2005) *The Global Politics of Sport: The Role of Global Institutions in Sport*, Routledge. An excellent case-based analysis of the hyper-commercialized aspects of world sport, and how television sponsorship and the celebrity athlete mutually reinforce each other's status and prestige, is provided by La Feber, W. (1999) *Michael Jordon and the New Global Capitalism*, WW Norton.

For a detailed analysis of how government impacts on sport development, see Green, M. and Houlihan, B. (2005) *Elite Sport Development: Policy Learning and Political Priorities*, Routledge. See also Stewart, B., Nicholson, M., Smith, A. and Westerbeek, H. (2004) *Australian Sport: Better by Design? The Evolution of Australian Sport Policy*, Routledge.

A comprehensive and highly instructive account of the finances and commercial foundations of the Olympic Games is contained in Preuss, H. (2000) *Economics of the Olympic Games: Hosting the Games 1972–2000*, Walla Walla Press (Chapter 2: 'Financing models', and Chapter 4: 'Aspects of business economy'). For an update of the economics of the Olympic Games, see Preuss, H. (2004) *The Economics of Staging the Olympics*, Edward Elgar.

For a succinct discussion of the J.League and its overall development see Watanabe, N. (2012) 'Japanese professional soccer attendance and the effects of regions, competitive balance and rival franchises', *International Journal of Sport Finance*, 7: 309–23.

A useful contrast between non-profit community sport and professional sport is contained in Hoye, R., Smith, A., Westerbeek, H., Stewart, B. and Nicholson, M. (2012) *Sport Management: Principles and Practice*, 3rd edition, Routledge (Chapter 3: 'Non-profit sport', and Chapter 4: 'Professional sport'). Additional contrasting commentaries can be found in Gratton, C. and Kokolakakis, T. (2012) 'Sport in the global marketplace', in Trenberth, L. and Hassan, D. (eds) *Managing Sport Business: An Introduction*, Routledge, and O'Beirne, C. (2013) 'Managing small and not-for-profit sports organisations', in Beech, J. and Chadwick, S. (eds) *The Business of Sport Management*, 2nd edition, Pearson.

To get a sharper insight into the financial operations of community sport enterprises, see Wicker, P. (2011) 'Willingness-to-pay in a non-profit sports club', *International Journal of Sport Finance*, 6: 155–69. See also Wicker, P., Breuer, C. and Pawlowski, T. (2010) 'Are sport club members big spenders? Findings from sport-specific analysis in Germany', *International Journal of Sport Finance*, 6: 122–33.

USEFUL WEBSITES

- An excellent analysis on sport's evolution, and the meaning it gives to its participants as both players and spectators, is contained in **www.epjournal.net/wp-content/uploads/EP100128.pdf**.
- The J.League website is worth a visit at **www.j-league.or.jp**.
- The financing of the upcoming 2016 Rio Olympics is nicely interrogated in **http://sevenpillarsinstitute.org/case-studies/financing-ethics-and-the-brazilian-olympics**. This site also contains a detailed account of the financing of previous Olympic Games.
- A good website for understanding the importance of financial literacy is **www.ourcommunity.com.au/financial/financial_article.jsp?articleId=4486**. It not only highlights the prevalence of poor financial knowledge in not-for-profit organizations, but also suggests what can be done to improve it.
- Another useful web-based resource on financial literacy in the not-for-profit sector is **www.philanthropy.iupui.edu/files/research/2012financialliteracy.pdf**. It contains a study of Canadian not-for-profit agencies, and discusses the importance they attach to financial skill, knowledge and know-how.

CHAPTER 2

Sport as a special form of business

LEARNING OUTCOMES

At the end of this chapter readers will be able to:

- explain the ways in which sport is both different from, and similar to, the world of business, and what its special features mean for effective financial management of sport enterprises
- describe sport's commercial transformation and the implications this has for the proper financial management of clubs, agencies, associations and leagues
- distinguish between funding arrangements that focus on capital works, and those funding arrangements that are geared to operational issues
- understand the ways in which sport can be organized to attract more funds and increase its attractiveness to members, fans and end users of the sports service.

CHAPTER SUMMARY

This chapter discusses the current status of sport, its special features and its financial operations. It begins with an examination of sport's structures and systems, and the ways in which it is similar to business on the one hand, but different from it on the other. It then uses these special features to contextualize the funding of sport, and how these funds are spent. It distinguishes between the different sources of funds (e.g. memberships, sponsorships, gate takings, social events, merchandising, broadcast rights, government grants and borrowings) and examines the strengths and weaknesses of each source. It also looks at the ways in which these funds are spent. It contrasts the use of funds by sport enterprises to undertake capital works (e.g. venues and grounds) with funds allocated to their ongoing operations (e.g. the club, association or league). It also confirms that all sport is capable of moving beyond member fees and fundraising function activities to finance its operations.

SPORT'S SPECIAL FEATURES

While all businesses, which include sport businesses, must manage their finances efficiently and balance their books, so to speak, there are some crucial differences in the weighting of funding sources, and how these funds are spent. For example, sport has a heavy dependence on human resources and their associated costs. This begs the question as to what distinguishes sport from business, and what it implies for sport's financial management. In Chapter 1 it was noted that, unlike business, sport generates a strong sense of tribal identity and fans have a passionate desire to see their club succeed. There are, as it turns out, many aspects of sport that make it a unique enterprise, and they are discussed below.

Additionally, sport's commercial development and growing financial complexity has been criticized on the grounds that increasing levels of professionalization, bureaucratization and specialization have undermined its localism and the community focus on sport. The ensuing debate about the future direction of sport has challenged many views about the nature and place of sport in society, but in the end has highlighted the commercial evolution of sport and crucial importance of having it well managed (Hoye *et al.* 2012).

Even though sport's commercialization has many detractors, even at the local or community level, it can no longer operate effectively in a cultural frame that focuses exclusively on amateurism and volunteerism, and that seeks to divorce sport from work and commerce. It has not taken long for most sport organizations to adopt the processes and practices of private sector business enterprises. Players and administrators are often paid employees, plans are designed, the sport product is branded and marketed, member and customer needs are monitored and alliances with corporate supporters are developed. But neither is sport just another form of private enterprise. Sport can be business, but it is a special form of business (Smith and Stewart 1999, 2013). In the remainder of this chapter we explore those features of organized sport that give it its special quality, and why these features need to be understood as a precursor to going about the 'building the sport business' and managing its finances.

Premierships over profits

The most significant difference between professional sport organizations and private business is the way in which they measure performance (Hoye *et al.* 2012). While business firms have many operational goals, their underlying purpose is to optimize profits. For example, BMW and Mercedes are fierce competitors, and by generating profits they can both claim a successful year. However, large profits will do little to convince sporting clubs of their success if they finish the season at the bottom of the ladder. While the BMW and Mercedes shareholders expect continuing profits, sport club members and fans judge performance mostly on the basis of trophies, premierships and pennants.

Sport clubs consequently face two prevailing models of organizational behaviour (Sandy *et al.* 2004; Buraimo and Simmons 2008). The first is the profit maximization model, which proposes that a club is simply a firm in a competitive product market, and profit is an indicator of success and long-term sustainability. The second is the utility maximization model, which emphasizes the desire to win as many games as possible, or the goal of meeting the needs of members for a satisfying sport experience. This 'utility' view of sport concedes that, while sporting organizations are by nature highly competitive, they are also status conscious, and use on-field success and 'quality' member experiences as their primary performance yardstick.

Changes in the sporting context and changing management practices have complicated this tension between profits and premierships. Expanding sporting options, increasing competition for the discretionary consumer dollar, and the professionalization of players and officials have forced clubs previously solely concerned with winning to focus more strongly on revenue profits and cash flow. This reinforces the need to implement quality financial management systems (Brown *et al.* 2010).

A level playing field

While sporting organizations are often prepared to do all that it takes to achieve on-field success, domination of a league or competition can be self-defeating. Highly predictable outcomes can produce low attendances and diminish the match-day, media and sponsorship revenue. The ongoing viability of the competition and the financial health of constituent clubs will be enhanced if rules are introduced that distribute playing talent equally between teams (Quirk and Fort 1992; Humphreys and Watanabe 2012). It is no surprise that two of the most successful professional sport leagues in the world, the American NFL and the Australian AFL, have implemented salary caps, player draft rules and ceilings on lists of contracted players. Outcome uncertainty and competitive balance is an important ingredient of the commercial success of team sport competitions, although as the English Premier League demonstrates, dominance by a few clubs does not always diminish its public support. While contrived uncertainty comes at the cost of a competitive marketplace, it can also improve the financial health of leagues and clubs.

Variable quality

As the above discussion suggests, fans are more attracted to games where the result is problematic and uncertain. By contrast, in the commercial world, predictability is important because customers demand both reliability and minimum quality standards (Hoffman and Bateson 2001; Rein *et al.* 2006). Consequently, this desire for uncertain outcomes in sport has its problems, since it brings with it enormous variability in the quality of sporting performances. Many factors contribute to this variability, including weather, player injuries, the venue, the quality of the opponents, the closeness of the scores and even the size of the crowd. The tactics employed by the opposing teams can also influence the level of game quality, and are exemplified in cricket. Captains can either make the contest dull and defensive by slowing down play and designing ultra-defensive field placements, or make it exciting by attacking batting. However, chronic fan boredom and unfulfilled expectations can place the financial health of a sport in jeopardy.

Fixed-supply schedules

Fixed short-run supply schedules also constitute a problem for sporting clubs (Tribe 2004). While private sector businesses can increase production to meet demand, sporting clubs have fixed, or highly inelastic, supply curves for many of their products and services (elasticity is discussed in detail in Chapter 10). Clubs can only play a certain number of times during their business cycle, or season. Where spectator demand for a game is high, the governing body may change the venue to allow a larger crowd to attend, but cannot decide to play the match twice. However, fans are unable to gain admission, and as a result revenue is lost.

This problem of fixed supply is particularly evident in the construction of stadiums and arenas. On the one hand, a large seating capacity will squeeze out any unmet demand. On the other hand, chronic under-utilization will increase the costs per spectator of delivering games. In the end, the problem of unmet demand can be resolved by providing more seats, or playing more games. For example, the steady increase in demand for cricket over the past thirty years has resulted in more limited-over games matches being played, thereby increasing productivity and supply.

Collaboration and cartels

Unlike the competitive benefits that a business firm can secure by forcing a rival out of the market, team sport clubs depend upon the continued viability of their opponents (Li *et al.* 2001; Quinn 2009). In short, clubs must cooperate with their rivals in order to deliver attractive sporting experiences to fans and customers. Clubs are mutually interdependent, and the division of clubs into wealthy and high performing on the one hand, and poor and low performing on the other, can damage all clubs by making the competition less interesting.

This interdependency can produce arrangements that constrain the activities of the most powerful clubs by cross-subsidizing the less powerful clubs. Such revenue sharing in the retail industry would be unthinkable, unless, of course, it was organized as a cartel. Cartel arrangements are common in sport, where clubs not only share revenue, but also prevent other clubs from entering the market, collectively fix prices and generally limit the amount of competition. The relationship between sport cartels and financial performance is discussed in more detail in Chapter 5.

Emotions and passions

Sport, commerce, culture and values are inextricably linked and, as noted in Chapter 1, sport has a symbolic significance and emotional intensity that is rarely found in an insurance company, bank or accounting office (Smith and Stewart 2013). While profit-centred businesses seek strong commitment from their employees, their overriding concern is efficiency, productivity and responding quickly to changing market conditions. Sport, on the other hand, is consumed by strong emotional attachments that are linked to the past through nostalgia and tradition (Crawford 2004; Bognon 2008). A proposal to change club colours in order to project a more attractive image may be defeated because it breaks a link with tradition. Similarly, coaches can be appointed on the basis of their previous loyalty to the club rather than because of a superior capacity to manage players. Sports administrators frequently allow tradition and history to dictate a sport's future, but being a slave to old practices can impede the capacity to adapt to changing circumstances and exploit new revenue opportunities. At the same time, passion can be used to sustain loyalty, attract fans, sell more merchandise and expand public support, all of which can increase revenue streams.

Product and brand loyalty

Sport engenders a high degree of loyalty at both the product (i.e. sport league or event) level and the brand (i.e. team) level, and there is consequently a low degree of substitutability between competing sport leagues and competitions. Match-day fixtures provide a clutch of entertainment benefits that attract spectators and television viewers, but these benefits are usually sport specific, and the satisfactions that come from watching one sport will not easily transfer to another (Tribe 2004; Bognon 2008). Even where fans are unhappy about game outcomes, they are unlikely to change their sporting preferences. In contrast, if consumers purchased computing equipment or a medical service, and were dissatisfied with the quality, then they would immediately consider changing providers or products, even if prices were higher. In sport, no such easy substitutability occurs. At the same time, a low degree of product substitution has its drawbacks, since it can limit a sport's ability to achieve quick market penetration. The customs and habits of sport fans make it difficult to attract them from one sport to another by using incentives or price discounts. Other inducements may therefore be necessary to build a fan base.

Many businesses use the power of sporting identification to market their products via endorsement from sporting heroes (LaFeber 1999; Quinn 2009). The aim is to capture some of the loyalty and charisma associated with players, rather than working through price, convenience or quality. This symbiotic relationship between sporting heroes, player identification and product promotion has a powerful influence on the spending patterns of consumers, and can be used by sport organizations to deepen their revenue pools.

DIFFERENCES AND SIMILARITIES

Foster *et al.* (2006) tackled the sport-as-business problem by compiling a list of things professional sport and business have in common, and areas where they differed. They concluded that, whereas sport and business shared a common concern for value creation, branding, funding new sources of revenue product innovation and market expansion, sport was significantly more concerned with beating rivals, winning trophies, sharing revenue and channelling the passions of both players (the employees) and fans (the customers). Table 2.1 lists these factors.

The other important point made by Foster *et al.* (2006) is that athletes are now business assets, who are instrumental in attracting fans, sponsors and media exposure. It therefore comes as no surprise that, unlike business, a sport's service deliverers (the players) earn far more than their immediate supervisors (the club managers).

TABLE 2.1 Models of business and sport

Areas of commonality	Areas of differentiation
Leadership and strategy matters	Winning on the field central
Value creation and value sharing	Diverse owner objectives
Search for revenue growth	Managing in the fishbowl
Value-chain fluidity	Supporting the weakest
New product innovation	Handicapping the strongest
Astute and creative contracting	Revenue pools and allocation rules
Quality of the product matters	Athletes as business assets
Branding matters	Managing the badly behaving player
Fans and customers as a business pillar	Limited financial disclosures
Globalization	Sports as an entertainment cocktail

Source: Foster *et al.* (2006: 2).

CASE STUDY 2.1

The specificity of sport

The idea that sport is qualitatively different from the world of 'normal' business has been given further impetus by the European Union's 2007 *White Paper on Sport* (Weatherill 2009: 109; Hassan 2012: 36; Beech and Chadwick 2013a: 19). When discussing the place of sport in contemporary society it gave special attention to its 'specificity'. It used this term to highlight significant features of sport that differentiate it from other fields of commerce and industry.

First, its activities are defined by a plethora of internal laws, rules and customs. These laws, rules and customs not only determine what is permissible and not permissible in different games and contests, but also set the parameters for who is permitted or not permitted to play. Moreover, all sorts of rules and regulations are used to ensure fair and balanced competitions, and thus avoid situations where the inequities are so severe that the outcome of the contest is never in doubt. Thus, tacit approval is granted by the broader community – and government especially – for the organizers of sport events to give the contest outcome a high degree of uncertainty that will attract both players and spectators. This can be done by giving the fastest runners a handicap (which they do in traditional forms of professional running), establishing a range of weight divisions (which they do in boxing, the martial arts and rowing) and segregating contests into male-only and female-only (which they do in 80 per cent of all sporting contests).

Second, sport is not only highly structured, but is also organized around clearly defined hierarchies. It conforms to a pyramid mode whereby the base of the pyramid includes community 'grass-roots' sport, the middle level involves those sports that are seriously competitive and sometimes played for money, while the peak of the pyramid includes all the elite players, many of whom will have an international reputation, and many of whom will be paid handsome retainers. The peak of every sporting pyramid will also have a single governing body that sets the planning and operational parameters for all the associations and clubs under its governance.

Third, this sporting pyramid is tightly bound by a set of interdependencies that connect its different levels, although not always in positive ways. For example, the young athletes at the bottom of the pyramid need constant nurturing because they will inevitably become the talent pool from which the next bunch of elite performers will be selected. At the same time, it is also important that retired elite players be encouraged to re-enter their chosen sport at the grass-roots level, since they can provide the experience and expertise to assist the establishment of the next talent pool of young players. Success at the top end of the pyramid can also assist those at the bottom, since the increases in revenue that often accompany the successes can be used to further develop all those people participating at the base of the sporting pyramid.

This is all well and good, but as we will see in more detail in later chapters, the practices that sport uses to control the conduct of its members may deliver greater 'outcome uncertainty', but may also be seen to be collusive, anti-competitive and against the public interest when implemented in the commercial arena. This is a dilemma that policymakers face when having to deal with the so-called special nature of sport.

STRIKING A BALANCE

To summarize, sport is not simply just another form of business enterprise, but neither is it so special that it has no connection to business. While the special features of sport referred to above suggest that it needs to be managed in ways that fit its idiosyncratic values and structures, it also works best under strong business models and sound management principles. One of the weaknesses of sport at the community level is its failure to grasp management theory and best practice models, and use them to improve the performance of the sport system. At the same time, sport's unique structures and practices have important implications for the management of sport organization finances, as the following chapters show.

MODELS FOR MANAGING SPORT

Sport is, by its very nature, a highly structured activity. It has rules that govern the ways games are played, and it sets conditions as to who can participate, and who cannot. It also demands a firm managerial hand to guide it along a sustainable path. Sport has been good at delivering all sorts of programmes, competitions, tournaments and leagues, but has been less successful in implementing strong financial controls. This has been due to the often obsessive desire to spend all that it takes to win, but is also in part due to the strong involvement of community volunteers in their local sport enterprises. While they generously offer their services, and provide a massive input to club and league operations, they are sometimes not well trained, and are almost always pressed for time. And, even where staff are paid and have prior experience, the financial management function has often been overridden by the drive for success and the desire for new and better facilities. At the same time, it is clear that new models for managing sport have evolved over recent times, and they are discussed below.

The kitchen-table model

Sport, like all other institutions in society, can only sustain itself if it has the resources to support its activities, programmes and events. Traditionally most sport was run on shoe-string budgets where the energies of volunteer officials and membership fees kept clubs and associations afloat. In short, the people who played and administered the game provided the bulk of the resources needed for sport's ongoing development. This is known as the kitchen-table approach to sport organization management, where the administration of the game was driven by a few officials making decisions from a member's home. This model of sport organization management has a number of strengths. It not only ensured the involvement of grass-roots players and members, and provided a strong local community club focus, but it also nurtured a strong set of values that centred on playing the game for its own sake, and the concomitant ideal of amateurism (Hoye *et al.* 2012). At the same time, it also perpetuated a primitive system of management driven by an administrative committee made up of a few elected members and self-appointed officials. There was a president who was the public face of the club or association, and a secretary who kept things ticking over by keeping a member register and organizing others to manage teams, run events and maintain the clubrooms and playing facilities. There was also a treasurer who looked after the financial affairs of the organization. The treasurer was more often than not unfamiliar with the theory and principles of accounting, but made up for a lack of expertise with a mind for detail, and a desire to ensure receipts ran ahead of expenses. Transactions were usually recorded as cash entries, where cash either moved out as a payment for something purchased and services rendered, or in as a bank account deposit.

The boardroom or corporate model

The widespread commercialization of sport around the world began in the 1970s, and transformed the ways sport organizations did business (Stewart 1984). As indicated in Chapter 1, sport, particularly at the elite end of the continuum, jettisoned its amateur values, and adopted many of the features of commercial business in its attempts to increase the scale of its operations and improve the standard of its competitions. Sport entered the age of professionalism, where players were handsomely paid for their services, old-time administrators morphed into general managers and chief executive officers, and a bevy of sport scientists, psychologists and sundry hangers-on provided all sorts of assistance to athletes. As sport became more commercialized and professionalized, it changed the way it did business, and in particular developed much stronger links with the corporate sector, which saw sport as a great vehicle for promoting its products and attracting audiences (Slack 2004). Some of the significant commercial developments in world sport over the last ten years are revealed in the following incidents:

- In 1998, the Dallas Cowboys football team became the most valuable sports brand in the world, at USD 274 million.
- In 1998, Nike made the biggest sponsorship deal ever; it signed the Brazilian Soccer team for ten years, and in return gave it USD 400 million.
- In 2000, the New South Wales Supreme Court ordered boxer, Kostya Tszyu, to pay damages of AUD 7.3 million to his former promoter, Bill Mordey, for breach of contract.
- By 2006, some Australian cricketers were earning AUD 1 million a year.
- In 2012, Real Madrid FC became the wealthiest sporting club in the world, having been valued at USD 400 million.
- In 2013, having just secured the rights to host the 2020 Olympic Games in Tokyo, the Japanese government announced that the showpiece of the Games would be an 80,000-seat stadium that would double as a major public work of art. It was estimated that the stadium would cost YEN 130 billion, or around USD 1.2 billion, to build.

Multi-phase models of sport's financial progress

The 'kitchen table to corporate boardroom' model of sport management's evolution is instructive, but it does not tell the full story. Andreff and Staudohar (2002) have extended the kitchen-table/corporate boardroom model of sport's financial progress by proposing a three-phase model that begins with amateur structures, moves into traditional professional structures and finishes with contemporary professional structures.

The amateur structure (phase one) is member-focused with an emphasis on participation at the community level, with a narrowly supported pathway to elite sport and the international sports arena. Its financial viability is sustained through gate receipts, members' fees, subscriptions, cash donations and food and drink sales (or what is called concession income in the USA). This is equivalent to the kitchen-table model of sport management referred to earlier. In contrast, the traditional professional structure (phase two) is more heavily dependent on sponsorship and government subsidies, while maintaining its gate receipts and local support. This structure, which is primarily concerned with sport development, is alternatively viewed as a sport-centred archetype and is the forerunner of the corporate sports model. The contemporary professional structure (phase three) is more heavily geared to corporate support as it develops its brand image and network of sponsors. The focus is on revenue generation rather than sport development and it is alternatively viewed as a business-centred archetype. In order to tap into the capital markets some clubs become public companies and, by listing their shares on the stock exchange, gain access to additional equity capital. The different financial arrangements for each structure are listed in Table 2.2.

Beech and Chadwick (2013a: 5–9) stretched things further by positing a seven-stage model of sport's commercial development. They viewed its progress as coming in fits and starts, with long periods of evolution punctuated by short periods of revolution. Their sport development model takes the following form:

TABLE 2.2 Sources of finance for different sport structures			
Revenue item	Amateur	Traditional professional	Contemporary professional
Gate receipts	✓	✓✓	✓✓
Members' fees and registration	✓✓	✓	✓
Cash donations	✓✓	✓	✓
Government subsidies	✓	✓✓	✓✓
Food and drink sales	✓✓	✓	✓
Sponsors and advertising	•	✓	✓✓
Merchandising	•	✓	✓✓
Television rights fees	•	✓	✓✓

Notes:
• = of no importance
✓ = of some importance
✓✓ = highly important

1 *Foundation* – in this evolutionary stage the rudimentary forms of sport are found in medieval community festivals and the various forms of folk football.
2 *Codification* – in this revolutionary stage sport becomes organized through the emergence of laws and rules that establish the structure and conduct of different sporting activities.
3 *Stratification* – in this evolutionary stage governing bodies are established, and leagues are formed.
4 *Professionalization* – in this revolutionary stage spectator sport expands and clubs can afford to pay players to play.
5 *Post-professionalization* – in this evolutionary stage amateur and professional sport move along together, each with its own 'sacred' space.
6 *Commercialization* – in this revolutionary stage the professionalization of sport explodes, amateurism loses its hold over sport fans, and even its cultural and ethical value is questioned. Sponsorship, product endorsements, merchandising, broadcast rights and venue-naming rights become massive sources of additional revenue.
7 *Post-commercialization* – in this stage things become uncertain as some sport brands increase in value (as leisure fads and fashions shift), while other sports have their brand value trashed (often being the result of some sex, drug-use, racism, homophobic or match-fixing scandal). The law and politics become intertwined with sport's often obsessive concern for performance enhancement. This stage is also associated with financial instability as clubs go in search of resources that will deliver success.

The increasing financial complexity of sport, and the instability it brings, is only one side of the sport management coin. The other issue to be dealt with is the escalation of player salaries and athlete assistance programmes, and the ever-increasing number of full-time support staff, such as coaches, trainers and sport scientists. In addition, any increase in revenue is immediately absorbed by staff and player salaries. While the revenue side of the sport finance equation has increased exponentially, so too has the cost side of the equation. The most newsworthy has been the escalating movement in player salaries, which was briefly noted in Chapter 1. The other major cost escalation has been in the area of stadium and arena construction (Sheard and Bingham-Hall 2005). These developments have at their core the need to establish appropriate systems of financial management and control. The other point to note is that the increasing funds available to sport are not shared equally, either between sport competitions and leagues or within them (Szymanski and Kuypers 2000).

FUNDING SOURCES

It is clear that the new business-based model of sport (the corporate boardroom/contemporary professional/post-commercialization structure) involves a massive expansion of income (Humphreys and Ruseski 2008). However, it is also important to not throw the baby out with the bathwater, and so traditional forms of revenue have been maintained, although in a slightly more sophisticated form. So, member fees are still important, as too are fundraising from social activities, and gate receipts. However, as was touched upon previously, new and varied revenue streams have opened up over the last thirty years that have transformed sport and the way it operates. The funding of sport organizations begs a number of questions, the main ones being:

- Where does the money come from?
- Where is the money spent?
- How are the movements of money monitored?

   In answering these questions it is important to distinguish between funds that are used to create infrastructure and facilities, and funds for use in managing the day-to-day activities of a sport organization. So, there are two types of basic funding uses. The first is funds for investment in capital development, and the second is funds for recurrent and operating activities.

Capital funding

Capital funding, which is money to finance *investment in assets*, can come from a number of sources:

- Government grants, which may be federal, state or local. The point to note is that there are differences between sports that reflect not only their scale of operation but also their likelihood of generating international success. Funding may also be subject to certain conditions being met, such as adopting certain policy requirements or working within a legislative framework.
- Loans and borrowing, which could be short term (up to a year) or long term (up to twenty years). Loans and borrowings are known as debt finance. The points to note are that, on the one hand, it provides ready cash for investment in facilities and income-producing assets. On the other hand, it can also increase the level of risk since

it also incurs an interest burden, and may not always generate the anticipated increase in income.

- New share issue or a public float, which is known as equity finance. The points to note are that, like borrowing, it provides ready access to cash, but unlike borrowing does not impose the burden of interest payment or repayment of the principal to lenders. However, it does hand over control to shareholders, and there is expectation that a dividend will be delivered.
- Retained earnings, which is money reinvested in the sport organization. The points to note are that there is no interest payment and control is retained over funds used. For non-profit sport organizations, the retention of earnings is mandatory, since this is a legal requirement.

Recurrent funding

The recurrent funding of sport involves money to fund day-to-day operations, which comes from a variety of sources depending on the type of sport enterprise. The main *revenue sources* are:

- Membership fees, which may be full adult, associate, family and similar categories. The point to note here is that they are usually upfront and relatively stable and therefore provide an immediate source of cash. Membership also serves a marketing function by establishing a core customer base.
- Spectator admission charge, which includes the categories of full adult, family, special groups and premium. The point to note is that, while there is a high degree of flexibility, it is subject to significant variation because of changing attendance patterns and differences in the scheduling of games.
- Corporate facilities, including boxes and hospitality. The point to note is that a large investment is required, but the strengths are that business connections are made and premium rental can be charged.
- Player fees and charges, including entry fees, facility charges and equipment hire. The point to note here is that revenue is dependent on demand, and the user pays for the experience.
- Special fundraising efforts are another source of recurrent funding and may include a dinner dance, rage-party, auction night, trivia night and so on. The point to note is that the burden is on staff and members to arrange and attend functions. However, these types of events can be profitable through large markups on food and drink.
- Lotteries and gaming such as raffles, bingo and gaming machines. The points to note are that permits are often required, margins are low and there is solid competition from other venues.
- Merchandising such as memorabilia, scarves, T-shirts, jackets and autographed equipment. The point to note is that while it can produce a significant short-run increase in revenue, it can plateau out with a fall in on-field success.
- Sponsorships and endorsement are another good source and may include naming rights, partnerships, signage, product endorsements and contra deals. However, the point to note is that the organization can lose control and become dependent on sponsor income and defer to its partnership demands.

- Catering may include takeaway or sit-down food or drink. The point to note is that it is labour intensive, but because it is delivered in a non-competitive environment higher profit margins can be sustained.
- Broadcasting rights, such as television and radio, and more recently internet and mobile phone streaming rights. The point to note is that this focuses on elite sports with a large audience base, and may be irrelevant for most sport associations and clubs. At the same time it provides the single largest revenue source for many professional sport leagues.
- Investment income such as interest earned and share dividends. However, the point to note is that share prices can vary at short notice and losses can be made, which increases the level of risk. In addition, interest rates may be low.
- Government grants, which may be federal, state or local. The points to note are that there are often marked differences between sports, they can vary from year to year and, like government capital funds, they are subject to certain conditions being met.

The *expenses incurred* in running a sport enterprise are also varied. They include:

- Wages and salaries, such as permanent, contract or casual administration staff and players. The points to note are that they are usually the largest expense item and are subject to inflation and competitive bidding as clubs aim to secure the best playing talent.
- Staff on-costs, which include insurance, training, leave and superannuation. The point to note here is that they are legally required, ongoing and linked to the employment contract.
- Marketing costs, including advertising, sales promotion, site visits, trade displays and give-aways. The point to note here is that it is easy to exceed budget estimates since there is always a tacit assumption that too much marketing and promotion is never enough.
- Office maintenance, including power and light, phone and fax, postage, stationery and printing. The point to note here is that it is ongoing and tight control is required.
- Venue maintenance, including the playing area, the viewing area and member facilities. The point to note here is that maintenance expenditure is ongoing and frequently absorbs a significant amount of revenue.
- Player management, including equipment, clothing and footwear, medical services, fitness and conditioning, and travel. The point to note is that, while this constitutes an essential investment in improved performance, it also requires tight budgeting.
- Asset depreciation, including facilities, buildings, cars and equipment. The point to note here is that assets lose value and must be replaced. Also, depreciation is a non-cash expense, and it is essential that assets be amortized as expenses over their lifetime.

The above discussion shows that, on the one hand, the sport sector is extremely diverse and, depending on its structure and level of popularity, will have access to either a broad or narrow range of funds. It also shows that all sport is capable of moving beyond member fees and fundraising activities to finance its operations. For instance, business and other partnerships have become integral to the financial sustainability of sport enterprises, no matter what their scale of operation.

On the other hand, even with these expanding opportunities there is still a significant risk in building a sport enterprise's infrastructure and profile. What is more, the 'risk exposure' problem is not confined to professional sport, where the pressure to succeed is immense (Brown *et al.* 2010). It is also an issue in community club-based sport. A 2010 study of German non-profit sport clubs reported that just under 4 per cent had experienced some type of financial hardship some time during the recent past (Wicker 2011). The sources of the problems were traced back to greater instability of government funding, greater competition from privately run facilities – especially gyms and fitness centres, the 2007–9 global financial crisis and escalating energy costs.

RECAP

Sport has gone through a radical overhaul over recent years, and there are now many parts of it that seem to be just another form of business. However, there are some fundamental principles about the operation and management of sport that still apply, no matter how complex or how rudimentary the enterprise might be. This is especially so when it comes to the financial management issue. Additionally, there are some features about sport that makes its management different from run-of-the-mill businesses, and these features need to be considered when constructing models for managing the finances of sport enterprises. Finally, it is also crucial to note that, when surveying a sport's funding arrangements, no matter what its scale or its commercial orientation, it is essential to distinguish between those funds earmarked to build up its capital stocks and infrastructure, on the one hand, and those funds for running its day-to-day operations, on the other.

REVIEW QUESTIONS

So, with all that in mind, many questions need to be posed about how sport works, and the financial implications that follow.

1 Having studied the ways in which sport has changed over recent times, what can you say about the features of sport (either community or commercial) that make it different from 'normal' business?

2 In what ways is sport similar to business?

3 Does sport have special features that impact on its management?

4 Do these special features pose additional problems for its financial management? And, if so, what are they?

5 In Europe especially, there is a lot of talk about the 'specificity' of sport, and how it can be used as a defence to give special treatment to sport. But what do people really mean when they talk about the specificity of sport?

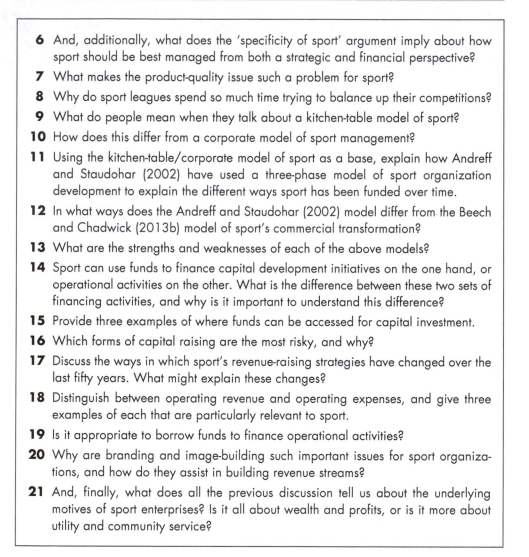

6 And, additionally, what does the 'specificity of sport' argument imply about how sport should be best managed from both a strategic and financial perspective?

7 What makes the product-quality issue such a problem for sport?

8 Why do sport leagues spend so much time trying to balance up their competitions?

9 What do people mean when they talk about a kitchen-table model of sport?

10 How does this differ from a corporate model of sport management?

11 Using the kitchen-table/corporate model of sport as a base, explain how Andreff and Staudohar (2002) have used a three-phase model of sport organization development to explain the different ways sport has been funded over time.

12 In what ways does the Andreff and Staudohar (2002) model differ from the Beech and Chadwick (2013b) model of sport's commercial transformation?

13 What are the strengths and weaknesses of each of the above models?

14 Sport can use funds to finance capital development initiatives on the one hand, or operational activities on the other. What is the difference between these two sets of financing activities, and why is it important to understand this difference?

15 Provide three examples of where funds can be accessed for capital investment.

16 Which forms of capital raising are the most risky, and why?

17 Discuss the ways in which sport's revenue-raising strategies have changed over the last fifty years. What might explain these changes?

18 Distinguish between operating revenue and operating expenses, and give three examples of each that are particularly relevant to sport.

19 Is it appropriate to borrow funds to finance operational activities?

20 Why are branding and image-building such important issues for sport organizations, and how do they assist in building revenue streams?

21 And, finally, what does all the previous discussion tell us about the underlying motives of sport enterprises? Is it all about wealth and profits, or is it more about utility and community service?

FURTHER READING

An extensive overview of the differences and similarities between sport organizations and business organizations is provided in Foster, G., Greyser, P. and Walsh, B. (2006) *The Business of Sports: Texts and Cases on Strategy and Management*, Mason, OH: Thomson (section 1.1: 'Business of sports – a perspective from Stanford'). For an alternative, if somewhat dated, analysis of the same phenomena, see Smith, A. and Stewart, B. (1999) *Sports Management: A Guide to Professional Practice*, Crows Nest, NSW: Allen & Unwin (Chapter 2: 'Special features of sport'). For an update of Smith and Stewart's 1999 discussion of the 'unique' nature of sport, and what makes it both similar to, and different from, the world of 'conventional' business, see Smith, A. and Stewart, B. (2013) 'The special features of sport: a critical revisit', in Soderman, S. and Dolles, H. (eds) *Handbook of Research on Sport and Business*, Cheltenham: Edward Elgar, pp. 526–47.

For an analysis of the variety of goals and motives pursued by sport organizations, see Li, M., Hofacre, S. and Mahoney, D. (2001) *Economics of Sport*, Morgantown, WV: Fitness Information Technology (Chapter 2: 'Economic motives of sport organizations'). See also Sandy, R., Sloane, P. and Rosentraub, M. (2004) *The Economics of Sport: An International Perspective*, Basingstoke: Palgrave Macmillan (Chapter 2: 'Club and league objectives'). Another solid examination of the tension between maximizing profits on the one hand, and maximizing utility on the other, is contained in Babatunde, B. and Simmons, R. (2008) 'The profitability of sports teams: international perspectives', in Humphreys, B. and Howard, D. (eds) *The Business of Sports, Volume 1: Perspectives on the Sports Industry*, Westport, CT: Praeger, pp. 33–58.

For a detailed account of the financial evolution of sport organizations, see Andreff, W. and Staudohar, P. (2002) 'European and US sports business models', in Barros, C., Ibrahimo, M. and Szymanski, S. (eds) *Transatlantic Sport: The Comparative Economics of North American and European Sport*, Cheltenham: Edward Elgar, pp. 23–49. It is also worthwhile to review the Beech and Chadwick interpretation of sports' commercial transformation, which is contained in Beech, J. and Chadwick, S. (2013) 'The commercialization of sport', in Beech, J. and Chadwick, S. (eds) *The Business of Sport Management*, 2nd edition, Harlow: Pearson, pp. 3–22. The distinction between the sport-centred archetype and the business-centred archetype is explored in detail in Cousins, L. (1997) 'From diamonds to dollars: the dynamics of change in AAA baseball franchises', *Journal of Sport Management*, 11: 11–30.

For an in-depth discussion of how sport organizations around the world secure funds for their operations, go to Forster, J. and Pope, N. (2004) *The Political Economy of Global Sporting Organisations*, Abingdon: Routledge (Chapter 4: 'Sources of sport revenue'). An extensive examination of revenue sources for USA sports is provided by Howard, D. and Crompton, J. (2004) *Financing Sport*, 2nd edition, Morgantown, WV: Fitness Information Technology. The relevant sections are Chapter 7 on stadium seating and naming rights, Chapter 10 on broadcast rights, Chapter 11 on food service and souvenirs, Chapter 12 on sponsorship and Chapter 16 on fundraising.

Two excellent studies on the finances of community sport enterprises are contained in Wicker, P. (2011) 'Willingness-to-pay in non-profit sports clubs', *International Journal of Sport Finance*, 6, 155–69; and Wicker P., Breuer, C. and Pawlowski, T. (2010) 'Are sports club members big spenders? Findings from sport-specific analysis in Germany', *International Journal of Sport Finance*, 13(3): 214–24.

The concept of risk, and its implications for prudent financial management, are expertly handled in Brown, M., Rascher, D., Nagel, M. and McEvoy, C. (2010) *Financial Management in the Sport Industry*, Scottsdale, AZ: Holcomb Hathaway. Chapter 3 is worth reading, especially the sections on 'sources of risk' and 'sharing the risk'. They make the important point that risk goes up whenever high-interest loans are incurred, but falls when guaranteed revenue streams such as members' fees and long-term sponsor agreements are increased. Risk also falls when leagues regularly distribute money to clubs from a centralized funding pool. Brown *et al.* (2010) also apply risk analysis to a discussion of the strengths and weaknesses of debt financing on the one hand, and equity financing on the other. This is all done in Chapter 3.

USEFUL WEBSITES

- To get more details on the 'specificity of sport' concept, readers should visit **http://ec.europa.eu/sport/white-paper/white-paper_en.htm**.
- The ways in which the 'specificity of sport' impacts on the funding of sport programmes is neatly summarized in **www.publications.parliament.uk/pa/ld201011/ldselect/ldeucom/130/13007.htm**. Box 6 is especially illuminating.
- Another useful website that signals sport unique features is **http://sportsagentblog.com/2008/06/15/should-ec-law-accommodate-the-unique-characteristics-of-sport**.
- Funding models for sport in France and the UK are discussed in **http://s3.amazonaws.com/zanran_storage/www.egba.eu/ContentPages/2504888886.pdf**.
- An excellent slide show on funding models for sport in the European Union is available in **http://ec.europa.eu/internal_market/services/docs/sport/conference2010 0216/2-the_different_grassroots_sports_funding_models_in_the_eu_en.pdf**.
- A broad-ranging analysis of soccer stadium design and funding can be found in **www.forbes.com/sites/chrissmith/2013/11/20/major-league-soccers-stadium-revolution**.

CHAPTER 3

Financing big time sport

LEARNING OUTCOMES

At the end of this chapter readers will be able to:

- articulate the main features of professional sport, and discuss its global arrangements
- explain the financial arrangements that underpin professional sport around the world, and identify the shifts that have occurred in the relative strengths of different revenue streams
- explain why, in spite of the massive growth in revenues, many sport enterprises have been unable to achieve any sense of financial sustainability
- reflect on the pressure impacting on big-time sport, and the problems that can arise from imprudent financial management.

CHAPTER SUMMARY

This chapter picks up on the 'business of sport' idea, and the 'special features of sport' concept, both of which were discussed in Chapter 2. It does this by addressing the financing arrangement of mega-sport events, such as the Olympic and Commonwealth Games, and professional sport leagues, such as the American National Basketball League (NBA), Major League Baseball (MLB) and National Football League (NFL), the Australian Football League (AFL) and National Rugby League (NRL), and the English Premier League (EPL). It highlights the differences and similarities in funding, and in particular how revenues are sourced and distributed. The chapter ends by making three points about these financing arrangements. The first is that big-time sport no longer depends on gate receipts to deliver most of its annual revenues. Sport has radically diversified its sources of funds. The second is that, no matter what the scale of sport's revenue base, its spending often runs ahead of its revenues. This problem becomes a constant theme in the following chapters, and thus a number of tools for managing it are addressed. The third is that big-time sport has to balance spending on capital and facility infrastructure against spending on ongoing operations and event management. Again, this crucially important point is followed up in the remaining chapters.

THE CONTEXT

As noted in Chapter 2, over the last fifty years there has been a transformation in the structure and operation of sport. Professional sport now occupies more space than it ever did, and the many hundreds of small-scale community sports activities with shallow funding pools, and an emphasis on participation, have been overshadowed by those sports with mass spectator appeal (Forster and Pope 2004; Rein *et al.* 2006). The demise of amateurism, particularly in those sports with a large following, has provided the space for professionalization where many more players can make a living from the game. According to Foster *et al.* (2006) and Winfree and Rosentraub (2012), this explosion in sport's commercial development is the result of the growth in four over-arching revenue streams that have taken over from match-day receipts as the key revenue sources. While gate revenues account for just under 40 per cent of the American National Hockey League's (NHL's) total revenues, the figures for MLB, the NBA and the NFL are now just 36 per cent, 31 per cent and 23 per cent respectively (Mason and Howard 2008: 126). As a further point of contrast, the AFL, Australia's wealthiest sport enterprise, was dependent on gate receipts for 60–70 per cent of its total revenues during the early 1990s.

First, broadcasting rights fees are a pivotal driver of sports' commercial growth. In the USA in 2006, the NFL secured a multi-network and cable television agreement that provides it with USD 1,800 million over eight years. This in turn provided each NFL team with guaranteed base revenue of around USD 70 million for each of the eight years of the agreement. The Olympic Games also have a heavy dependency on income from the sale of broadcast rights. According to Dawson (2012) it has been the single largest revenue stream for the last twenty years.

Second, sponsorship has also become a major income source. Large multinational businesses not only provide financial support in return for the use of a team or league as a promotional vehicle, but the arrangement also allows participating organizations to create a co-branding strategy. The team or league gets the benefit of being linked to a successful business partner, while the business firm secures a promotional benefit from being associated with a high-profile sport organization and its supporter and viewer base. The Olympic Games is, once again, an exemplar. Dawson (2012) noted that it had mostly accounted for just over 20 per cent of total revenues, which was second to broadcast rights fees, which took up more than 50 per cent of total revenues.

A third emerging revenue source is various in-stadium and arena arrangements that can be secured by sport venue managers. These range from stadium naming rights and corporate box leasing, to preferential seat bookings, catering franchises and car parking facilities. In American professional sports especially, sales of prestige seating and stadium naming rights have become important sources of revenue (Mason and Howard 2008: 132–4).

Finally, professional sport has over recent times expanded its store-based sales of team- and league-related merchandise. This merchandise can take the form of branded apparel, gifts and mascots, and books, magazines and journals that provide statistics and inside stories on fans and favourite teams. There are finally videos and DVDs that provide mementos of special incidents and events. These items are listed in Table 3.1.

TABLE 3.1 Incremental revenue sources (beyond ticket sales)

1	Broadcasting rights fees (over-the-air, cable, direct)
	– national
	– local
	– internet (as a medium)
2	Sponsorships
	– teams
	– arenas
	– in-stadium/arena (signage, 'official' stadium concession brands)
	– broadcast ads
3	In-stadium/arena arrangements
	– naming rights
	– luxury boxes
	– personal seat licences
	– concessions
	– parking
4	Stores
	– branded retail partners
5	Licensed merchandise/equipment
6	Publications/videos

Source: Foster *et al.* (2006: 12).

These trends were first documented by Szymanski and Kuypers (2000) in their study of Premier League and professional world football in England between 1972 and 2000. They found that, while gate receipts have traditionally been the single most important income source, their relative importance has fallen over the last twenty years. While they were anywhere between 79 and 90 per cent of total annual revenue in the late 1970s, they fell as low as 40 per cent in the late 1990s. This figure is now around 35 per cent. This was not so much the result of falling attendances, but rather the result of the emergence of new sources of revenue.

CASE STUDY 3.1

The big American sport leagues

The home of big-time sport is the USA where professional sport leagues have been operating since the 1950s. The four dominant professional sport leagues are the National Football (gridiron) League (NFL), Major League Baseball (MLB), the National Basketball Association (NBA) and the National (ice) Hockey League (NHL).

These leagues are organized around governing Commissions, which coordinate the leagues' operations. They schedule games, negotiate broadcasting rights, set player salary limits and, most importantly, decide who can and cannot play in the leagues. That is, they control the sale of new franchises, although they allow franchise holders to move their teams to other cities and sell their franchises to a new owners. These features are common to cartels, and Chapter 5 will cover this theme in more detail. In addition, teams are for the most part privately owned by a coterie of investors and, unlike Australian professional sport, there is little room for non-profit, member-based clubs. Moreover, unlike some English Premier League clubs, they are not listed on the stock exchange, and therefore have very concentrated ownership.

The USA professional sport leagues are some of the most commercialized sport competitions in the world. According to Plunkett Research Group (2013), the NFL has the largest commercial support, with its thirty-two teams generating total revenues of just under USD 9 billion. The total revenue for MLB and its thirty teams is around USD 7 billion, the thirty NBA clubs deliver a total revenue of USD 4 billion, while the thirty NHL clubs provide revenues of just over USD 3 billion. The NFL also leads the attendance race, with an average game attendance of 68,000. MLB average attendance is 31,000, while NBA and NHL attendances come in at around 17,000.

A large part of these revenue streams is used to pay player salaries. In the NFL, salaries on average account for around USD 80 million, or 47 per cent of total club revenue. In MLB average club salaries are USD 70 million, which is 54 per cent of average club revenue. NBA average club salaries are USD 60 million, or 63 per cent of revenue, while NHL average club salaries are about USD 40 million, or 62 per cent of revenue (Plunkett Research Group 2013). The most profitable league is the NFL, despite its hefty wage bill. Its big advantage is that it has the highest capacity to pay, and has also successfully managed the wage demands of players through the application of a club salary cap. Figures for a sample of professional sport league club revenues and salaries are given in Table 3.2.

TABLE 3.2 Professional sport league clubs' average annual revenues and average player salaries, 2004

	USD million				GBP million	AUD million
	NFL	MLB	NBA	NHL	EPL	AFL
Average team revenue	170	130	95	70	65	25
Average team player salary bill	80	70	60	40	35	10

Sources: Howard and Crompton (2004); Stewart *et al.* (2005); Foster *et al.* (2006).

While the use of average figures to highlight the commercial scale of USA professional sport leagues can be quite revealing, it can also be misleading by hiding the differences between clubs. The differences are greatest in those leagues that do not have a broad-based revenue redistribution scheme. The NFL and NBA have for some time had regulations that provide for the sharing of major revenue items such as broadcasting rights fees and gate receipts, but this has not historically been the case with MLB and the NHL. As a result, MLB clubs that represented large urban centres such as New York and Chicago had commercial advantages over clubs that were situated in regional America. It therefore came as no surprise to find that, whereas in 2001 the New York Yankees generated revenues of USD 240 million, the Minnesota Twins and the Kansas City Royals took in USD 56 million and USD 64 million respectively (Howard and Crompton 2004). It was noted that, as a result of these huge revenue disparities, only one-third of all league teams had a real chance of reaching the play-offs (or World Series, as they like to be called in the USA). In 2002, a new MLB collective bargaining agreement provided for both a salary cap and a system for redistributing gate monies from richer to poorer clubs, but inequities still occurred. In 2005, for example, the Atlanta Braves, the Kansas City Royals and the Houston Astros, on the one hand, all made profits of more than 20 per cent. On the other hand, the Florida Marlins and the Boston Red Sox incurred losses of more than 20 per cent (Buraimo and Simmons 2008: 34). It was also clear that some clubs that had previously been profitable were now making losses.

CASE STUDY 3.2

The Olympic Games – financial constraints and strategic opportunities

As noted in Chapter 1, the Olympic Games is an exemplar of the financial complexity that underpins the planning and management of professional sport in general, and mega-sport events in particular. The Olympic Games no longer involve the expenditure of millions of dollars, but rather the spending of billions of dollars. Moreover, they rely on many funding sources for both the construction of facilities and stadia and the operation of the events themselves. The other thing to remember is that the International Olympic Committee (IOC) awards the Games to a city and not a private organization. The onus is consequently on the host city and its organizing committee to raise sufficient funds to ensure a quality event. A host city contract is negotiated, which makes the host city responsible not only for all facility development and operational activities (including the opening and closing ceremonies), but also for ensuring that every event meets the standards set by the appropriate international sporting governing body (Preuss 2000, 2004).

At the general structural level there are four possible funding sources for the host city. The first source of funds is local government and the city itself. There are good reasons to expect the city to provide either cash or in-kind support, since it will be the recipient of enormous international media exposure, and for the most part it will also be favourable unless there is a major management catastrophe. In practice though, the host city only ever provides a small percentage of funds to support the Games, although in 1996 the city of Atlanta spent around USD 294 million on facility improvement. For the most part the host city will invest in facility upgrade, traffic infrastructure and security. The second source of funds is the regional or provincial government within which the host city is located. In the case of the Sydney Olympic Games the State Government of New South Wales was the major source of funds for facility construction. The large-scale funding of facility development is defended on the grounds that the taxpayers will not only benefit directly from the Games themselves, but also benefit from the legacy of having international standard sport facilities for later use. The third source of funds is the national government. National governments have been important contributors over time, and have justified their spending on the grounds that a mega-sport event such as the Olympic Games provides many broad benefits, ranging from international prestige and more tourists, to the construction of social and economic infrastructure and urban renewal. The final source is the private sector, which involves all those profit-based businesses that manufacture and distribute goods and services to the community. The private sector not only provides funds in the form of sponsorship, but also designs, constructs and operates facilities for use during the Games. In short, the Olympic Games can be funded either through the public purse (i.e. the various levels of government) or through the private sector. Or, it could be a mix of both.

In practice, there has been a wide variety of funding arrangements used to finance the Olympics over the last forty years. On the one hand, the most heavily government-funded Games were the 1976 Montreal Olympics, 1990 Moscow Olympics and the 2004 Athens Games. In fact, it was estimated that the National Government of Greece had spent nearly USD 10 billion on getting the infrastructure in place (Humphreys and Zimbalist 2008: 104). On the other hand, the most heavily privately funded Games were the 1984 Los Angeles Olympics. Table 3.3 summarizes the different funding sources for the Olympics.

TABLE 3.3 Funding mix for a sample of Summer Olympic Games

Host city	Private funding percentage	Public funding percentage
Munich 1972	19	81
Montreal 1976	5	95
Moscow 1980	0	100
Los Angeles 1984	98	2
Seoul 1988	56	44
Barcelona 1992	62	38
Atlanta 1996	85	15
Sydney 2000	30	70

Source: Preuss (2000: 33).

The use of a private–public divide to explain the funding for the Olympics is interesting, but it only illuminates part of the funding problem. It is also important to examine the more focused questions of how much income or revenue was secured, what form it took and what it was used for. For instance, while the Sydney Olympic Games cost around AUD 3,500 million to mount and run, it is also crucially important to see if total incomes matched the costs. The next task is to identify the revenue breakdown and see, for example, what proportion came from ticket sales, and what proportion came from broadcast right fees, and how much came from sponsorships. The other interesting question to ask is how much was allocated to facility construction, and how much was allocated to the management and overall operation of the Games themselves.

The most obvious thing to note is that the Games are expensive to organize, wherever they are held. In real terms, every Olympic Games since the 1990s has cost at least USD 4,000 million to set up and conduct. Until recently the two most expensive Games were Barcelona in 1992 and Athens in 2004. However, the spending bar was raised at the 2008 Beijing Games and 2012 London Games. At last count it was calculated that the London 2012 Olympic Games cost just under GBP 9,000 million to stage and operate. The least expensive was Los Angeles in 1984, where a large proportion of events were run in existing facilities. The capital investment and operating costs of selected Games between 1972 and 2004 are listed in Table 3.4.

TABLE 3.4 Capital and operating costs for selected Olympic Games (USD millions)

	Munich	Montreal	Moscow	Los Angeles	Seoul	Barcelona	Atlanta	Sydney	Athens
	1972	1976	1980	1984	1988	1992	1996	2000	2004
Capital	*	*	*	*	700	1,500	1,000	2,200	2,400
Operation	546	399	*	467	512	1,610	1,200	1,300	3,100
Total funds	*	*	*	*	1,212	3,110	2,200	3,500	5,500

Source: Preuss (2000: 33, 197).

Note: * Figures not available.

In discussing the total costs of mounting the Olympic Games, the key point is to distinguish between the costs of investing in facilities and venues and overall infrastructure (i.e. the capital costs) and the costs of actually running the Games (the operating costs or expenses). The capital costs can vary significantly since there may be a need, on the one hand, to build most of the sports infrastructure from scratch, while, on the other hand, it may be just a matter of upgrading and improving existing facilities. This accounts for the massive costs of mounting the Athens Games, since not only did operating costs escalate mainly because of the increase in security costs,

TABLE 3.5 Facility construction for selected Olympic Games

	Munich 1972	Montreal 1976	Los Angeles 1984	Seoul 1988	Barcelona 1992	Atlanta 1996	Sydney 2000	Athens 2004	Beijing 2008
Main stadium	new	new	existing	existing	existing	new	new	new	new
Swim centre	new	new	new	new	existing	new	existing	new	new
Velodrome	new	new	new	new	existing	new	new	new	new
Main arena	new	existing	existing	new	new	existing	new	new	new

Source: Preuss (2000: 203).

but capital costs were also high because most of the venues had to be built from the ground up. The capital costs also exploded because of their very complex architectural design requirements. The IOC bid document guidelines make this distinction very clear in order to ensure both comparable submissions and transparent figures on each cost dimension. Table 3.5 compares the extent to which different host cities constructed new facilities for the Games, or alternatively used existing facilities.

As far as operating expenses are concerned, the IOC also requires bidding cities to break down the expenses into the following categories:

- in-Games venue and event operations;
- pre-Games events;
- opening and closing ceremonies;
- general administration of the Games;
- technology;
- advertising and promotion;
- security;
- catering;
- medical;
- transport.

Again, this allows the IOC to obtain a clear and comparative picture of what the operating budget will look like, and also highlights areas where there are either very conservative estimates, or where spending seems to be extravagant.

When comparing total Games operating expenditures, two distinct phases emerge over the 1972 to 2012 period. The first phase begins with the 1972 Munich Games and ends with the 1988 Seoul Games. During this phase operating expenses plateaued. Whereas Munich cost USD 546 million to run, Montreal cost USD 399 million, Los Angeles cost USD 467 million and Seoul cost USD 512 million. The second phase begins with Barcelona in 1992 and goes through to the present time. In Barcelona operating expenses more than doubled to USD 1,610 million. The figure fell to USD 1,200 million in 1996 in Atlanta, but increased to USD 1,300 million in Sydney and USD 3,100 million in Athens. According to Preuss (2004) the main reasons for the increase are multi-fold. Contrary to what some critics had to say about the extravagance of the Games, it was not due to higher opening and closing ceremony costs. The real reasons had more to do with the growing complexity of Games resulting from more participants, more sport disciples, more test or pre-Games events, more technical requirements for events and greater security.

When Games total fundings are addressed it is not surprising that this figure has also increased dramatically over the last thirty-five years. Whereas the organizers of the Munich Games raised USD 1,000 million, it had risen to USD 1,300 million by Seoul and nearly USD 3,500 million in Sydney. This increase arose out of tapping into new sources of revenue while also increasing existing sources. In addition, some traditional sources actually fell over this period. The most dramatic increases occurred in revenue raising from sponsorship and broadcasting rights fees.

The revenue sources for both Munich and Montreal are in stark contrast to current revenue-raising arrangements. At both of these Games most of the revenue was raised from the sale of commemorative coins and stamps and the proceeds from a Games lottery. In the case of Munich it was close to 90 per cent. Both television rights fees and ticket sales accounted for less than 10 per cent each, while sponsorship income was less than 5 per cent of total revenue. The traditional revenue-raising mould was seriously broken in Los Angeles, when broadcast rights fees accounted for 30 per cent of revenue raised, while sponsorship accounted for around 20 per cent. The proportion of revenue raised from ticket sales had also increased to 20 per cent. The contribution of sponsorship, broadcast rights fees and ticket income is more significant when the Atlanta Olympic Games are examined. In this case sponsorship accounted for 30 per cent, broadcast rights fees now accounted for 30 per cent (the same as Los Angeles), while ticket sales were now 25 per cent of total revenue. Sydney, Athens, Beijing and London were similarly dependent on broadcast rights fees, sponsorship and ticket income (Preuss 2004; Dawson 2012).

CASE STUDY 3.3

English Premier League

Another example of sport's financial and commercial transformation over the last twenty years is world football in England. During the 1980s, English football faced a variety of crises that ranged from falling attendances and rampant hooliganism to decrepit, unsafe stadia (King 1998). In 1991, in an attempt to solve some of the game's structural problems, the governing body of English football, the Football

Association (FA), published its *Blueprint for the Future of Football*, which recommended the reinvention of its first division competition as the Premier League. One of the first things the Premier League did was to renegotiate the television broadcast contract, which was previously held by the Independent Television network, ITV. Coincidentally, around this time Rupert Murdoch's News Limited had consolidated its pay television station, BSkyB, and was seeking programmes that would not only rate well in the first instance, but also provide the catalyst for an expansion of pay television subscribers. After spirited bidding and legal challenges, BSkyB finally secured the rights to broadcast sixty live games of Premier League a year for AUD 50 million a year (Gratton 2000). This was substantially higher than the AUD 11 million annual rights fee paid by ITV between 1998 and 1991. The English Premier League (EPL) has now become one of the wealthiest sport competitions in the world on the back of its broadcast rights agreement with BSkyB, which delivers to the EPL around GBP 1 billion a year (Gratton and Solberg 2013). This approximates to around AUD 2 billion or USD 1.8 billion.

Some of the EPL's member clubs are public companies and listed on the stock exchange, but most of the wealthiest are now owned by private investors. Annual revenues for the richest clubs, such as Manchester United, Chelsea, Liverpool and Arsenal, now exceed GBP 300 million, and players can earn up to GBP 3 million for a single season of play.

Like the US professional sport leagues, the EPL has been able to increase its wealth through accessing a broad base of revenue streams. At the big-end of the professional sport league spectrum, Manchester United's revenue comes principally from match-day receipts (30–35 per cent), media rights fees (35–40 per cent) and commercial sponsorship and merchandising (25–35 per cent). The main revenue items for EPL clubs are illustrated in Figure 3.1.

At the same time there are other clubs in the EPL that earn significantly less. Whereas in 2002 Manchester United generated revenues of GBP 148 million, Aston Villa could only secure GBP 47 million to fund its operations. Ten years later, in 2011–12, revenues exploded, but the inequalities still abound. Whereas Newcastle United had built up its annual revenue base to just over EUR 115 million, Manchester United's revenue had weighed in at EUR 395 million, which is three times that of Newcastle United. Aston Villa was struggling to reach EUR 90 million (Deloitte Sports Business Group 2013). The revenues and tangible assets for a sample of EPL clubs in the early 2000s are listed in Table 3.6.

This earnings discrepancy can be explained by the simple fact that the wealthiest clubs are also the most successful, and have a much broader and deeper fan base. In short, commercial success breeds on-field success, which in turns generates additional commercial success, which further feeds on-field success. A study of the EPL by Szymanski and Kuypers (2000) and a follow-up review by Szymanski (2010a) found a very close correlation between a club's average annual revenue and league performance. For example, between 1972 and 1990 the highest-earning clubs were Liverpool, Manchester United and Tottenham Hotspur. They also filled three of the top five performance spots throughout this period. This state of affairs is even more evident today. The only thing that has altered is that the order has slightly changed.

FIGURE 3.1 Revenue sources for English football clubs

Source: Szymanski and Kuypers (2000: 39).

TABLE 3.6 Total revenues and tangible assets for a sample of EPL clubs, 2002 (GBP millions)

Clubs	Revenue	Tangible assets
Arsenal	91	46
Aston Villa	47	42
Chelsea	115	180
Leeds United	99	40
Liverpool	82	43
Manchester United	148	130
Newcastle United	71	94
Tottenham Hotspur	65	46
Average	89	78

Source: Gerrard (2004b: 74).

Over the last ten years Manchester United has taken over from Liverpool as the most financially powerful club and not surprisingly also as the best-performing club. As Arsenal and Chelsea have deepened their pool of funds, so too has their performance improved. All of this begs the question as to how the EPL's financial resources might be spread more evenly to allow more clubs to share the on-field spoils.

CASE STUDY 3.4

Australian Rules football and Australian rugby league

Australia's leading professional sport leagues are the Australian Football League (AFL) and the National Rugby League (NRL). Neither league has clubs listed on the stock exchange, although some NRL clubs are owned by private consortia. The AFL comprises a majority of member-controlled clubs constituted as companies limited by guarantee, which means they do not have to pay income tax, but cannot distribute any profits to external stakeholders. So it can be said that both leagues are essentially non-profit entities, where surplus funds are reinvested in league and club development.

TABLE 3.7 AFL and NRL revenues and valuations, 2005 (AUD millions)

AFL club finances			NRL club finances		
Team	Total revenue	Value	Team	Total revenue	Value
Collingwood	39	44	Brisbane	20	18
Brisbane	32	37	St George	15	14
Hawthorn	29	34	Melbourne	13	13
West Coast	29	33	Canterbury	13	12
Essendon	28	33	Newcastle	13	12
Sydney	28	32	Sydney City	12	12
Geelong	27	31	Parramatta	12	11
Fremantle	26	29	Canberra	11	11
Port Power	24	27	North Queensland	11	10
Richmond	23	27	New Zealand	10	9
Melbourne	24	26	West Tigers	10	9
Adelaide	22	25	Penrith	9	9
St Kilda	21	25	Cronulla	9	9
Carlton	20	24	Manly	9	5
Kangaroos	22	24	South Sydney	9	4
Western Bulldogs	21	23			

Source: *Business Review Weekly*, 16–22 March 2006, p. 39.

The AFL has historically generated more revenue than the NFL, which is the result of its larger match attendance, broader base of sponsorship and greater broadcasting rights fee. Whereas the AFL annual TV rights fee in 2005 was AUD 156 million, the NRL TV rights fee was just under AUD 80 million a year. However, they were both significantly in excess of the newly established world-football A-League, which, because of its smaller fan base, could only negotiate an AUD 17 million a year agreement with FOX Sports, the pay TV network.

Table 3.7 compares the annual revenue and valuation figures of AFL clubs with those of NRL clubs for 2005. While the median revenue for AFL clubs was around AUD 25 million, it was only AUD 11 million for NRL clubs. This reflects not only the higher broadcast fee for AFL, but its much larger average game attendance figure (35,000 compared with 15,000). In fact, the average game attendance for the AFL was the fourth largest for sport leagues around the world. This is a startling figure in view of the fact that Australia has a population of only 23 million, which is nearly 300 million fewer than the USA. The USA's NFL is ranked first, with an average game attendance in excess of 65,000, followed by the German Bundesliga with 40,000 and the EPL with 36,000.

The table also contains a valuation of clubs, in which a much higher value is placed on AFL clubs. These valuation figures also beg the question as to how the valuations are calculated, why some clubs will be valued more highly than others, and the relationship between a club's annual stream of revenues, its business value and its overall level of wealth. This will be discussed in the next chapter.

RECAP

Professional sport leagues around the world have not only built massive fan support, but also created a complex set of demands on their management teams. The drive to succeed has led to a constant search for funds to secure a competitive edge. The pressure that comes from the availability of competing entertainment experiences has also forced venue managers to deliver the highest-quality service to spectators. This means that too much money is never enough. This presents a troublesome dilemma for finance officers and managers. Should they do all that it takes to accommodate the demands of CEOs, coaches and fans, or should they say that enough is enough, and suggest that frugality is not always a bad thing?

REVIEW QUESTIONS

With the above points in mind the following questions arise. There are many issues that demand attention in the light of the explosive commercial growth of sport around the world in recent times.

1 What are the most important revenue sources for professional sport teams? Where does gate revenue rank as a source of revenue? Is it more or less important than it once was?

2 Explain how sport stadia and their design features are used to generate revenue for stadium owners, teams and leagues.

3 Rank American sport leagues on the basis of their average team revenues.

4 How can these revenue differences and income inequalities be explained?

5 To what extent do revenue inequalities exist within leagues?

6 Which leagues have the greatest levels of inter-club inequality, and how can it be explained?

7 Calculate the proportion of total team revenues accounted for by player payments. Is there a common theme here, or is there not?

8 What scales of salaries are paid to professional team sport players around the world? In which sport leagues do you find the highest paid, and in which sport leagues do you find the lowest paid?

9 How do you explain these differences?

10 Explain how the Olympic Games are funded, being careful to point out the strengths and weaknesses of their financial arrangements.

11 Over the last thirty years how important has government been as a funding source for the Olympic Games?

12 Compare the capital cost of hosting the last four Olympic Games with their operating costs.

13 Explain the origins of the EPL, and the source of its commercial growth.

14 How wealthy are EPL clubs, and how do the revenue streams compare to North American professional sport teams?

15 Contrast the revenues of the main professional sport teams in Australia. How would you explain the revenue gap between the AFL and NRL? How do they compare with clubs in professional football leagues in America and Europe?

FURTHER READING

A detailed analysis of the operation of big-time sport is contained in Humphreys, B. and Howard, D. (eds) (2008) *The Business of Sports, Volume 1: Perspectives on the Sports Industry*, Westport, CT: Praeger. Readers should give special attention to the chapters written by (1) Babatunde and Simmons, who look at the profitability of sports teams, (2) Humphreys and Zimbalist, who examine the financing and economic impact of the Olympic Games, and (3) Mason and Howard, who discuss new revenue streams in professional sports.

An additional discussion of the business of American sport is contained in Winfree, J. and Rosentraub, M. (2012) *Sports Finance and Management: Real Estate, Entertainment, and the Remaking of Business*, Boca Raton, FL: CRC Press. Of special interest are Chapter 2 ('Structures of ownership'), Chapter 8 ('What are teams worth?') and Chapter 3

('Financial statements, revenues and costs'). For another revealing overview of the structure and operation of American professional sport leagues, see Brown, M., Rascher, D., Nagel, M. and McEvoy, C. (2010) *Financial Management in the Sport Industry*, Scottsdale, AZ: Holcomb Hathaway (Chapter 15: 'Professional sport').

An extensive discussion of the finances of North American professional sport leagues is also found in Howard, D. and Crompton, J. (2004) *Financing Sport*, 2nd edition, Morgantown, WV: Fitness Information Technology, which provides a chapter-by-chapter breakdown of revenue sources, with special attention to ticket sales and broadcasting rights' fees. See also Foster, G., Greyser, P. and Walsh, B. (2006) *The Business of Sports: Texts and Cases on Strategy and Management*, Mason, OH: Thomson (section 2 on leagues, including a discussion on women's professional sport in the USA, section 3 on clubs, which includes comparative studies of sport clubs in different leagues, section 8 on broadcasting, media and sports, and, finally, section 10 on financial valuation and profitability). An additional overview of the key commercial issues being addressed in American sport is contained in Rosner, S. and Shropshire, K. (2004) *The Business of Sports*, Sudbury, MA: Jones and Bartlett.

One of the most comprehensive studies of the commercial evolution of the Olympic Games has been undertaken by Barney, R., Wenn, S. and Martyn, S. (2002) *Selling the Five Rings: The International Olympic Committee and the Rise of Olympic Commercialisation*, Salt Lake City, UT: University of Utah Press. See also Preuss, H. (2000) *Economics of the Olympic Games: Hosting the Games 1972–2000*, Petersham, NSW: Walla Walla Press. For a more political analysis of the commercial expansion of the Olympics, see Pound, R. (2004) *Inside the Olympics*, Mississauga, Ont.: Wiley. The most relevant sections are Chapter 6, which looks at corporate partnerships, and Chapter 7, which addresses broadcast rights.

One of the most detailed analyses of EPL finances is provided in Szymanski, S. and Kuypers, T. (2000) *Winners and Losers*, London: Penguin. Chapter 2, which provides detailed data on revenue, and how it impacts on performance, is particularly illuminating. Also see Morrow, S. (2003) *The People's Game? Football Finance and Society*, Basingstoke: Palgrave Macmillan. Other references on the commercial expansion of EPL include Gratton, C. (2000) 'The peculiar economics of English professional football', in Garland, J., Malcolm, P. and Rowe, M. (eds) *The Future of Football*, London: Frank Cass, pp. 11–28. An earlier critique of the commercialization of English football can be found in Horton, E. (1997) *Moving the Goal Posts: Football's Exploitation*, Edinburgh: Mainstream.

USEFUL WEBSITES

- An excellent overview of player salaries in American sport leagues is contained in **http://sports.yahoo.com/nba/news?slug=ycn-10423863**.
- The average salaries paid to players in European football are listed in **http://soccer lens.com/highest-football-club-wages/69045**.
- *Forbes* carries many well-researched articles on football finances. See, for instance, **www.forbes.com/sites/christinasettimi/2012/04/18/the-worlds-highest-paid-soccer-players**.

- A longitudinal analysis of American pro-sport finances is contained in **www.wrham brecht.com/wp-content/uploads/2013/09/SportsMarketReport_2012.pdf**.
- An excellent analysis of global sport's commercial future, and likely trends in revenues, has been undertaken by PricewaterhouseCoopers. The 2011 report can be found at **www.pwc.com/en_gx/gx/hospitality-leisure/pdf/changing-the-game-outlook-for-the-global-sports-market-to-2015.pdf**.
- A commentary on the EPL blueprint 'twenty years on' is contained in **www.soccerex. com/media-centre/soccerex-blog/the-premier-league-at-20-the-saviour-of-football**.
- The following website contains an instructive commentary on the 2009 Football Association's proposal for a new 'blueprint', and how it was undermined by EPL clubs: **http://andersred.blogspot.com.au/2011/02/exclusive-fa-blueprint-for-reform. html**.

CHAPTER 4

Wealth, profits and inequality in sport enterprises

LEARNING OUTCOMES

At the end of this chapter readers will be able to:

- understand the meaning of wealth and value, and how these concepts can be used to calculate the financial worth of sport enterprises
- additionally understand the meaning of income and profits, while appreciating the fact that they are quite distinct from wealth and value
- explain how wealth is accumulated, how wealth is measured, the different forms wealth can take, and the virtuous cycle of wealth creation
- discuss the wealth inequalities that exist in sports throughout the world, and how these sometimes obscenely unfair differentials have come about.

CHAPTER SUMMARY

This chapter introduces a basic concept for understanding the financial status of sport enterprises, and their likely future viability. It is wealth, which can also be interpreted as value. The chapter first of all defines what wealth is, and then assesses how it can be used to measure the financial well-being of sport enterprises. It shows that, while wealth is a good indicator of long-term financial performance, it does not say much about the current, or day-to-day, operations of clubs, associations and leagues, or explain much about their profitability. The chapter goes on to discuss the notions of revenue and profit, and the ways in which revenues, and especially profits, impact on wealth. Evidence is provided in support of the claim that wealth and profit differentials in the sports world are enormous, and are frequently problematic. An effort is made to explain these differences. Special emphasis is given to how wealth is accumulated, how wealth is measured, the different forms wealth can take, and the virtuous cycle of wealth creation where profits are used to build more income-earning assets, which can in turn be used to deliver even more profits. The chapter ends with a detailed discussion of the essential differences between wealth and value on the one hand, and between wealth and revenue and profits on the other, and thus why it is critically important to carefully define any financial concepts or terms before using them to explain the performance of sport enterprises.

WHAT MAKES SOME SPORT ENTERPRISES WEALTHY AND PROFITABLE, AND OTHERS NOTHING MORE THAN PAUPERS?

As the previous chapters show, not only has sport in general become more commercialized and professionalized over the last fifty years, but it has also delivered significant inequalities (Deloitte Sports Business Group 2013). Many clubs, associations and leagues have become very wealthy, but many other sport enterprises are barely making ends meet, and as a result are just managing to provide the most basic of services to players and members. Moreover, even within the same league or competition, a few clubs can snare more than what seems to be their fair share of funds and resources. This begs the question as to what factors and forces impact on the wealth of a club, league or competition, and why some clubs become increasingly profitable and wealthy, while others stagnate.

MAKING SENSE OF WEALTH INEQUALITIES

An illuminating explanation of the wealth disparities between sport enterprises is provided by Szymanski and Kuypers (2000), who begin by making the salient point that, while sport is not just another form of business, since it frequently privileges winning over profits, it has a strong interest in building the brand and increasing its wealth. Rein *et al.* (2006: 50–1) take a similar line when they talk about the 'elusive fan', and how important it is to build sport brands that connect with the increasingly demanding aspirations of sports' customers. Szymanski and Kuypers (2000) go on to say that, in sport, just like business, financial success in general and profitability in particular come about from two core generic sources.

Different industry structures and conduct

The first source of financial success has to do with industry structure and conduct. Industry structure is crucially important since it includes the demand for the product or service. In sport, the demand conditions vary enormously and, generally speaking, the higher the demand, the greater the revenue streams that will ensue (Winfree and Rosentraub (2012). This is why clubs located in densely populated spaces have a 'revenue generation' advantage over clubs facing a dispersed population.

Industry structure also includes the issues of costs and how technology is used to deliver the service to the public. In sport, cost-cutting is not usually used to secure a strategic edge and, in any case, costs are often the same for different clubs. Sport technology is a little more problematic, since it has changed little in some areas, but in other respects has changed a lot. These days, social media can be used to secure a financial edge by claiming the interest of young people who delight in building relationships with others via Facebook and Twitter. Some clubs have been highly successful in capturing this fan segment, while others have not.

Industry structure also influences the barriers to entry into the industry. In sport leagues the barriers to entry are usually very strong since the governing body or central administration will have sole control over the structure of the league, and which new teams will be allowed to enter. High entry barriers will often protect member teams by enabling existing clubs, for example, to extract the same income share from an ever-increasing financial pie.

On balance, the structure of sport leagues not only protects member clubs from the threat of entry of competitors, but also guarantees teams a captive fan base – or market, if you like – by ensuring both a broad spatial spread of teams, and minimal levels of geographical overlap. In theory this means that all member clubs will be able to secure expanding revenues, big profits and a strong bundle of assets.

The consequent opportunity to engage in a diverse range of industry conduct is also important since it establishes the competitive environment and determines the level of rivalry between businesses and what form the rivalry takes. In some sport leagues the rivalry between clubs is always strong in respect of on-field success. However, when it comes to revenue expansion and wealth creation there is a wide variety of behaviours, as well as constraints on those behaviours. While sport leagues such as the EPL have few constraints on the behaviour of member clubs and teams, the NFL and AFL are much more severely constrained by rules about player salary caps, player recruitment and transfers, ticket prices and the distribution of league revenues. As Chapter 5 shows, heavily regulated sport leagues will diminish inter-team rivalry in their off-field activities and also create more centralized control, which can in turn lead to cartel-type behaviour. Also, cartel behaviours are often used to restrict supply, increase prices and increase revenue, which may run counter to the interests of fans and other external stakeholders.

This structure–conduct approach to business behaviour – which says that structures impact on the behavioural possibilities for clubs and teams, both good and bad – also underpins the five-force model first developed by the international business consultant, Michael Porter, in the 1980s. Porter argues that an industry's potential for generating a competitive advantage and long-term profitability depends upon the degree of inter-firm rivalry, the threat of new entrants, the availability of substitute products, the power of buyers and the power of suppliers. This means, on the one hand, that a business operating in an industry where new firms can easily enter and substitute services are freely available, competition is fierce, and so buyers have a high degree of bargaining power and suppliers can dictate prices; these businesses will only make slim profits. On the other hand, where entry of new firms is difficult, key resources are scarce, and both buyers and sellers are fragmented, the potential for profit will be high (Mauws *et al.* 2003).

Different levels of resources and capabilities

The second source of financial success has to do with a company's strategic resources and capabilities. Sport clubs can secure a competitive advantage through a number of tactical focal points. The first tactical focal point is innovation, and in the case of professional sport clubs it can take the form of improved administrative processes or the use of science and technology to improve player rehabilitation programmes, player decision-making and on-field performance. The second tactical focal point is access to strategic assets, which, in the case of sport, includes coaching skills and tactical know-how. It can also include the recruitment of outstanding players whose abilities cannot be easily replicated. The third tactical focal point is the reputation of the club and its capacity to attract fan support outside its surrounding geography, and meet the aspirations of potential corporate sponsors. The reputation of the club can also be strengthened by a branding campaign that aims to secure a strong identity and image that has mass public appeal. This is the point that Rein *et al.* (2006) rate highly. The fourth tactical focal point is the strength of a club's architecture, which comprises its internal management structures, its strategic aspirations and the relationships that it can build up with its stakeholders. This might involve a high degree of trust between club officials, players and the players' union, or strong links between coaching staff and the sports science department at a nearby university. This becomes the essence of partnership building.

This 'asset building' approach to business strategy and corporate behaviour is encapsulated in the resourced-based view (RBV) of the firm, and how it can be used to gain an edge over competitors. According to Barney (1991), a competitive edge, additional success and greater profits are most effectively gained by not so much reducing the level of intra-industry competition, but rather by assembling an array of quality resources. First, that they are valuable (that is, they generate greater efficiencies), second, they are scarce (that is, they are not easily available to competitors) and, third, they are inimitable (that is, unique) and not easily copied. In short, superior performance will result from a strong endowment of resources that cannot be matched by competitors, enables greater efficiencies to be achieved and delivers greater product quality. The RBV is thus particularly relevant to sport where access to the best player talent, quality coaches and strong support systems can quickly secure a winning edge (Smart and Wolfe 2000; Mauws *et al.* 2003; Gerrard 2012).

The ways in which these factors impact on league and team profitability are illustrated in Figure 4.1. This model is instructive in the way it highlights both the context in which sport organizations operate and their scope to implement strategies that may secure a competitive advantage. However, its foundations are set in the commercial and business world, and not in sport. It is therefore important to design a more sport-specific model of profit generation and wealth creation that takes into account the special features of sport as discussed in Chapter 2. Gerrard's (2005) model of sport-team ownership value, and Gerrard's (2012) model of effectiveness and efficiency in professional team sports, provide a good explanatory framework since they have as their starting point the crucial proposition that profit and wealth creation in sport result from both on-field or sporting performance and off-field or financial performance. Gerrard also makes the important point that the two components are closely linked. That is, improved on-field success will produce a financially healthy outcome, while a sound financial base is likely to produce an improvement in on-field performance. Szymanski and Kuypers (2000) also make this point clearly in their research. This, of course, begs the question as to what specifically underpins strong on-field performance, and what drives better off-field performance.

According to Gerrard, the key to better on-field performance is the availability of playing talent and quality coaching, while the key to better off-field performance is, as Rein *et al.* (2006) reiterate, a strong fan base – which includes both community and corporate support – and managerial efficiency. Dolles and Soderman (2013: 380–2) bring player performance and managerial efficiency together when they talk about 'value capture', which is all about getting a competitive advantage through attracting additional

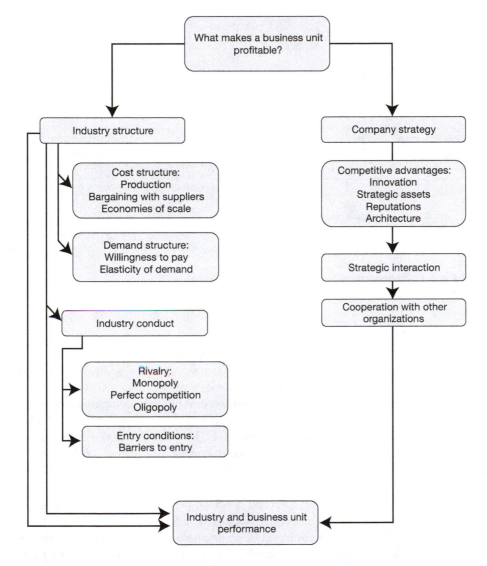

FIGURE 4.1 Contextual and strategic influences on organizational profitability

Source: Szymanski and Kuypers (2000: 132).

resources and utilizing them cleverly. This can occur on both the supply side (experienced administrative staff and skilled coaches) and the demand side (more fans and more corporate partners). Thus, the strong fan base will provide a lucrative revenue stream, while managerial efficiency will contain costs. This sports-specific model of profit generation and wealth creation can be illustrated as in Figure 4.2.

This model provides a succinct picture of what drives sport club performance, what enables a competitive advantage to emerge and why some clubs regularly outperform others.

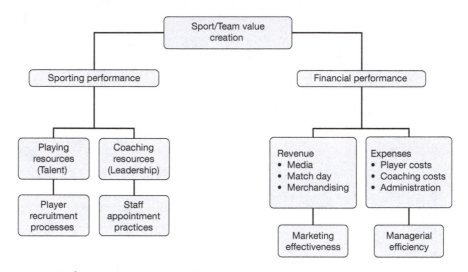

FIGURE 4.2 Profit generation and wealth creation in sport

Financial sustainability

Another explanation of what underpins a sporting club's financial sustainability is provided by Foster *et al.* (2006). They claim that the financial strength of a sport club is linked to six drivers. The first driver is the scale and strength of the league to which the club belongs. In Australia the superior financial position of AFL clubs compared to other pro-sport league clubs, such as world football and rugby league, is in part the result of a larger spectator base and much higher television rights fees. In Great Britain the clubs and teams that comprise the Premier League have a similar advantage over teams and clubs in lower-status world-football leagues, as well as clubs playing in the elite but less popular rugby league and rugby union competitions.

The second driver is the club's current level of performance and the scale of its supporter base. Specific performance-related factors include its on-field ranking, the quality of its coaching staff and player roster, and current marquee players. Some of the more important off-field factors include membership levels, the club's sponsor portfolio and its capacity to control the post-game behaviour of problem players.

The third driver is the club brand and its associated history and traditions. In every major sport league there is a coterie of clubs whose rich history of success give them a major branding advantage over other clubs. In the EPL, Manchester United and Liverpool have the strongest brands, which in large part are based on their rich tradition of iconic players, on-field achievements and fan support (Andrews 2004), and, as Rein *et al.* (2006) demonstrate, strong sports brands can deliver escalating levels of profits and wealth.

The fourth driver is the stadium in which the club plays it home matches. As Winfree and Rosentraub (2012: 113–38, 175–202) explain, the stadium capacity, the quality of its facilities and its location and accessibility all impact on the attendances and revenue. The Melbourne Cricket Ground (MCG) is one of the world's best-known sport venues, and the combination of a rich history, proximity to the central business district, public transport and quality facilities enables it to attract more fans than any other sport stadium in Australia. Clubs that play out of the MCG consequently have an advantage over clubs that use less glamorous venues.

The fifth driver is the city or region in which the club is located. In some cities sport fandom is a peripheral cultural practice, whereas in other cities sport watching and sport participation in general are embedded within the community's social fabric. Also, a one-city team will have an advantage over teams that have to compete against other teams in the same city for the loyalty of fans and the support of sponsors (Winfree and Rosentraub 2012: 98). In addition, the size of the surrounding population will affect a club's financial viability. A team that has a catchment of 500,000 potential fans will have a significant commercial advantage over a team with 200,000 likely supporters.

The final driver is the owner's attributes and the club culture. While, on the one hand, owners and managers may be completely committed to doing all it takes to win, on the other hand they may be so conservative and frugal that they will not risk excessive outlays to achieve on-field success. Gerrard (2012) highlights this crucially important point by noting that, unlike commercial businesses, sport enterprises can choose to maximize profits, on the one hand, or maximize utility – that is winning and on-field success – on the other. Teams are thus faced with a performance trade-off. According to Gerrard, as teams 'enhance the quality of their playing squad', there comes a point where the 'increased revenue from the expected improvement in sporting performance' will not be enough to cover the 'increased wage cost incurred in recruiting more talented players' (2012: 303). Two important points come out of this argument. First, clubs who put most weight on performance will tend to buy more talent even when doing so will erode their profitability. Alternatively, clubs that want to keep profits up, and costs down, will stop buying talent well before the costs of doing so outweigh the benefits. A summary of the drivers together with examples of strong and weak features are provided in Table 4.1.

TABLE 4.1 Financial drivers in professional sport clubs

Driver	Strong	Weak
Scale of competition	National competition	Regional competition
Level of performance	Regular appearances in final series	Regularly sits in bottom half of league ladder
Supporter base	Broad national support	Narrow provincial support
Club brand	Broad awareness, strong impact	Narrow awareness, weak impact
Stadium quality and size	New generation – all seats covered, clear sight lines	Ageing – limited seating, limited cover
Scale of host city support	Single team in large city	Competing with other teams in same city
Culture and values of club	Primary concern for revenue growth	More concerned with cost containment

Source: Foster *et al.* (2006).

CASE STUDY 4.1

What comes first . . . profits or wealth?

The above discussion raises the issues of, first, how profits contribute to wealth creation and, second, the difference between profitability and wealth. The first point to note is that profitability results from the difference between flows of revenue and flows of expenses. Wealth, however, has more to do with a sport organization's value at a point in time. Value is heavily dependent on the assets owned by the club or association, its levels of long-term debt, and its earnings potential, although, as will be noted in the following section, value is ultimately determined by how much someone is prepared to pay to secure ownership.

All things being equal, continued profitability will increase a sport organization's wealth and value. In other words, a wealthy sport organization such as Real Madrid Football Club or the Washington Redskins NFL team will have built up its wealth through reinvesting its profits and increasing its revenue earning capacity over a number of years. By contrast, a club that has a very low market value would most probably have a history of poor performance, a weak revenue base and running deficit budgets. In the AFL at least three clubs have negative value. That is, total liabilities exceed assets and, as a result, the level of the accumulated funds is negative. In 2005, the Western Bulldogs' total tangible asset base of around AUD 5 million was undermined by total liabilities of AUD 9 million. The Carlton Blues club has exhibited a similar sluggish state of affairs over the last five years, and has built up debt levels well in excess of its tangible assets. It is therefore important to understand how profits are linked to wealth creation, how sport clubs and associations can be valued, and why some are highly valued and others have much lower values.

CASE STUDY 4.2

What makes sport clubs valuable?

As regularly noted in this book, many aspects of sport are now big business. Mega-sport events such as the Olympic Games and world-football World Cup have operating budgets of hundreds of millions of dollars, while professional sport leagues such as the American NFL and NBA turn over thousands of millions of dollars a year. Many professional sport clubs have annual earnings of more than EUR 100 million, while the most successful clubs, such as Manchester United, Real Madrid, the New York Yankees Baseball Club and the Washington Redskins Football Club, all generate annual earnings of more than EUR 300 million. At the other end of the professional sport club continuum, AFL clubs (which are the wealthiest sport clubs in Australia) earn between AUD 30 million and AUD 60 million a year.

Not surprisingly, some leagues and clubs are much wealthier than others, and even within the same league there are significant differences in respect of revenues, profits and wealth. It was suggested in the early part of this chapter that these differences can be explained by (1) differences in industry structure and industry conduct, and (2) a club or league's ability to secure a competitive advantage through access to more productive resources. It is also important to note that annual earnings provide only a very rough estimate of the wealth of a professional sport club. So how might we go beyond annual earnings and profits to secure a more reliable indicator of a club's wealth or value?

Market capitalization

The simple answer to the question 'what is the real worth or value of a sporting club?' is the amount someone is willing pay to obtain ownership of the club. In other words, it is the current market value of the club. But this immediately begs the question as to how the market value of a sport club can be best calculated.

In the broader business world the market value of a publicly listed company (which is owned by shareholders) is found by multiplying the number of ordinary shares by their average sale price. So, if the company has one million shares trading at $10 a share, the market value is $10 million. Using this approach, which goes under the name of market capitalization, it is possible to quickly establish the value of all those EPL clubs that are listed on the stock exchange. For example, the value of Manchester United in 2003 – when it was a listed company – was GBP 610 million (Foster *et al.* 2006), but by 2012 this had increased to more than USD 2 billion. However, this is not a feasible way of calculating the market value of most sport clubs since, with a few exceptions in European football leagues, their shares are not normally traded on the stock exchange.

Market multiples

In North American professional sport leagues, where clubs (or franchises, as they are usually called) change ownership fairly regularly, the valuation of the franchise is revealed through the cost of acquisition. Over the last ten years, for example, there has been an explosion in the valuation of NFL clubs. Whereas the asking price was around USD 150 million for a club franchise in the 1980s, it is now around USD 1 billion at the minimum. A decade ago the record sale price for an NFL club franchise was USD 805 million for the Washington Redskins, which included not only the team, but also its stadium (Howard and Crompton 2004). The Redskins are now valued at just under USD 2 billion.

Moreover, this acquisition cost can be used to estimate the market value of other clubs in the league. For example, the fictitious Little Rock Lions may have been sold to a new owner (and to be called the Long Island Lions) for $50 million, having earned an average of $25 million per annum over the previous three years. By dividing the acquisition price by the average annual earnings, an acquisition price-to-earnings multiple of 2 is calculated. This multiple of 2 can then be used to estimate the market value of other similar clubs. If, for instance, the Rapid Bay Rhinos' annual earnings were $15 million, then by applying the acquisition price to earnings multiple of 2, the Rhinos' estimated market value is around $30 million.

At the moment the rule of thumb for American professional sport clubs is to use a multiple of around 3 to calculate the market value of clubs (Winfree and Rosentraub 2012: 287). Using 2010 revenue figures for NBA teams, one of the most highly valued was the Los Angeles Lakers ($643 million), while one of the lowest valued was the Indiana Pacers ($268 million). Among NFL teams the most highly valued was the Dallas Cowboys ($1,800 million), closely followed by the Washington Redskins ($1,600 million) and the New England Patriots ($1,400 million). Teams with low valuations included the St Louis Rams ($780 million) and the Oakland Raiders ($ 760 million). In the MLB, the most highly valued by a large margin was the New York Yankees ($1,600 million), while the low-value teams included the Florida Marlins ($318 million) and the Tampa Bay Devils ($316 million).

Book value of assets and shareholders' equity

Another way of calculating a club's market value is to dissect its balance sheet. One approach is to measure its total assets to determine its book value. However, this can be unreliable since it does not take into account the club's level of indebtedness. It is one thing to have a total asset base of $60 million, but the market value of the club will be severely undermined by $30 million of long-term borrowings. It is therefore more realistic to measure the club's net worth, which is the difference between assets and liabilities. In the case of profit-centred sport organizations, and sport clubs that are structured as public companies, net worth is also referred to as shareholders' equity. In the case of non-profit clubs, the terms 'accumulated funds' and 'members' equity' are also used.

However, no matter what term is used, this can still be a fairly loose measure since it may not include some important intangibles that are not listed on the balance sheet. For example, in European world-football leagues, players are traded. They are in effect assets since they have a resale value. However, in many instances the real value of players is severely discounted. First, players who are recruited through the club's domestic junior development pathways are usually not listed as assets, since they did not come through the player transfer market. Second, in line with standard depreciation principles, the price paid for players on the transfer market is amortized over the contract life of the player. A player who was bought for $1 million, and contracted for five years, could have his value reduced by around $200,000 a year until the player has, technically, no value when the contract is up for renewal. In reality this is patently false. Indeed, if players are competing at this peak by the end of the fifth year, their trading value could be in excess of the $1 million purchase price. While the balance sheet has the player valued at zero at the end of five years, the player's market value could be anything between $1 million and $2 million. Another problem resulting from using the book value of assets to establish a club's value is that many assets are listed as the purchase price. In reality many property-based assets are undervalued. A revaluation would provide a much higher set of figures.

The impact of expected future earnings

The other complicating thing about a professional sporting club's market value is that it is not only a function of past successes and earnings, but also about future successes and earnings (Brown *et al.* 2010: 270). So, if a club is expected to perform at a high level, and this increase in performance will strengthen its profile and attract additional resources, its market value is likely to increase. A simple method for linking earnings to market value is to calculate an average rate of return on capital invested. If, for example, the current market value of $20 million is based on annual earnings of $5 million and an average rate of return of 25 per cent, then an increase in earnings to $8 million with the same expected rate of return of 25 per cent will produce a revised market value of $32 million.

CASE STUDY 4.3

Club comparisons for England, the USA and Australia

Table 4.2 provides valuation data for a sample of professional sport clubs. The compounding successes of Manchester United, together with its strong global presence and massive support base, have allowed it to accumulate profits and build up its asset base, hence its great wealth is not surprising. The Washington Redskins' substantial wealth reflects a similar set of circumstances. However, unlike Manchester United, it is a one-team city, but it also occupies a stadium that offers quality facilities and more than 60,000 seats a game. While the value of the Collingwood Magpies is

TABLE 4.2 Valuation of sporting clubs, 2003 (USD millions)

Club name	League	Valuation
Manchester United	EPL	1,200
Washington Redskins	NFL	1,100
New York Yankees	MLB	832
Juventus	Italian 'A'	828
Bayern Munich	Bundesliga	617
Atlanta Falcons	NFL	603
Los Angeles Lakers	NBA	447
Chicago Bulls	NBA	356
Toronto Maple Leafs	NHL	263
Collingwood Magpies	AFL	45

Source: Foster *et al.* (2006: 440–1).

relatively low by international standards, it is Australia's wealthiest professional sport team, which is largely due to its strong brand name and large and loyal supporter base.

The market value of clubs, events and leagues will continue to grow so long as they can secure stable profits and reinvest them in the improvement of player quality, venue quality and the overall public attractiveness of tournaments and leagues. While market value can be quite different from profitability levels, continued profits through revenue growth and cost containment will increase the asset base of a club, enhance its reputation and generally increase its financial sustainability.

RECAP

There is a clear link between profits and wealth, with wealth being all about the value placed on a club, association or league. Profits are fairly straightforward to calculate, but wealth is a bit messier to deal with. What is more, there are vast differences between the profits and wealth of different clubs, even when they are in the same league or competition. In the case of MLB some teams are at least three times better off – that is wealthier – than others. Why is this so, and what can be done about it? Alternatively, does it matter? Yes, it does matter because, as we have already noted, clubs that hold more resources, and have a deeper reservoir of special competencies, are usually going to outperform clubs with a meagre resource and shrinking competency base. It not only makes for an unbalanced competition, but also undermines the financial viability of the poorer performing clubs.

REVIEW QUESTIONS

The following questions address the wealth inequality issue. They also focus on what enables some enterprises to build their wealth so readily, while others stumble around for years.

1 A profitable sport organization is not the same as a wealthy sport organization. Please explain.

2 Profitability in sport can come from a number of factors. One factor is the sport's surrounding industry structure and conduct. Please explain.

3 According to Szymanski and Kuypers (2000), some sport organizations are more profitable than others because they have a superior competitive strategy. Identify four tactical focal points that can be used to establish a competitive advantage.

4 Another way of looking at how sport organizations can secure a continuing profit is to examine the contributions made to sporting performance and financial

performance. Explain how Gerrard (2005) goes about linking sporting performance to improved financial performance. Also identify how other factors identified
by Gerrard can improve financial performance.

5 Foster *et al.* (2006) have listed six drivers that impact on sport clubs' financial
sustainability. What are they, and how do they influence revenues and costs?

6 How is profitability linked to value and wealth?

7 Compare the use of market capitalization and market multiples as tools for
estimating a sport organization's market value.

8 What 'multiple' is currently used to value professional sport teams in the American
leagues?

9 How can assets values and shareholders' equity be used to measure a sport
organization's market value?

10 To what extent is a sport club's market value affected by expected future earnings?
Give an example.

11 Is there any indication that in some sport leagues there is a vast difference in the
amount of wealth accumulated by clubs?

12 Are wealth inequalities between clubs a bad thing?

13 If severe inequality is a bad thing, then what can be done about it?

FURTHER READING

An excellent examination of wealth creation in sport, and how to value a sport enterprise,
is contained in Winfree, J. and Rosentraub, M. (2012) *Sports Finance and Management:
Real Estate, Entertainment, and the Remaking of Business*, Boca Raton, FL: CRC Press
(Chapter 2: 'Structures of ownership' and Chapter 8: 'What are teams worth?'). An
equally illuminating analysis is available in Brown, M., Rascher, D., Nagel, M. and
McEvoy, C. (2010) *Financial Management in the Sport Industry*, Scottsdale, AZ: Holcomb
Hathaway (Chapter 10: 'Valuation').

For more details on models for examining the market value of sport organizations, see
Szymanski, S. and Kuypers, T. (2000) *Winners and Losers*, London: Penguin (Chapter 2:
'Revenue' and Chapter 8: 'The future'). See also Gerrard, W. (2004) 'Why does
Manchester United keep winning on and off the field?', in Andrews, D. (ed.) *Manchester
United: A Thematic Study*, Abingdon: Routledge, pp. 65–86. Another useful discussion on
the drivers of sport club finances is contained in Foster, G., Greyser, P. and Walsh, B.
(2006) *The Business of Sport*, Mason, OH: Thomson (section 10: 'Financial valuation and
profitability').

To get a detailed explanation of the background to how industry structure and conduct
and company strategy affect profitability in sport organizations, go to Gerrard, B. (2005)
'A resource utilization model of organizational efficiency in professional team sports',
Journal of Sport Management, 19(2): 143–69. A solid exposition is also contained in

Mauws, M., Mason, D. and Foster, W. (2003) 'Thinking strategically about professional sports', *European Sport Management Quarterly*, 3: 145–64. See also Smart, D. and Wolfe, R. (2000) 'Examining sustainable competitive advantage in intercollegiate athletics: a resource-based view', *Journal of Sport Management*, 14(2): 133–53.

The link between the theory and practice of wealth creation in English world football is extensively examined in Szymanski, S. and Kuypers, T. (2000) *Winners and Losers*, London: Penguin (Chapter 6: 'Competitive advantage in football'). In addition, Rosner, S. and Shropshire, K. (2004) *The Business of Sports*, Sudbury, MA: Jones and Bartlett (Chapter 12: 'Sport franchise valuation') has a useful discussion on the valuation of intangible assets, including player contracts and acquired goodwill.

For a succinct introduction to sports branding and how brand equity can be used to increase a sport organization's value, see Ferrand, A. and Torrigiani, L. (2005) *Marketing of Olympic Sport Organizations*, Champaign, IL: Human Kinetics (Chapter 1: 'Branding'). See also Amis, J. and Cornwell, T. (2005) *Global Sport Sponsorship*, New York: Berg (Chapter 4: 'Global brand equity, FIFA and the Olympics').

For an analysis of how the video-game industry might be used to enhance the value of sport clubs, see Rosson, P. (2005) 'SEGA Dreamcast: national football cultures and the new Europeanism', in Silk, M., Andrews, D. and Cole, C. (2003) (eds) *Sport and Corporate Nationalism*, New York: Berg, pp. 167–85. See especially p.175, where it is put into the context of a value-chain for football business.

For an explanation of how the discounted cash flow (DCF) technique can be used to calculate the value of a sport organization's assets, see Beech, J. and Chadwick, S. (eds) (2004) *The Business of Sport Management*, Harlow: Pearson (Chapter 7: 'Sport finance').

USEFUL WEBSITES

- An excellent website for finding out more about the value of sport clubs is **www. forbes.com/sites/kurtbadenhausen/2012/07/16/manchester-united-tops-the-worlds-50-most-valuable-sports-teams.**
- A succinct overview of Australian professional sport club valuations is available in **www.smh.com.au/rugby-league/league-news/moneyball-how-is-your-club-placed-20130830-2swhv.html.**
- There is a massive amount of data on sport club finances on the Deloitte website at **www.deloitte.com/assets/Dcom-UnitedKingdom/Local%20Assets/Documents/ Industries/Sports%20Business%20Group/uk-sbg-football-money-league-2013.pdf.**
- Additional material on the brand value of European sport clubs can be found at **www.brandfinance.com/images/upload/top_30_european_football_brands_2011_ final_website.pdf.**
- A succinct examination of the value creation process in American sport is contained in **www.srr.com/assets/pdf/professional-sportsthe-next-evolution-value-creation.pdf.**
- For a thoughtful analysis of the ways in which fans add value to sport enterprises, see **http://bmsi.ru/doc/50533886-7c56-4d1e-b654-9729c4277f7a.**
- A brief analysis of what causes financial inequalities in sport is contained in **http:// mg312.wordpress.com/2011/11/08/inequalities-in-professional-sports.**

- Another insightful discussion on wealth inequality in sports is included in **http://philosophyatwestern.typepad.com/equality_matters/2012/11/exploring-wage-inequality-in-professional-sports.html**.
- An additional website on financial inequalities in sport, and especially tennis, is **http://usatoday30.usatoday.com/sports/tennis/story/2012-03-14/bnp-paribas-open-indian-wells-pay-disparity-on-the-atp-tour/53538094/1**.

CHAPTER 5

Profiteering from sport cartels

LEARNING OUTCOMES

At the end of this chapter readers will be able to:

- understand the nature of cartels, and discuss their place in sport leagues and competitions
- explain how sport cartels can use their monopoly power to increase revenue, constrain costs and generate large, and sometimes exploitative, profits
- reveal the costs that sport cartels can impose on many of their stakeholders, especially players
- appreciate the ways in which some aspects of cartel structures and conduct can be usefully employed to stabilize the financial operations of both clubs and leagues.

CHAPTER SUMMARY

This chapter looks at the ways in which sport competitions and leagues can organize themselves into cartels, and then considers the financial implication of these arrangements. It begins by explaining what a cartel is, how it gets to build its monopoly power, and how this monopoly power can be used to further the commercial and financial interests of its members. It then focuses on sport leagues in particular – with American leagues front and centre – and discusses the ways in which they can go about building a cartel, and use their consequent monopoly power to increase revenue, constrain costs and generally ensure their long-term financial viability. Specific attention will also be given to the Australian Football League (AFL), which has established many cartel-like features over the last thirty years. Using the models of wealth creation and profit-making discussed in the previous chapters, it will be shown that the AFL created a cartel structure that allowed it to regulate the sale of the football product, control its supply, manage its pricing, give clubs a minimum guaranteed income and restrict the entry of new clubs, all of which enabled it to become Australia's wealthiest sport enterprise.

WHAT IS A SPORT CARTEL?

Many professional sport leagues (especially those in the USA and Australia) operate as joint ventures or cartels. It is a far less common feature in European sport leagues where they are less regulated, and where they use a system of inter-league promotion and relegation to deliver incentives for doing well, and demotion to lower-level competitions for doing poorly. European sport also relies on hierarchical systems of governance to manage their affairs, while American sport focuses more on league 'Commissions' to organize its affairs (Nafziger 2009).

A cartel is a collective of firms who, by agreement, act as a single supplier to a market and, in doing so, pursue a number of joint policies. As a result, cartels are able to minimize competition, restrict the entry of new firms, control the supply and cost of their products, coordinate advertising and promotion, set prices and, most fundamentally of all, protect the interests of member organizations. In order to secure member compliance, a cartel will normally impose sanctions and penalties for the violation of its rules and regulations.

In most countries cartels are illegal, since they act against the public interest by increasing monopoly power and limiting competition. Trade practice and 'anti-trust' legislation aims to break up cartel behaviour by prohibiting collusive conduct by firms in the same industry. It will aim to prohibit conduct that denies new firms entry into an industry, prohibit mergers and takeovers that will substantially reduce competition, and prohibit suppliers from agreeing to fix prices. The main features of cartels are listed in Table 5.1.

TABLE 5.1 Features of a cartel

Feature	Business application
Decisions on cartel composition	Erection of high entry barriers in order to control competition
Decisions on the spread of the cartel	Relocation/merger of firms to expand markets and reduce competition
Control over input and labour costs	Exclusive arrangements with suppliers and internal labour markets
Control over prices	Fixed wholesale and retail prices to guarantee markup
Decisions on growth maximization	Entry into new markets in order to expand sales
Decisions on revenue sharing and income distribution	Guaranteed minimum income for cartel members to secure compliance

Source: Stewart *et al.* (2005: 97).

CASE STUDY 5.1

Does the NCAA fit the cartel model?

Sport leagues have a natural tendency to adopt cartel-like behaviour since they depend upon the cooperation of many teams to ensure a viable competition (Quirk and Fort 1992; Leeds and von Allmen 2011). This is evident in the evolution of professional sport leagues in basketball, baseball, ice hockey and football in the USA. While member teams will be highly competitive, and primarily concerned with on-field dominance, they also understand that their long-term viability depends on a high-quality competition where teams are of comparable strength and ability. Therefore, for a sport cartel to operate effectively, it must enforce policies that constrain member behaviours and maximize the league's public appeal and long-run sustainability.

In America, the National Collegiate Athletic Association (NCAA) is the league most often charged with engaging in cartel-like behaviour (Fleisher *et al.* 1992; Tollison 2012). At first glance this is a surprising claim to make since the NCAA is recognized for two admirable qualities. First, it is seen to be the 'benign administrator of the rules of college athletics' and, second, it 'promotes the ideals of amateurism' in sport (Tollison 2012: 339). However, the NCAA is also a tightly run enterprise whose rules and regulations benefit the cartel members (all the colleges and universities it represents) at the expense of other stakeholders (mainly the participating athletes and the broadcast media). The first thing the NCAA does is to tightly organize the schedule of games and tournaments so that it can secure the best array of matches at the best time of day or night. This is easy to do because it has no significant competitor to deal with. The NCAA also monopolizes the sale of broadcast rights to the media, which allows it to play off each potential rights purchaser against the others. The usual result is the best possible broadcast rights fee arrangement for the NCAA. But it does not end there because the NCAA does not only maximize its revenues, but it also minimizes its costs. It does this in the most blatant – and, some would say, most exploitative – of ways by demanding that its players compete as amateurs. The NCAA easily legitimizes this practice by arguing that it is not dealing with employees, but rather with player-athletes. That is to say, these young men and women are first and foremost getting a college education, and for the most part at a heavily discounted rate. Moreover, the sports side of their education is viewed as a bonus. It is, if you like, an add-on reward for building up their athletic prowess while doing it all under the watchful auspices of the colleges and their highly professionalized staff. If only everyone else could be so lucky!

CARTEL POWER

For the suppliers of sport services, cartels are in many ways something to aspire to, since they offer stable and secure environments where the room for independently collective action is spacious. But they do not come naturally, or through highly developed imagination or creative fantasizing. Their realization demands thoughtful planning, managerial efficiency and effective controls over wayward behaviour from member organizations. It is about regulations that allow leagues to not only put on quality sports entertainment, but also do it in a profitable way. There are a number of guiding principles, which are discussed below. So, effective sports cartels will be able to sustain their dominant positions by the following means:

- Having a centralized decision-making organization that regulates constituent teams and clubs, and disciplines members who breach the league's rules and regulations. This is a core requirement, since cartels will maximize their returns only if they act as single enterprises.
- Expanding profits by imposing cost minimization regulations. These regulations include rules that restrict competitive bidding for players and set ceilings on total player wage payments.
- Expanding the market by admitting new teams to the league, extending the playing season or playing games at different times of the week.
- Enhancing their product in order to improve the absolute quality of the game. This may involve the development of player skills, making stadiums more comfortable and securing safer and more predictable playing surfaces.
- Enhancing their product in order to improve relative game quality by providing uncertain game outcomes, which is often referred to as competitive balance. This can be achieved by drafting the best recruits to the worst-performing clubs at the end of the season, and redistributing league income so that all member teams can afford minimum standards of administration, coaching and sport science support. The additional imposition of salary caps can also improve competitive balance in some situations.
- Heightening the league's reputation and status through centralized promotion campaigns that aim to improve the public image of the sport. Rules are put in place to regulate the conduct and behaviour of team administrators, coaches and players.
- Using their monopoly power to maximize broadcast rights fees. This will involve negotiating as a single entity, and avoiding any arrangement that allocates the rights to individual teams.

The policies and rules that characterize sport cartels are listed in Table 5.2.

Unlike more traditional industries, the sport industry is often allowed by government to pursue what are effectively anti-competitive practices. This occurs because there is tacit agreement that restrictive practices are essential for the sport league to sustain its public interest and long-term viability. In other words, a completely unregulated sport league will be unsustainable since a few clubs will use their superior fan and revenue base to capture the best players and dominate the premiership race. This argument is supported by the claim that, while the resulting conduct may be anti-competitive or a restraint of trade, it is not unreasonable, or against the public interest (Leeds and von Allmen 2011). It is claimed, therefore, that unlike the world of commerce and industry, sport leagues often perform poorly under free market conditions, and some form of self-regulation is essential to produce the outcome uncertainty that attracts fans, sponsors and media interests (Sandy *et al.* 2004).

TABLE 5.2 Features of a sport cartel

Feature	Examples and cases
Policies for managing league structure, composition and team location	Admit new teams into league, provide incentives for clubs to merge or relocate, set league fixtures and playing schedules
Policies to prevent the entry of rival leagues	Establish long-term contracts with media organizations, stadia owners and star players
Policies for increasing relative game quality and improving competitive balance	Establish recruiting zones, create player draft, and implement salary caps and player wage ceilings
Policies to regulate league costs	Design regulated player transfer market, implement salary caps and wage ceilings for member club staff
Policies to regulate league prices	Control admission prices, set prices for league merchandise and publications
Policies for increasing absolute game quality and improving general appeal of game to public	Develop programmes to optimize player skill and abilities, improve spectator facilities and stadium design, refine rules of game
Policies to ensure the reputation of the game/league	Design rules to protect the good name of the game, implement codes of conduct for players, and rules to restrict public comments of officials
Policies for expanding the market for the game	Conduct centralized promotional and advertising campaigns, manage player participation and game development programmes
Policies for maximizing broadcast right agreements	Be the sole supplier of broadcast rights to television and radio stations
Policies for redistributing revenue	Pool TV rights and redistribute to member clubs, implement income equalization schemes
Policies for increasing revenue streams	Sell brand name and logo to merchandisers, sell advertising and promotional space to sponsors

Source: adapted from Stewart *et al.* (2005: 99).

CASE STUDY 5.2

The Australian Football League cartel

In the following section the recent performance of the Australian Football league (AFL) will be examined through the prism of cartel structure and conduct. In doing this, the sport cartel template illustrated in Figure 5.2 will be used to address the following questions. First, to what extent has the AFL established structures that enable it to govern its affairs, and regulate the conduct of member teams as if it was a single entity? Second, how successful has the AFL been in reorganizing the competition so that it can capture new markets and attract new fans? Third, has the AFL been able to increase its revenue base by both broadening and deepening its income streams. Fourth, in what way has the AFL been able to control costs by fixing player wage bills and operational expenses, and to fix prices by setting common admission and merchandise prices? Fifth, in what ways has the AFL managed demand by influencing game quality, where quality has both an absolute dimension (the competition has many star players and comfortable venues) and a relative dimension (games are exciting where the outcome is uncertain)? Sixth, what schemes have been put in place to pool income and redistribute it to ensure a guaranteed minimum income for member teams? Finally, to what extent has the AFL used rules, agreements and threats to manage the behaviour of administrators, coaches and players, and to protect the good name and reputation of the game?

Centralized governance

The Victorian Football League (VFL), from which the AFL emerged, was formed in 1897. It expanded during the 1920s, and by 1980 had become a competition of twelve teams based in Melbourne. Throughout the post-Second World War period the VFL was governed by a Board of Directors that comprised delegates from each of the twelve clubs, with the day-to-day management conducted by a central administration. During the early 1980s the VFL faced many threats and problems. The South Melbourne club, which relocated to Sydney in 1982 in order to avoid liquidation, was finding it difficult to attract a viable fan base, attendances were falling and eight of the twelve clubs were technically bankrupt.

Two task-force reports commissioned by the VFL in the mid-1980s were the catalysts for a major restructuring of the league. It was clear that a system of governance that relied on member clubs nominating delegates to the Board was inappropriate in such a turbulent environment. In late 1985 the VFL Board of Directors was replaced by a football Commission elected by member clubs. This Commission structure has continued to the present day, and has been used to provide centralized decision-making and a set of rules and regulations by which the clubs have to abide.

League expansion

During the 1980s world football was considered a threat to Australian football, and the new Commission also became aware that the New South Wales Rugby League

(NSWRL) competition, after many years of neglect, had increased its public support and reach. It had already admitted teams from the ACT and Wollongong, and was investigating the possibility of admitting teams from the Gold Coast and Brisbane, which it did in 1987. The AFL Commission report, *Establishing the Basis for Future Success*, recommended interstate expansion as a way of both managing the threats from world football and rugby league, and extending the reach of the VFL beyond Melbourne and Sydney. It was agreed to establish VFL clubs in Brisbane and Perth, thus producing a fourteen-team competition covering four of Australia's seven states.

The Commission's national ambitions led to the Adelaide Crows being admitted in 1991 and the Fremantle Dockers in 1995. These were strategically important decisions, since they provided a better national balance, curbed the growing financial dominance of the West Coast Eagles, and reduced the impact of rugby league decisions to locate teams in Adelaide and Perth. In 1997, Port Power, a second Adelaide club, was admitted to the league, which coincided with the merger of Fitzroy and Brisbane. This created a sixteen-team competition covering five states, which continues through to the present day. The national spread of the AFL competition during this time is illustrated in Figure 5.1.

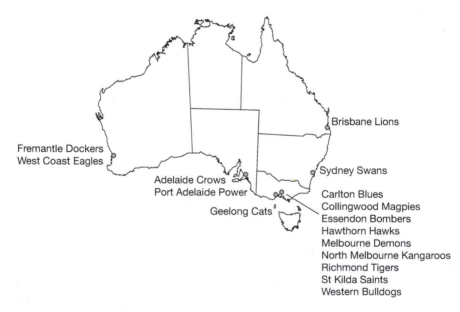

FIGURE 5.1 Location of AFL teams, 1997 to 2006

Source: adapted from Hess and Stewart (1998: 236).

The AFL's cartel structure allowed a more centralized management model to emerge, in which the interests of the league as a whole were of primary concern. Support for the national expansion from existing member clubs was reinforced by the distribution of the AUD 4 million licence fee paid by newly admitted clubs.

Flexible scheduling of games

The Commission's centralized control also allowed further restructuring to occur at the end of 1990, when the VFL changed its name to the Australian Football League (AFL). This national expansion strategy was accompanied by a plan to improve the quality of the competition by rationalizing the use of playing venues, upgrading facilities and playing games over the whole weekend as a way of giving broadcasters greater programming opportunities. By 1989, Sunday football received state government approval, and the MCG progressively became the home venue for most Melbourne-based clubs, and with the construction of the Docklands stadium in 2000 (which was renamed Telstra Dome, and subsequently the Etihad Stadium) further relocations and rescheduling occurred, and the MCG and Telstra Dome (come Etihad Stadium) became the only Melbourne venues to regularly host AFL fixtures.

Creating a level playing field

The AFL also used its cartel structure and monopoly power to implement a raft of policies to achieve a balanced competition. In the early 1980s, players were regulated by rules that tied them to their club until such time the club decided to grant a transfer. This master–servant relationship was reinforced by a geographic zoning system that tied all likely recruits to a specific club. In 1983, the VFL's player transfer policy was challenged in the Victorian Supreme Court, where it was concluded that the clearance, transfer and zoning rules were an unreasonable restraint of trade and that they be replaced by a system of player drafts and contracts. Player transfer rules were amended so that, by 1986, a national player draft was in place. Player transfer fees were removed and player lists were reduced, all of which stabilized the cost structure of clubs, but gave players little choice as to where they would like to play.

Controlling player costs

Player payments have also been a vexing issue for the AFL. Rules for containing player payments were first established by the VFL in 1930, when a maximum wage was implemented. However, the rule was flouted so often during the 1970s that escalating player wages had undermined the financial viability of many clubs.

To protect the league against a wage-cost explosion, a salary cap was introduced in late 1984, which was modelled on the American National Basketball Association (NBA) wage ceiling policy of 1983. The cap not only constrained the player wage costs of member clubs, but also helped redistribute playing talent more evenly. The salary cap subsequently became the pivotal strategy for controlling player payments. In 1983, it was set at AUD 0.5 million per member team, but since then has steadily increased. In 1996, it was AUD 2.5 million and is now just under AUD 9 million per team. The Commission sets the salary cap, which it recently retitled 'total player payments', based on movements in broadcast rights fees, revenue from finals games, and club membership income. This means that the salary cap will increase in line with the league's revenue and, by implication, the club's capacity to pay. The scale of the

TABLE 5.3 Payments to AFL players, 1980 to 2005 (AUD)

Year	Salary cap ($ millions)	Average player earnings ($ thousands)	Percentage of players earning more than $100,000
1980	Not applicable	11	0
1985	1	15	0
1990	2	45	2
1995	2.5	75	18
2000	5	127	62
2002	6	167	68
2005	8	203	75

Source: AFL *Annual Reports* 1981 to 2005.

expansion in player payments is illustrated in Table 5.3. The salary cap dampened the bargaining strength of recruits, and eliminated the player-hoarding by rich clubs that occurred in the 1970s and early 1980s.

The AFL Commission has also implemented sanctions that impose penalties on clubs that breach the salary cap provisions. In 2002, Carlton, Richmond, Fremantle and St Kilda were all found to have breached the salary cap, and were penalized through a combination of fines and denial of national draft choices.

Improving absolute game quality

The AFL Commission also developed policies and strategies for improving the overall quality of the game. From the 1990s, the AFL used sport science and improved technologies to develop the skills and athleticism of players. Just as there had been an increase in the corporate logic that dominated decision-making in the off-field AFL, a similar logic underpinned the development of the on-field side of the AFL. The game became faster with the players being taller and heavier, and possessing a greater aerobic capacity than previously. Sport science, underpinned by physiology, biomechanics and psychology, became an integral part of the AFL landscape. Tactically, the game advanced considerably, and during the 2001–12 period this resulted in an increase in the number of full-time assistant coaches.

The same innovative approach was applied to stadium development. The pivotal place of the MCG in the national league was reinforced in 1992 when its AUD 150 million Great Southern Stand was completed. The comfortable new seating and improved sight lines were instrumental in increasing the average MCG attendance from 25,000 to more than 40,000 during the next few years. Stadium redevelopment peaked in the late 1990s when the AFL helped construct a new-generation stadium in Melbourne's inner west Docklands precinct, complete with retractable roof.

Strengthening the brand

Although the AFL expanded its fan base substantially during the 1980s and early 1990s, it was aware of the growing national presence of rugby league. It was particularly aware of how rugby league's cleverly constructed marketing campaigns during the early 1990s had increased the game's national profile. The Australian Rugby League's Tina Turner promotional campaign, which began in 1989, aimed to soften the game's hyper-masculine, blue-collar image by selling the game's sociability and excitement to a white-collar audience.

By contrast, the AFL had historically let the media promote the game through its game reporting. But all this changed in 1993 when it contracted the leading advertising agency, Campaign Palace, to design a promotional campaign that would not only update the game's public image, but also capture the attention of people with little exposure to the traditions of Australian football. The campaign brief was to promote the AFL as a national game, and gear it heavily to New South Wales and Queensland. To this end it was decided to feature overseas athletes and celebrities who would express congratulatory amazement about some aspect of the game using the tag line 'I'd like to see that'. In one feature, Russian cosmonaut, Sergei Avdeev, said 'Australia launching men into space every few minutes? I'd like to see that'.

The campaign ran from 1994 to 1998, and by the fourth year had achieved a national recall rate of 97 per cent. It also coincided with an increase in total season attendance from 4.7 million in 1994 to 6.1 million in 1998. This was followed by the 'I was here' campaign in 1999 and the 'For the Love of the Game' campaign in 2002. The 'For the Love of the Game' campaign highlighted the community roots of Australian football, and how the AFL was assisting community football throughout the nation. This has remained a constant theme through to the present day.

Improving the league's reputation

For a cartel such as the AFL, it is not enough to strengthen the brand and extend its exposure. It is also important to use its monopoly power to improve the league's overall standing and reputation in the sport world. This standing and reputation is not only a function of the quality and balance of the competition, the skill of players and the standard of stadiums. It is also a function of the behaviour of the league's administrators, coaches and players.

The lengths the AFL has gone to in order to protect its reputation is revealed in the collective bargaining agreement (CBA) between the Commission and the AFL Players Association (AFLPA), which covers issues related to players and their perform- ance. The most recent collective bargaining agreement includes sections on player payments, injury and veteran lists, contracts, use of player images and choice of player footwear. The Commission helped fund the implementation of CBA programmes, and in 2003 allocated AUD 5 million to support professional development and player welfare programmes, including provision for players in their retirement.

The CBA also incorporates a code of conduct, which has been jointly formulated by the Commission, the AFLPA and member clubs. The purpose of the code is to promote the good reputation of Australian Rules football, the AFL competition, AFL clubs and players by establishing standards of performance and behaviour for AFL footballers. In addition, it seeks to deter conduct that could have an adverse effect on the standing and reputation of the game. The code of conduct also incorporates rules and regulations related to doping and racial vilification, which reinforces the AFL's desire to maintain a clean image, as well as provide positive role models for children.

The AFL introduced an anti-doping code in 1990 as a result of a growing public awareness of the effects of performance-enhancing drugs on both the health of athletes and the image and appeal of the competition. The Justin Charles case of 1997, where he tested positive for anabolic steroids, provided the catalyst for entrenching the league's anti-doping policy. In 2005, the AFL extended its policy by introducing penalties for the use of illicit recreational drugs. Any player who tests positive for cocaine or ecstasy on match day can now expect a twelve-match suspension for the first offence and a two-year suspension for the second. In 2013, the anti-doping code was brought into play when the Essendon Football Club, one the most successful and wealthiest clubs in the competition, was found not only to have used substances that were banned, but also to have put the health and welfare of players at risk. As well as having the coach sacked, the club was fined more than AUD 1 million.

Expanding participation

Throughout the 1990s, the AFL had used its monopoly power to expand the market, substantially increase its annual revenue and net worth, maintain control over player wages and transfers, achieve competitive balance, and establish codes of conduct that guided the behaviour of players. However, there was a growing concern that, while it had managed the national competition very well, it had been less successful in pursuing its role as the keeper-of-the-code, and developing the game in the northern markets of New South Wales, Queensland and the Northern Territory.

AFL administrators were acutely aware that Queensland and New South Wales would soon be home to more than half of Australia's population. The northern markets were considered integral to a national competition, and the AFL developed a three-pronged approach to sustain its dominant position in the sporting market-place. The first prong aimed to ensure that the Brisbane Lions and Sydney Swans were both financially stable and successful on the field; the second prong aimed to ensure greater television exposure of the AFL competition; while the final prong involved heavy investment in game development and junior participation.

By 2013, the national spread had been consolidated when two new teams were admitted to the competition. The first were the Gold Coast Suns, who were located about 90 kilometres south of Brisbane, and the second was Greater Western Sydney, situated in the heartland of Sydney's rapidly expanding western suburbs. These expansion teams were not the result of a whim or an optimistic wish from some enthusiastic local benefactors. They were carefully thought-out decisions to secure new markets and maintain the AFL's position as not only the nation's most popular sport league, but also its most profitable.

Managing the sale of broadcasting rights

Television has always had a strong relationship with the AFL, and throughout the forty-five years of negotiating broadcast rights, the VFL/AFL always acted on behalf of member clubs. The AFL was the jewel in the crown of the Seven Network's programming, and their relationship created significant corporate synergies. While the AFL praised the breadth and quality of Seven's football coverage, the Seven Network provided saturation levels of promotion for the AFL. The Seven Network valued the relationship so highly that, in 1998, it agreed to pay the AFL AUD 40 million a year until the end of 2001 for four weeks of pre-season competition and twenty-six weeks of the premiership league. However, the Seven Network's relationship with the AFL was severed in December 2000, when a consortium headed by Rupert Murdoch's News Limited secured the broadcast rights to all AFL fixtures for a fee of AUD 500 million over five years. In a complex arrangement, the rights were spread across one pay TV and two free-to-air providers, namely Foxtel, the Nine Network and the Ten Network respectively. In the latest round of negotiations held in early 2006, the Seven and Ten networks colluded to outbid the Nine Network and thus secured the rights to broadcast the AFL's fixtures for five years in return for a then record payment of AUD 750 million. In 2011, a new rights agreement was struck, which gave the AFL Commission just over AUD 1 billion for the following five years. This may have been modest by American and European standards, but was a massive revenue stream by Australian standards. The growth in TV broadcast rights income is illustrated in Table 5.4.

In the aftermath of these agreements there were rumblings within member clubs and venue managers such as the MCG that it may be possible to challenge the monopoly power of the Commission over broadcast rights. It was noted, for example, that in Major League Baseball in the USA, member teams could negotiate their own local free-to-air and cable television broadcast rights. However, the AFL Commission also noted that this tactic had resulted in some clubs obtaining up to a USD 50 million

TABLE 5.4 Trends in AFL broadcasting rights fees, 1980 to 2007

Agreement year	Fees (AUD million)	Fee as percentage of total commission revenues
1980	1	4
1985	4	22
1990	8	27
1995	17	24
2000	40	36
2002	100	63
2007	150	70

Source: AFL, *Annual Reports* (1981–2005) and Stewart (1984).

advantage over rival teams. The AFL Commission declared its intention to be the sole negotiator in order that the competition as a whole would benefit, rather than a few powerful clubs.

Redistributing the pool of revenue

The VFL and AFL have a history of pooling part of the league revenue and redistributing it, through a system of cross-subsidization, to member clubs in equal amounts. In the early 1980s, 20 per cent of net match proceeds was put into an equalization fund, together with broadcasting rights income as well as the net proceeds from the final series. Over the following twenty years the revenue pooling policy was strengthened, and by 2012 included all broadcasting rights fees, all corporate hospitality income, the net income from the finals series and the profits from the *Football Record*, the match-day publication. Overall, around 40 per cent of all league revenue is now pooled and redistributed to member clubs. The AFL's revenue-pooling policy is a powerful tool for controlling the behaviour of member clubs. While the AFL claims it is not a banker to the clubs, and does not guarantee club debts, its pooling policy has allowed a number of member clubs to survive serious financial crises. Consequently, the AFL's policy, by protecting weaker clubs, has been able to preserve the viability of the league and ensure the operational sustainability of member clubs.

Cumulative financial impact

As a result of the above practices the AFL's revenue base (comprising both Commission and club income) has exploded exponentially. This reflects its ability to set admission prices, attract large at-ground crowds and generate high-rating television audiences. In 1990, total Commission revenue was AUD 30 million, by 2003 had increased to AUD 171 million, and by 2006 had reached around AUD 220 million. A large part of this growth came from broadcasting rights fees. Whereas these contributed just under AUD 8 million in 1990, this had increased to AUD 17 million in 1995, AUD 100 million in 2003, AUD 150 million a year in 2010, and just over AUD 250 million for 2012. Sponsorship and merchandising income also increased rapidly over this period, although on a much smaller scale. Club incomes grew at a similar rate. Average member club income was AUD 4 million in 1990, had increased to AUD 8 million in 1995, and escalated to AUD 25 million in 2005. By 2012, total annual league revenues exceeded AUD 500 million, with the broadcasting rights fees stream accounting for 25 per cent of the total revenue river. The growth in AFL income and at-ground attendances is illustrated in Table 5.5.

Overall, the establishment of a centralized Commission enabled the AFL to better control its member clubs, regulate fixtures and pursue its national expansion agenda. It continued to regulate the movement of players by replacing its zoning rules with a national player draft. The draft not only ensured an even spread of playing talent across the teams, but because it reduced the competition for players, it also dampened the ability of young recruits to negotiate a starting salary commensurate with their

TABLE 5.5 AFL income and attendances, 1980 to 2005

Year	Commission revenue (AUD millions)	Av. club revenue (AUD millions)	Total season attendance (millions)
1980	15	1.2	3.7
1985	18	1.5	3.1
1990	30	4.0	4.1
1995	72	8.2	5.9
2000	111	12	6.6
2002	160	17	6.4
2005	220	25	6.5

Source: AFL *Annual Reports* (1981 to 2005).

abilities. The Commission also extended its reach over player payments by introducing a salary cap, which established a ceiling on the total player wage bill. It used its monopoly power to enhance game quality by improving stadium facilities, rationalizing venues and developing player athleticism and skills. It continued to negotiate broadcasting rights as a single entity. It also introduced an array of coercive agreements and codes of conduct that increasingly constrained the behaviour of administrators, players and coaches as a way of maintaining the reputation of the league. Finally, it increasingly pooled league income and redistributed it to member clubs to ensure they had a guaranteed minimum income to sustain their financial viability. There is no doubt the AFL's financial success, in large part, resulted from its cartel structures and conduct, which are illustrated in Figure 5.2.

Figure 5.2 confirms that profit-making in professional sport leagues is a function of both the drive to expand revenue and the need to control costs. In the case of a sport-league cartel both revenue expansion and cost-containment strategies can be secured through a centralized body that regulates its member clubs by a combination of incentives and coercion.

CASE STUDY 5.3

What happens when sport cartels are absent? Spanish football in the spotlight

As noted above, the AFL is heavily regulated by its controlling body and so are America's NFL and NBA. As such they take on many of the monopoly-like features described above. One of the benefits of this structure – at least in theory – is

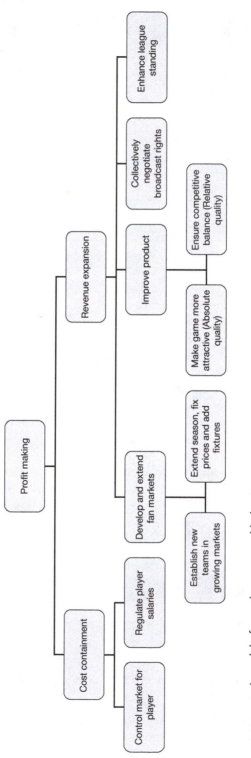

FIGURE 5.2 A model of sport-league cartel behaviour

that member clubs are guaranteed a minimum income. This approach makes a lot of sense if the major Spanish football leagues are anything to go by. A recent study showed an alarming amount of financial instability in the two top divisions of Spanish League Football.

At first glance this is surprising, given that the Real Madrid and Barcelona clubs are two of the wealthiest in the world. According to a 2012 survey, Forbes feature writer Kurt Badenhausen calculated that Real Madrid's market value was around USD 1.9 billion, just a little short of Manchester United's USD 2.2 million. The New York Yankees, Dallas Cowboys, Washington Redskins, Los Angeles Dodgers and New England Patriots all had market values in excess of USD 1 billion, with Barcelona not far behind.

Most Spanish football clubs are registered as limited companies, which means they are not listed on the stock exchange. Only four clubs are owned and controlled by their members, and they are Athletico Bilbao, Barcelona, Real Madrid and Osauna. There is very limited income sharing, and there is also a wide disparity of membership, gate takings and corporate partner support between clubs. It is also the case that there is an enormous disparity in total revenues and wealth between the clubs. In fact, there are more clubs in financial strife than there are clubs performing well (Barajas and Rodriguez 2010). It therefore comes as no surprise to find that 88 per cent of all clubs had incurred operating losses over recent times. Additionally, 71 per cent of all clubs had debts that exceeded total revenues, while 34 per cent of clubs had more debts than assets. In the Spanish League's second division the financial position was close to being catastrophic, with 51 per cent of clubs reported to be technically insolvent. While these challenging results cannot be solely attributed to the loose structure of the Spanish League, the governing body's lack of tight controls and the slapdash monitoring of financial performance, they are clearly part of the explanation for this sorry state of affairs.

RECAP

Sport cartels can deliver both good and bad outcomes. As the cases above illustrate, a well-organized sport cartel can deliver its members healthy profits and long-term viability. It can therefore protect member clubs from bankrupting themselves, while making sure no single club dominates the competition for any great length of time. The absence of cartel-type agreements can deliver a lot of individual club autonomy, but can also create a lot of inequality, as the Spanish Football League case study indicates. So, what is it about sport cartels that make them so problematic for many sport officials and commentators?

REVIEW QUESTIONS

These problematic issues raise many questions. Are sport leagues better off with cartel-like arrangements, or are they better off without them? So, we need to go a bit further in understanding just how sport cartels come into being, what they deliver to their stakeholders and what social costs they might impose on the wider community.

1 What are the main features of a cartel?

2 In what ways is a cartel similar to a monopoly?

3 What do cartels do in order to restrict competition, contain costs and increase revenue?

4 What are the main features of a sport cartel, and how might it go about constraining the conduct of its member clubs in order to secure its financial future?

5 What is it about the NCAA that leads critics to argue that it is a cartel?

6 Is there any social good that comes out of the NCAA rules and arrangements?

7 What cartel-like features does the AFL possess?

8 How does the AFL go about restricting competition, constraining its costs and increasing revenue?

9 Why is the concept of competitive balance so important in the AFL, and what does it do to secure a more balanced competition?

10 Why is reputation and brand image important to the AFL, and how does it use its monopoly power to improve it?

11 How does the AFL use its monopoly power to maximize its income from broadcasting rights fees?

12 Does the English Premier League (EPL) have any cartel-like features? And, if it does, what are they and how do they work in practice?

13 Would the EPL be better off if it had a strong cartel arrangement? And, if it would, what might these benefits be?

14 Contrast the cartel-like conduct of the NFL with the operation of the EPL.

15 How would you rank the AFL, EPL and NFL in terms of their cartel structure and conduct?

16 The Spanish Football League is an interesting case to look at. While Real Madrid and Barcelona FC are two of the wealthiest sport clubs in the world, most of the other elite professional teams in Spain are facing serious financial problems. How can this be explained, and how might this financial inequality problem be solved by having stronger cartel-like arrangements?

17 Cartels might be good for leagues and member clubs, but are they good for players and other stakeholders? What do you think, and why?

FURTHER READING

An instructive introduction to cartel behaviour in sport is contained in Fleisher, A., Goff, B. and Tollison, R. (1992) *The National Collegiate Athletic Association: A Study in Cartel Behavior*, Chicago, IL: University of Chicago Press. See also Downard, P. and Dawson, A. (2000) *The Economics of Professional Team Sports*, Abingdon: Routledge. Chapter 3, which looks at league structures, is particularly insightful.

For a succinct coverage of how professional sport leagues go about restricting competition and regulating member clubs, see Leeds, M. and von Allmen, P. (2011) *The Economics of Sport*, 4th edition, Boston, MA: Addison-Wesley. Chapter 4 looks at monopoly and anti-trust, while Chapter 5 focuses its attention on competitive balance. See also Brown, M., Rascher, D., Nagel, M. and McEvoy, C. (2010). *Financial Management in the Sport Industry*, Scottsdale, AZ: Holcomb Hathaway (Chapter 15: 'Professional sport'). The special case of America's MLB, and how it came to be exempt from the nation's anti-competition laws, is also discussed by Blair, R. and Haynes, J. (2012) 'Baseball's anti-trust exemption', in Kahane, L. and Shmanske, S. (2012) *The Oxford Handbook of Sports Economics – Volume 1: The Economics of Sports*, Oxford: Oxford University Press, pp. 81–96.

Another excellent source is Sandy, R., Sloane, P. and Rosentraub, M. (2004) *The Economics of Sport: An International Perspective*, Basingstoke: Palgrave Macmillan. Chapter 7 provides a sharp insight into sport team conduct and league structures from a regulatory and cartel perspective.

For an expansive analysis of the economic organization of professional world-football leagues in Europe and England – which covers cartel-like conduct – see Dobson, S. and Goddard, J. (2001) *The Economics of Football*, Cambridge: Cambridge University Press, especially Chapter 2 on professional football, Chapter 3 on competitive balance and Chapter 9 on current issues and future prospects. This leads nicely into a discussion of the benefits and costs of highly regulated leagues on the one hand, and unregulated leagues on the other. For more details see Rosner, S. and Shropshire, K. (2004) *The Business of Sports*, Sudbury, MA: Jones and Bartlett, especially Chapter 2 on league structures and their evolution and Chapter 3 on revenue sharing in professional sport leagues.

One of the most detailed accounts of the long-term effects of sport league regulation in the USA, even though it is now slightly dated, is Quirk, J. and Fort, R. (1992) *Pay Dirt: The Business of Professional Team Sport*, Princeton, NJ: Princeton University Press. See, especially, Chapter 5 on the reserve clause and anti-trust, Chapter 6 on why it is that professional athletes make so much money, and Chapter 7 on the 'old chestnut' of competitive balance.

A concise comparison of the structure and conduct of European and North American professional sport leagues is made by Szymanski, S. (2004) 'Is there a European model of sports?', in Fort, R. and Fizel, J. (eds) *International Sports Economic Comparisons*, Westport, CT: Praeger, pp. 19–38.

For a detailed analysis of Australian football's structure, conduct and financial progress, see Stewart, B. (ed.) (2007) *The Games Are Not the Same: The Political Economy of Football in Australia*, Melbourne, Vic.: Melbourne University Press. Rugby is covered in Chapter 6 by James Skinner and Allen Edwards, world football – or soccer, as it is referred to in

Australia – is examined in Chapter 7 by Braham Dabscheck, while Australian Rules football is interrogated in Chapter 8 by Robert D. Macdonald and Ross Booth.

For an exposé on the fragile financial state of Spanish soccer in the 2008–10 period, see Barajas, A. and Rodriguez, O. (2010) 'Spanish football club finances: crisis and player salaries', *International Journal of Sport Finance*, 5: 52–66.

USEFUL WEBSITES

- *Forbes* has a short but insightful discussion on who wins and who loses from a sport cartel arrangement. American leagues are contrasted with European leagues. See **www.forbes.com/sites/timworstall/2013/01/14/why-american-sports-are-organised-as-cartels**.
- For an analysis of American college sport through the lens of cartel theory, see **http://ftp.iza.org/dp2186.pdf**. It provides a very detailed and revealing study of a complex sporting structure.
- *The New York Times* is also a useful source of material on sport as a cartel. See **www.nytimes.com/2011/12/31/opinion/nocera-the-college-sports-cartel.html?_r=0**.
- The financial statements for the NCAA operations in 2008 and 2009 are contained in the following website. Begin at p. 50: **http://catalog.proemags.com/publication/cc5da338#/cc5da338/52**.
- The annual reports for the Australian Football league (AFL) from 2005 to 2012 can be found at **www.afl.com.au/afl-hq/annual-reports**. The reports contain sections on (1) the structure, rules and operation of the league and (2) the league's financial performance, including detailed reporting on the balance sheet, the profit and loss statement and the cash flow statement.

Foundation competencies

CHAPTER 6

Complying with financial standards

LEARNING OUTCOMES

At the end of this chapter readers will be able to:

- explain the history and evolution of bookkeeping and accounting systems
- understand the key principles, conventions and standards that frame contemporary accounting and finance practices
- compare and contrast the different financial entities relevant to sport enterprises by highlighting their core features, strengths and weaknesses
- reflect on the ways in which sound financial management underpins the effective operations of sport enterprises.

CHAPTER SUMMARY

This chapter discusses the structures and operating principles that underpin the effective financial management of sport enterprises. It begins with a brief history of bookkeeping and accounting systems, and the ways in which the financial affairs of organizations have been traditionally managed. Special attention is given to the different financial entities relevant to sport enterprises, and the core features of each entity are discussed in detail. These entities involve sole traders, partnerships, non-profit incorporated associations, companies limited by guarantee, private companies and public companies. The remainder of the chapter focuses on the importance of good financial management, and the key principles and conventions that frame contemporary accounting and finance practices. They include the ideas of the going concern, materiality, conservatism and historical costing. Special attention is paid to the development of global reporting standards, and how they may improve the financial management systems of sport enterprises. The chapter ends with a brief analysis of profit-making and dividend allocations on the one hand, and the retention of operating surpluses on the other.

A BRIEF HISTORY OF ACCOUNTING

There has always been a need to manage the financial affairs of groups and organizations. This is not surprising in the light of a deep-seated propensity of most populations to spend money on things they may later not want with money they have not got. There is also a deep-seated desire to monitor spending that involves the use of funds that are sourced from other populations.

The need to control the flow of funds has a long history. In ancient Greece and Rome the use of money in the form of coins enabled rulers of states, the leaders of communities and the owners of businesses to calculate their wealth by listing the money they owned, and comparing it with the money they owed. It led to the establishment of banks, which set up account books and loaned money to citizens. Around 600 BC the ancient Greeks also used systems of accounting to assess the efficiency of government programmes. The civil servants of the time were required to keep a list of their receipts and expenditure, which could be examined by an appointed group of so-called public accountants. Ancient Rome had a similar system of controls over government spending. Auditors were used to verify spending by the treasury, and to review spending on public works and the operation of the Roman army.

During the eleventh and twelfth centuries in England, financial management focused more on the feudal manor and the local tradesperson. Subsequent to his invasion of England in 1066, William the Conqueror conducted a survey of every estate from which taxes to be paid were calculated. This led to the creation of the Domesday Book, which, for the very first time, provided detailed information for the annual listing of rents and taxes payable to the King of England. This was called the Pipe Roll. County sheriffs were appointed to collect the rents and taxes, and the monies paid to the King were recorded through the marking of a hazelwood stick. These 'tally sticks' were notched and marked to indicate how much income had been received from each estate or business, and when it was paid. When the sheriffs had collected their money, they would meet with the King's treasurer, who would take the money; the Pipe Roll entry would be marked accordingly and a receipt would be issued. This occurred at a table covered by a chequered cloth, hence the term 'exchequer' to describe the treasurer's role in modern British politics.

However, it was not until the fifteenth century that what we now know as double-entry bookkeeping was invented. The Italian Renaissance was a period of enormous artistic and commercial vitality, and one of its many innovations was the introduction of double-entry bookkeeping. In 1494, Luca Pacioli, a mathematician and monk, published a book titled *Everything About Arithmetic, Geometry and Proportion* (or *Summa*, its abbreviated Italian title). One of his chapters (called 'Reckonings and writings') was on the topic of accounting, and in it he described the fundamentals of an accounting system that we still use today. Pacioli identified the journal as the foundation document that lists the details of every financial transaction. It includes the date it occurred, the nature of the transaction, and whether it was a payment or a receipt. He also invented a system of ledger entries. The ledger provided a radical departure from previous bookkeeping systems since it enabled the compiler of the books to include an offsetting entry for every transaction. That is, for every entry on the left side of the ledger (a debit entry), there had to be an equivalent entry on the right side of the ledger (a credit entry). Pacioli also discussed the concept of the trial balance, where all the debit entries were tallied and compared with the summary of all the credit entries. His double-entry system required that the debits would equal credits. The Venetian System, as it was subsequently called, allowed Italian merchants to do business efficiently because of its superior bookkeeping outcomes. As trade expanded it spread across Europe and became the standard model for keeping the books thereafter (Pacioli, cited in Gleeson-White 2012). The Pacioli accounting model will be discussed in more detail in Chapter 7.

Another major bookkeeping development occurred in England during the Industrial Revolution in the eighteenth century. This time it revolved around the management of costs in manufacturing industries. Josiah Wedgwood, one of England's major pottery producers, found that he could better manage his production costs by calculating detailed costings for materials and labour. He also distinguished between overhead costs, fixed costs and variable costs. He identified the ways in which these costs changed as production levels changed, and explained how unit costs would fall as total production increased. He could then calculate the savings resulting from large production runs. We now use the term 'economies of scale' to describe this process.

In the nineteenth century accounting became a profession through the establishment of the Institute of Chartered Accountants in Edinburgh and, as the Industrial Revolution accelerated, the demand for accountants increased exponentially. During the twentieth century the globalization of commerce, increasing inter-firm competition, the increasing complexity of corporate taxation and stringent government regulation have all increased the demand for accounting systems that allow businesses to manage their financial affairs efficiently, ensure a competitive advantage and provide appropriate information to owners and regulators.

ACCOUNTING AND SPORT MANAGEMENT

Unfortunately, sport has, for many years, lagged behind the business sector from a financial management perspective. This is due to a number of reasons. First, it has a history of amateurism, which meant that money management was not as important as participation and the pleasure of competition. Second, most sport organizations were traditionally run on a small scale, where budgets were constrained by the funds available from memberships, fundraising events, donations and generous benefactors. Third, sport was seen as something different from business and, as a result, there was no need for sophisticated systems of financial management. However, this has all changed over the last fifty years, as Chapters 1 and 2 explain. Even small-scale sports now have to ensure their financial viability in the face of competition from other sporting activities. Moreover, governments now require sport associations to manage their affairs efficiently in order to qualify for grants and subsidies. In addition, there has been a massive growth in professional sport around the world, which in turn requires sound financial management for its overall sustainability (Bourg and Gouguet 2007).

For the most part, sport management education has centred on planning, strategy and marketing. While this approach has fostered the emergence of many sophisticated development and marketing plans for sport organizations, it has undervalued the importance of good financial management competencies. There are still many sport managers who have difficulty reading balance sheets and profit and loss statements, and who would be unable to distinguish between the 'investing' section of a cash flow statement and the 'financing' section of the same statement.

There are a number of facets to being a good financial manager. The first is to be systematic in the way one runs the organization, and to provide resources for the proper keeping of the books. The second is to understand the difference between the reporting function of the accounts (which is to provide financial summaries to stakeholders) and the management function of the accounts (which is to generate data that can be used to strategize, monitor and control the financial affairs of the organization). The third is to become financially literate, which means not only being able to understand and speak the language of accounting and bookkeeping, but also being able to accurately interpret financial documents. These documents include budget papers, economic impact statements, project evaluation reports, cash flow statements, profit and loss statements and, finally, balance sheets.

The need for financial management skills is increasingly important when having to accommodate a range of legal and reporting requirements. In most nations around the world there are generally accepted accounting principles, which go under the acronym of GAAP. The aim of GAAP is to make financial statements consistent and comparable, and consequently allow investors and other stakeholders to make judgements about the relative performance of businesses. This principle applies equally to sport organizations. Attempts have also been made to develop international standard accounting principles, and in recent times an International Accounting Standards Board (IASB) has been established. The Board has set international financial reporting standards (IFRS) for the format and content of balance sheets, the definition and valuation of assets, the classification of liabilities, and how profits should be defined and calculated.

KEY ACCOUNTING PRINCIPLES

There are a number of accounting principles that underpin financial management and reporting around the world. These principles allow for a standard framework by which accounting records are created and displayed. Unless otherwise noted, the following principles will apply to accounting documents discussed in subsequent chapters of this book.

The business entity

The first principle is that for legal and financial purposes the business is separate from its owners or proprietors. This means that, even where the owner of the business and its management may be the same people, there is a clear distinction between the business or organization as an entity and the ownership. This also means that, even in an owner-operated business, all transactions involving the owner are designated and recorded. So, if the owner injects her own funds into the business, this is recorded as an increase in the owners' equity, and an increase in the cash assets of the business. Alternatively, if the owner decides to take money out of her business, it is recorded as a decrease in the owners equity and a fall in the cash assets of the business.

The going concern

The second principle is that the business or organization has a life of its own independently of what happens to the owner. So, the business continues to operate and is a going concern until it is wound up or liquidated. This means also that assets will be valued at their purchase price or market value, and not at a forced sale price.

The accounting period

The third principle is that the business life of the organization is divided into distinct accounting periods. For each period, usually of one year in length, accounts are prepared and made available to all stakeholders. Under this principle the aim is to include all transactions that occur in the period, and not to exclude relevant items of revenue and expenditure.

Historical cost

The fourth principle is that, unless designated otherwise, all transactions will be recorded at their historical cost. This applies to not only all recurrent expenses such as wages and overheads, but also to assets such as merchandise, buildings, machinery and other equipment. Assets will be valued at their historical cost, unless there has been a revaluation, in which case a brief comment about their depreciation or increase in value will be provided in notes attached to the financial statements.

Conservatism

The fifth principle is that financial information will be reported conservatively. This means that expenses and liabilities will never be underestimated and, where there is any doubt, the higher figure will prevail. The opposite applies to revenue and assets. Being conservative means that, where there is any doubt, they will be underestimated. That is, in this instance the lower figure will prevail. This is an important principle to follow since there is always an optimistic propensity to exaggerate revenues, and push some expense items to the side.

Materiality

The sixth principle is that financial reports should contain everything that is significant and relevant. In particular, any significant shifts or changes in assets, liabilities, revenues and expenses should be noted. This principle, which is called the doctrine of materiality, also means that, where there is variability between annual reports – be it a change in format and design, or a change in the amount of detail provided – these differences should be made clear and transparent.

Reliability

The seventh principle is that the same methods and practices should be used in constructing the accounts. This is also called the principle of consistency, and it means that methods for distinguishing between different types of assets and liabilities should be the same, depreciation should be calculated on a uniform basis, cash flow statements should follow the same format, and the processes for calculating operating and net profits should be consistent.

CASE STUDY 6.1

Setting standards for clubs, associations and leagues

As noted above, the IASB has taken on the role of setting international financial reporting standards (IFRS) for the compilation, formulation and presentation of financial information. In the light of the globalization of nearly all economic activity, it was felt there needed to be a common international language for the conduct of business affairs in general, and the production of financial documents in particular. Sport was viewed to be no exception, since sport enterprises are now building a host of international networks and partnerships. It is therefore more important than ever before that business accounts are not only understandable across international boundaries, but can also be properly compared and contrasted. There is also an emerging problem around the issue of what exactly should be made available to the public, and what can be legitimately kept in confidence. Sport is an especially interesting sector in this respect since it has been notoriously renowned for not disclosing sensitive financial information on the grounds that it would undermine any competitive advantage a club, association or league had built up over time. And, what is more, the sometimes paranoid concern for secrecy in these clubs, associations and leagues often occurred in situations where public – that is, taxpayers' – money was being used to prop up their financial operations. There has consequently been a strong movement – with professional sport leagues being the focus of attention – to make organizations more transparent and accountable when it comes to the disclosure of problematic practices, the release of financial documents and the public interrogation of financial data.

   In recent times Transparency International (TI), an international agency that looks at public policy around the world, has championed the cause of greater levels of public disclosure for not only profit-based organizations, but also not-for-profit ones as well. TI has spent a considerable amount of resources highlighting the social problems that sport enterprises create through their desire to do things in secret, and only disclose information when they are forced to. In 2011, TA examined the governance practices of FIFA (Fédération Internationale de Football Association), the international governing body for world football, and found a number of weak reporting processes, especially when it came to the discussion of bribery and match fixing. It recommended that FIFA's commitment to a public policy of zero tolerance of bribery be 'backed up by a transparent implementation process that is monitored and evaluated' (Schenk 2011: 3). In 2013, TI completed a similar analysis of the International Cricket Council's (ICC's) structures and systems. It found that cricket needed 'greater transparency and "accountability"' throughout all its operations,

which, in turn, demanded 'transparent governance structures, policies, and procedures, and a commitment from the top (the ICC, that is) to adhere to these policies'
(Barrington *et al.* 2013: 4).

As the TI reports show, IFRS initiatives have not always delivered the sort of
changes that were desired. However, it has on balance been a good thing. This is
because it demands that organizations, no matter what their legal status, or what
industry sector they operate in, have an obligation to deliver appropriate and professionally documented financial information to their stakeholders. These standards
revolve around two foundation statements that comprise both the structure and
framework for the following chapters:

- The *financial position* of an enterprise should be provided in the Statement of
  Financial Position, or what used to be called a balance sheet. The main items are
  (1) Assets, which are a resource controlled by the enterprise as a result of past
  events from which future economic benefits are expected to flow to the
  enterprise, (2) Liabilities, which are a present obligation of the enterprise arising
  from the past events, the settlement of which is expected to result in an outflow
  from the enterprise's resources, and (3) Equity, which is the residual interest in
  the assets of the enterprise after deducting all the liabilities under the historical
  cost principle. Equity is also known as owners' equity, and is the constant real
  value of shareholders' equity.
- The *financial performance* of an enterprise is primarily provided in the Statement
  of Comprehensive Income, or what used be called the income statement or profit
  and loss accounts. The main items that measure financial performance are (1)
  Revenues, which are the increases in economic benefit during an accounting
  period in the form of inflows or enhancements of assets, or decrease of liabilities
  that result in increases in equity (however, this does not include contributions
  from equity participants in the form of proprietors, partners and shareholders),
  and (2) Expenses, which are decreases in economic benefits during an accounting
  period in the form of outflows, or depletions of assets or incurrences of liabilities
  that result in decreases in equity. Additionally, revenues and expenses should be
  measured in nominal monetary units under the historical cost accounting model
  and, where appropriate, in units of constant purchasing power where an
  'inflation-adjusted' index is applied to the numbers.

The other important point to remember here is that these reporting standards
apply equally to non-profit business as to profit-centred businesses. This means that
sport enterprises that do not have shareholders cannot absolve themselves from
responsibility from issuing proper financial accounts on the grounds that they are not
in the business of making profits. This improperly narrow view of what information
needs to be made public, and what should not, has been addressed in many forums
around the world. A publication of the Institute of Chartered Accountants of
Australia (ICAA 2013) titled *Enhancing Not-for-profit Annual and Financial Reporting,*
takes up this issue in some detail. It gave special attention to annual reports, and how
they should be best prepared. It makes the crucial point that all financial reporting

issues should be framed by the organization's governance system, mission and vision statements, and strategic plan. Once this is done the organization is then in the position to document its achievements, while also discussing any problematic outcomes. It also suggests that organizations err on the side of more rather than less disclosure, and not only provide all relevant data, but also discuss it in a thoughtful manner. In short, the aim is not only to attend to the detail, but also to be accountable and transparent in one's dealings with key stakeholders (ICAA 2013: 13–22).

UNDERSTANDING THE ORGANIZATIONAL CONTEXT

As the above discussion shows, there is a concerted attempt around the world to standardize accounting and financial management functions, ensure that statements and reports adhere to a common set of rules and guidelines, and ensure that all financial data relevant to the organization's performance are disclosed. At the same time it should be remembered that accounting and financial management will take place in many different settings and contexts. In particular, organizations can take on different legal forms.

Single proprietor

The simplest business entity is one that is owned and operated by a single person. They are known as sole traders. The owner supplies the cash and other assets to establish the business, and is also able to draw money out of the business, which is effectively the profits. The owner can also borrow funds to build up the asset base of the business. At the same time, the personal affairs of the owner are kept separate from the financial transactions of the business. While from an accounting viewpoint the owner is separate from the business, from a legal viewpoint the owner is not. This means the owner or operator is liable for all debt of the business.

Partnership

A partnership has a similar structure to that of a single proprietor organization. The key difference is that it can be owned by two or more people. No specific legal requirement is needed to form a partnership, other than a written agreement to say that a partnership has been organized. Like a single proprietor business, the partners are liable for the debts of the business. Single proprietorships and partnerships are easy to establish, although they must be registered as businesses, and provide for a unique business name. However, they provide little legal protection for the owners, and in situations where large debts have been accumulated the claims of creditors may have to be met in part from the owners' personal assets.

Company

In order to provide a stronger business structure and greater legal protection a company can be formed. A company will cost more to form than a single proprietorship or partnership, but it has the benefit of creating a legal separation between the owner or owners and the business. Because the business is a separate legal entity the owners are not liable for its debts. However, the owners are the designated shareholders in this form of business, and their shareholding or equity in the business may be used to meet creditors' demands, but their losses cannot exceed their shareholdings. This feature is known as limited liability.

There are different types of companies. The first is a proprietary company, which is allowed no more than fifty shareholders. In addition, it cannot raise funds from the public. However, its shares can be transferred to some other person. It is also allowed to pay dividends to shareholders. A second type of company is the public company. A public company has no limitation on the number of shareholders, and can raise capital by inviting the public to subscribe to an issue of shares, debentures and loans. Public companies are listed on the stock exchange, and their shares can be traded at will. In the EPL world-football competition some clubs are registered as public companies, their aim being to ensure access to a larger funding base. Like a private company, a public company can distribute dividends to shareholders. The benefit of its structure is that it allows access to large amounts of funds or capital. The cost is that it is subject to stringent reporting requirements, and must provide detailed reports for both its shareholders and appropriate government agencies.

A third type of company is the company limited by guarantee. In this case the investors in the business are liable only for the funds they have contributed. This structure is often used in situations where an entity is established to undertake a specific mission to generate revenue, but does not wish to distribute profits. While there are no restrictions on the ability of the company limited by guarantee to earn profits (which is why commercially oriented sport clubs find it an appropriate legal structure), it is not able to distribute its surplus to members or issue shares. Companies limited by guarantee must use the word 'limited' or the abbreviated 'ltd' after their names. In addition, the setup costs are high and, because they must be registered under the Corporations Act in Australia, they are required to disclose significant financial information. A majority of Australian Football League clubs have adopted this legal structure.

Non-profit associations

The above business structures may be suitable for people wishing either to make money from sports, or to distribute the profits to their owners or shareholders. However, the majority of sport organizations, unlike the privately owned professional sport teams in the USA, or most of the public company-based football clubs in the EPL, are not interested in maximizing profits for their owners. Rather, they are more concerned with servicing their members, developing the sport and improving their on-field performances. These types of organizations are consequently interested in having an organizational or business structure that gives non-profit status, while at the same time protecting their members from creditor demands and threat of litigation.

Governments now have in place legislation that allows community sport organizations to register as incorporated associations. This allows the members to be legally separated from the entity while allowing tax-free status by virtue of their non-profit operations, whereby operating surpluses are reinvested in the development of facilities, improvement in services to members and general development of the sport.

PROFIT OR NON-PROFIT?

Sport organizations consequently take on a number of different legal forms, depending on what their aims are, and how structured and extensive they want their businesses to be. The most basic structure is to be a non-profit organization that has no legal identity separate from its owners. Small community sport clubs traditionally took on this form. In another instance, the organization may be profit-centred, but also a small sole trader or partnership. While sport clubs do not fit this model, it is particularly suitable for sport consulting firms, player agents and sport retailers. The third possibility is to have an incorporated structure, but operate as a non-profit entity and therefore not be required to pay company tax. Most sport clubs and associations have adopted this structure, and some clubs in professional football leagues have also taken on a variation of this form by registering as companies limited by guarantee.

The final possibility is to adopt a company structure that enables an extension of funding options, and allows the club to optimize revenue and return dividends to shareholders. As noted previously, this model characterizes many European and USA professional sport clubs. In Europe many clubs are registered as public companies, while

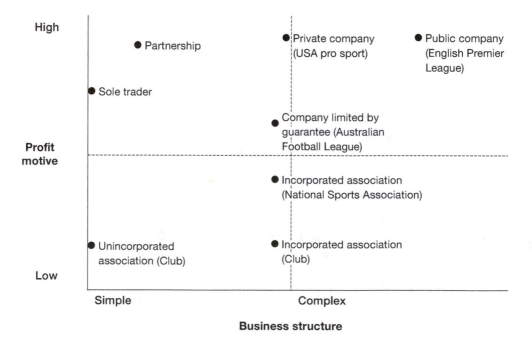

FIGURE 6.1 Legal structures for sport organizations

in the USA most are private businesses with only a few independent shareholders. These different legal arrangements are illustrated in Figure 6.1.

Each of the above structures has its strengths and weaknesses, but as sport becomes more complex and commercialized there is growing pressure to become incorporated, and where the need to access a larger funding base is strong, to change to a private or public company structure, which enables the 'sport business' not only to raise capital funds through large-scale borrowings – which goes under the name of debt financing, but also to issue shares to the public – which is referred to as equity financing. This important distinction is neatly summarized in Brown *et al.* (2010: 5–9).

RECAP

Financial management in sport does not happen in a social or legal vacuum. It is conducted in enterprises embedded with many unique features, but it is also framed by a number of accounting principles and practices that have stood the test of time. What is more, accounting theory has a strong methodological base, which gives it a rationality and logic that is beyond reproach. It also operates a variety of legal structures that need to be clearly understood. As a result it is actually in the best interests of sport clubs, associations and leagues to comply with both foundation accounting principles and international reporting standards. It constitutes an essential first on the pathway to professional financial management practices.

REVIEW QUESTIONS

These comments raise many questions, with the key ones being identified below.

1 What is bookkeeping all about, and where and when did it originate?

2 From a commercial perspective, why is it important to have a good set of books?

3 What makes for an effectively organized financial management system?

4 How does the reporting function differ from the management function when it comes to the financial management function?

5 What does Transparency International say about the reporting practices of FIFA and the ICC? What does it recommend to make things better?

6 What is the primary role of the International Accounting Standards Board (IASB)?

7 Identify four important accounting principles and how they can be used to frame accounting structures and systems.

8 The proper public disclosure of financial information is an important issue in sport enterprises. At the very minimum, how much financial data should be made available to a sport organization's stakeholders?

9 What might go wrong when financial data are regularly not disclosed to the stakeholders of a sport enterprise?

10 The financial management function can take place in many types of organizational settings. Identify the different legal form an organization can take, and indicate which forms are most used in the sport industry.

11 Why are so many sport organizations set up as non-profit entities?

12 What are the strengths and weaknesses of setting up a sport organization as a company limited by guarantee?

13 Under what circumstances would it be appropriate to have a sport organization set up as a public company, and what might the benefits be?

14 The compilation of financial accounts is doubly important for people running sport enterprises. This is not only because they have a 'reporting' role, but also because they have a 'strategic management' function. Please explain.

FURTHER READING

For a general historical study of the role of money in business and commercial affairs, see Davies, G. (2005) *A History of Money from Ancient Times to Present Day*, 3rd edition, Cardiff: University of Wales Press. For a concise review of generally accepted accounting principles, see Horngren, C., Harrison, W. and Oliver, M. (2011) *Accounting*, 9th edition, Upper Saddle River, NJ: Prentice Hall (Chapter 1: 'Accounting and the business environment').

There is an excellent discussion of accounting principles and reporting standards in Wilson, R. (2011) *Managing Sport Finance*, London: Routledge (Chapter 2: 'Regulatory standards'). And, for a detailed discussion of how non-profit organizations (which includes most sport enterprises) can deliver 'best practice' annual reports, and what type of financial data should go in them, see Institute of Chartered Accountants of Australia (ICAA) (2013) *Enhancing Not-for-profit Annual and Financial Reporting*, Sydney, NSW: ICAA.

For a sport-specific discussion of legal structures for sport organizations, see Fried, G., DeSchriver, T. and Mondello, M. (2013) *Sport Finance*, 3rd edition, Champaign, IL: Human Kinetics (Chapter 5: 'Business structures'); and Fried, G., Shapiro, S. and Deschriver, T. (2003) *Sport Finance*, Champaign, IL: Human Kinetics (Chapter 4: 'Business structures'). An additionally instructive discussion of legal structures in sport organizations is contained in Brown, M., Rascher, D., Nagel, M. and McEvoy, C. (2010) *Financial Management in the Sport Industry*, Scottsdale, AZ: Holcomb Hathaway (Chapter 5: 'Financial management').

For a thorough examination of the formation and operation of partnerships and companies, see Hoggett, J., Edwards, L. and Medlin, J. (2006) *Accounting*, 6th edition, Milton, Qld: John Wiley and Sons (Chapter 15: 'Partnerships' and Chapter 16: 'Companies'). The strengths and weaknesses of incorporating as an association or a company are discussed in Healey, D. (2003) *Sport and the Law*, 3rd edition, Sydney, NSW: University of New South Wales Press (Chapter 3: 'The legal nature of sporting organisations').

USEFUL WEBSITES

- For a discussion of the origin and evolution of accounting theory and practice see Giroux, G. (1999) *A Short History of Accounting and Business*, College Station, TX: Mays Business School, Texas A&M University. It is accessible on **http://acct.tamu. edu/giroux/Shorthistory.html**.
- A brief introduction to GAAP and IFRS, and some problems they face, are contained in **www.economist.com/node/21559350**.
- The following website contains an instructive slide show on GAAP: **www.youtube. com/watch?v=-MFV2lYjwcY**.
- The European Commission's 'take' on the push to have common international accounting standards is presented in **http://ec.europa.eu/internal_market/accounting/ias/index_en.htm**.
- A useful guide for understanding the different legal structures available for both profit-centred and not-for-profit enterprises is included in **www.gov.uk/business-legal-structures/overview**.
- For a detailed discussion of the sport and transparency problem it is worth taking a visit to the Transparency International website at **www.transparency.org/global_priorities/private_sector/business_principles**.

CHAPTER 7

Constructing the accounts

LEARNING OUTCOMES

At the end of this chapter readers will be able to:

- understand the principles of double-entry bookkeeping
- explain the difference between cash accounting and accrual accounting models
- articulate the distinction between asset accounts, liability accounts, revenue accounts, expense accounts and capital/owners' equity accounts
- construct a set of simple accounts for a sport enterprise using the above knowledge.

CHAPTER SUMMARY

This chapter introduces readers to the theory and practice of double-entry bookkeeping and its use of debit and credit columns to build financial statements. This will be done by dissecting the simple equation that underpins it. This equation – where assets will always be balanced by an equivalent amount of liabilities and owners' equity (or proprietorship, as it is sometimes called) – will be scrutinized. This will, in turn, lead into a discussion of the five core account types that drop out of the accounting equation. They are asset accounts, liability accounts, revenue accounts, expense accounts and capital – that is, owners' equity – accounts. At this point a careful distinction will be made between cash accounting processes (simple but often misleading) and accrual accounting processes (more complicated but more meaningful). Financial data from fictitious sport club examples using a 'simulation exercise' approach will be used to establish a simple set of accounts using the five account types listed above.

SPORT AND FINANCE

As the earlier chapters have noted, significant segments of sport are now big business. And, as indicated, this trend to commercialized sport has been succinctly addressed by Bourg and Gouguet (2007: 7–35). At the same time it was also noted that most sport organizations are relatively small, and depend on the support of club members, volunteer officials, community businesses and local government to sustain their operations. While high-profile professional sport leagues turn over hundreds and, in some cases, thousands of millions of dollars a year, the majority of sport clubs and associations are lucky to secure any more than a million dollars for their operations. A majority of sport is really a form of small business. A suburban supermarket turns over more money than most sport clubs and associations.

ISSUES TO ADDRESS

However, no matter what the scale or size of sport organizations, they all need to be managed in a sound and responsible manner. Many sport administrators do not feel comfortable handling money, or planning the financial affairs of clubs and associations. This often arises out of poor background knowledge and a lack of experience in managing complex financial issues. In practice, there are many financial questions that sport managers need to answer. They include:

- What do we own?
- What do we owe?
- What did we earn?
- What did we spend?
- Did we make a profit?
- Do we have enough cash to pay debts when they fall due?
- How big is our interest bill?
- Are we borrowing too much?
- Did we improve upon last year?
- How do we compare with other similar sport organizations?

There is also the problem of making sense of the vocabulary of accounting. The distinction between assets and liabilities is mostly clear, with assets amounting to all those things we own, and liabilities being all those things we owe to others. However, the distinction between tangible and intangible assets and current and non-current liabilities may often be less clear. There can also be additional consternation when someone is asked to explain the difference between liquid assets, current assets, non-current assets and fixed assets. The concepts of owners' equity, proprietorship, shareholders' funds and accumulated funds can also cause confusion, while further difficulties can arise when contrasting operating profits with net profits. When listening to how financial ratios operate, the confusion may be compounded. The distinction between a working capital ratio, a debt to equity ratio and a return on capital ratio usually needs careful explanation. A further spanner in the conceptual works arises when the terms 'depreciation' and 'amortization' have to be explained and operationalized. This raises the additional thorny question of how assets might be best valued.

FINANCIAL RECORDS

A good first step in improving financial management skills is to become familiar with the fundamental data used to create financial records. While most sport organizations may not be as big as the average commercial business enterprise, they still engage in hundreds of exchanges and transactions every day. These transactions include the payment of wages and salaries to staff, the purchase of equipment, the sale of merchandise to members and fans, the refurbishment of offices, the ordering of stationery and the receipt of monies from members, government and sponsors. Also, these transactions are embedded in specific documents that include:

- the purchase order, which is a statement requesting supply of a good or service in which payment is now (cash) or later (credit);
- the invoice, which is a statement requesting payment for sale of a good or service;
- the receipt, which is a statement that confirms payment for a good or service (this can also take the form of a paid invoice);
- the bank statement, which is a statement of the trading account transactions that summarizes the movement of cash in and out of the business, and the amount of cash held in the cash account at a point in time.

While the above transactions are external to the organization (i.e. they involve an exchange with an outside entity) transactions can also be internal. A good example of an internal transaction is the depreciation of assets, where the wear and tear on computer equipment, and the speed with which it becomes obsolete, make it less valuable as time goes on. This needs to be accounted for, and internal transactions provide a visible way of revealing these changes.

It is one thing to identify the transactions that will impact on the financial position of a club or association, but it is another to put a value on them. For the most part this issue is easily resolved since transactions involve the exchange of products (including tangible goods and less tangible services) for money. Money is both a medium of exchange and a store of value. It is the common currency by which all sorts of items (e.g. the services of a physiotherapist, or the purchase of sport equipment) can be priced and valued.

Once the transaction has been identified, priced and valued, the next step is to record and classify these transactions. Without a system of recording and classifying, the organization is left with a mass of data that means nothing more than that things were either busy or slow in one week, or that a lot of money passed hands in some other week. It is therefore crucial to set up systems for sorting transactions on the basis of some common theme or type. A simple first step is to distinguish between assets and borrowings, and revenue and expenses, and then to further divide them into subcategories or specific accounts. The final step is to compile the different accounts, and create summary financial statements that reveal how the organization is going. Two sorts of reporting can occur here. First, it can be an internal report, which includes an analysis of specific issues such as trends in salary costs, merchandise sales, membership income, maintenance expenses and equipment costs. Second, it can be an external report, which is more general, and can take the form of a set of accounts comprising a profit and loss statement, balance sheet and cash flow statement. These concepts will be covered in more detail in Chapters 8 and 9.

FOUNDATION PRINCIPLES OF SOUND BOOKKEEPING

An additional thing that financial managers of sport organizations need to understand is the basics of double-entry bookkeeping (which was briefly discussed in the previous chapter and is examined in more detail here). Once this step has been taken, the issues of how accounts are compiled, and how they can be used to construct a financial statement, can be addressed. However, before this is done it is appropriate to look at the difference between a cash method of accounting and keeping the books, and the accrual method of keeping the books.

Cash method

Traditionally, most small sport clubs and associations operated using the cash accounting method where revenue and expenses are reported when they are actually received or paid. As a result, with the cash-based system, the revenue and expense patterns of the organization are an exact match with their cash flow pattern. So, under this approach, when a cheque is banked it is recorded as the receipt of revenue, and when a cheque is written as payment to a creditor, it is recorded as the incurring of an expense. The same goes for all cash-based transactions. As a result, the cash method of accounting is just a matter of recording all receipts and all payments of the club or association over a period of time, and calculating the difference to see if there is a surplus or deficit. However, while the cash method is uncomplicated and appeals to our common sense, it does not accurately measure an organization's financial performance over specific time periods. Because the cash system is based on cash as it is spent or received, it can lead to quite inaccurate summaries of a sport organization's overall financial performance.

It can therefore be quite misleading to record all payments or receipts for the period in which they actually occur, and then use them to measure current financial performance. As noted previously, when we discussed the core accounting principles and conventions, only those transactions directly relevant to the period under consideration should be included in the accounts for that period. In short, a list of cash receipts and cash payments is not a good measure of income earned for the period and expenses incurred for that period.

It is thus instructive to reflect on the following examples. Using the cash method of bookkeeping, if an organization were to pay a professional indemnity insurance premium of $5,000 in advance (i.e. for the following year) it would be recorded as part of the current year's transactions (cash payment) despite the fact that the benefits would be obtained next year. Similarly, under the cash method of bookkeeping, the purchase of a $6,000 computer system would be recorded in the year it was bought (as a cash payment), even though it would provide benefits in many subsequent years as well. According to the cash method, expenses for the year would now total $11,000, although most of the benefits from these transactions would not be realized until the following year. On the revenues side, if club members paid $10,000 of their registration fees in advance (i.e. for next year), then, under the cash method, these monies would be recorded as cash received for the current year. The same result would occur if a sponsor wrote a $90,000 cheque for a three-year arrangement commencing this year, and it was received and recorded in the current period. Under the cash method these two transactions produce an addition to revenues for this period of $100,000. But, again, this is misleading, since only $30,000 was directly relevant to the current period. The cash method of bookkeeping can therefore distort the real financial position of a sport organization by overstating the profit position if receipts are bunched in the current year, or understate it if payments are bunched in the current year. There must be a way of adjusting for these distortions, and the accrual method of accounting provides the solution.

Accrual method

In contrast, the accrual system is based on the notion that the real issue to be addressed is how to measure revenue earned for the current period, and to compare it to expenses incurred for the current period. This approach highlights two important principles. First, revenues and expenses need not involve the payment or receipt of cash at the immediate moment of transaction. Second, not all receipts and payments will relate to revenue and expenses for the current period. Instead, it is all about the use of resources to deliver a benefit or to impose a cost for a particular period of time. So, under the accrual model of bookkeeping, revenue is recognized when it is earned instead of when it is collected, and expenses are recognized when they are incurred, instead of when they are paid for. The accrual system consequently provides more accurate details on the financial status of a sport organization than the cash-based system, and therefore is of more effective use for management decision-making.

However, the accrual accounting system is also more complex than the cash accounting method. As already explained, with the accrual method expenses and revenues are identified independently of the movement of cash. So, in the case of the $5,000 insurance premium paid in advance, there needs to be a way of ensuring this $5,000 is not recorded as an expense for the current year. It is obviously an expense for the year that has not yet arrived. Similarly, with the member income and sponsorship funds received in advance, there needs to be a way of making sure they are not treated as an increase in revenue for the current year. This is because it is revenue for the following year. The resolution to this problem is addressed in the following section on double-entry bookkeeping. It will be shown that the insurance premium will be recorded as an asset under the heading of prepaid expense, while member and sponsor income will be recorded as a liability under the heading of income received in advance. But, more about this later.

In addition, under the accrual system, revenue earned during a specific period must be matched with the expenses linked with that revenue, thus making revenue the driving force dictating the documentation of expenses. The chief purpose of the matching procedure is to ensure that an accurate picture of profit or loss for the period under review is reported. In order for the matching process to be as accurate as possible, recording adjustments are made prior to the final preparation of financial statements. Consequently, a good initial step in improving financial management skills is, first, to understand how accounts are compiled and, second, to identify the ways in which double-entry bookkeeping can be used to construct a set of financial statements.

PROCESSING TRANSACTIONS

To repeat, there are two basic reasons why it is important to keep records of a sport organization's financial transactions. The first is to monitor the organization's ongoing performance to ensure that costs are properly managed, and that income is sufficient to cover costs and pay bills when they are due. The second is to provide a summary of its financial affairs to its stakeholders. For small sport clubs and associations there are few financial transactions, leaving summaries of total receipts and total payments as the only details to consider in calculating overall financial performance. However, other sport organizations are faced with a large number of daily transactions that influence both their profitability and wealth. They include not only commercial enterprises such as fitness centres and gymnasiums, but also non-profit professional sporting clubs such as those in professional sport leagues. In these situations, transactions are recorded on a daily basis in journals that are subsequently totalled into ledgers, which in turn are compiled to form trial balances that form the basis for financial statements. The flow chart in Figure 7.1 illustrates this process.

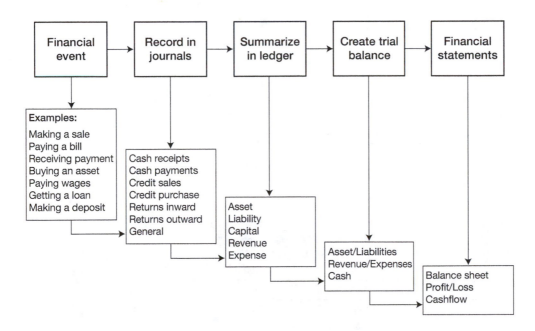

FIGURE 7.1 The bookkeeping process

Source: adapted from Smith and Stewart (1999).

Journals

To get the accounting process off the ground, transactions are recorded in chronological order, and are compiled as books or electronic files. Although financial events can be documented in a single all-encompassing journal, there are typically several subdivisions that can be used to record specific transactions. They include:

- cash receipts journal, which records all cash received;
- cash payments journal, which records all cash paid;
- credit sales journal, which records all sales of goods or services that are paid for by credit;
- credit purchase journal, which records all purchases of goods or services bought with credit;
- general journal, which records purchases of assets other than stock on credit, and any other transaction that is not entered elsewhere.

These subdivisions are not always necessary, but the need for systematic record-keeping remains a fixed principle. Some simple examples of journal entries are listed in Tables 7.1 and 7.2.

TABLE 7.1 Sample journal entry – cash payments, South Wales Indoor Polo Association

Item	Details	Amount ($)
1	Office stationery	25
2	Advertising	150
3	Postage-paid envelopes	1,500
4	Staff T-shirts	225
5	Promotional caps	300
		2,200

TABLE 7.2 Sample journal entry – cash sales, North Shore Swim Centre

Item	Details	Amount ($)
1	G. Hackett – full membership	550
2	L. Lenton – swim suit	50
3	T. Blair – gym membership	300
4	Ocean View City Council – corporate membership	20,000
5	J. Howard – protein powder	100
		21,000

Ledgers

The totals from journals are transferred to ledgers, which comprise a database of transactions grouped under a number of account categories. Moreover, for each account type there are two columns. The left-side column is designated as the debit column, while the right-side column is designated as the credit column. These accounts of credit and debit are typically represented by a T-account. The T-account includes debits on the left side and credits on the right, as can be seen in Figure 7.2. It is important to note that, when it comes to the models of accrual accounting and double-entry bookkeeping, debits and credits have nothing to do with gains and losses, or positive or negative balances.

In order to understand how transactions are recorded in the T-account, it is necessary to understand the foundation principles of double-entry bookkeeping. As indicated previously, it is built around the concept of debits and credits, where a debit entry involves locating it on the left side of a ledger account, while a credit entry involves locating it on the right side of the account. In other words, debit equals a left-side entry, and credit equals a right-side entry. The other important thing to remember about double-entry bookkeeping is that there are five standard groups of accounts. They are asset accounts, liability accounts, capital accounts, revenue accounts and, finally, expense accounts. The main features of each of these account types are listed below.

Name of account	
Debits	Credits

FIGURE 7.2 The T-account

Account group 1: assets

Assets are items of value owned by the business. They constitute a benefit to the business, and are categorized as follows:

- cash or money held in a trading bank account;
- debtors or people who owe money to the business (e.g. purchased branded T-shirt but yet to pay), also known as accounts receivable;
- prepaid expense (e.g. property insurance paid for in advance);
- stock and merchandise (e.g. branded T-shirts for sale to members);
- furniture and equipment;
- investments;
- motor vehicles;
- land and buildings.

Assets can also be current, which are those assets more easily converted to cash at short notice, or non-current, which are those assets that are fixed and thus a little slower to liquidate. This is always an important distinction to make.

Account group 2: liabilities

Liabilities comprise the amounts owed to others by the business. They constitute a claim against the business and are categorized as follows:

- creditors or people who are owed money (e.g. a computer purchased on credit), also known as accounts payable;
- accrued payments or monies earmarked to pay future claims (e.g. provision for superannuation or employee sick leave);
- bank overdraft whereby the business is able to overdraw on its trading account;
- short-term loans;
- long-term loans.

Like assets, liabilities can be current or non-current.

Account group 3: capital

Capital is the amount of funds invested in the business, and is otherwise known as proprietorship or owners' equity:

- it comprises the owners' contribution to the business;
- it includes startup capital, retained profits and additional cash injections.

Owners' equity can change due to an injection of capital into the business, profits, losses or when the owner draws money out of the business.

Account group 4: revenue

Revenue comprises the amount earned through the business's trading activities and includes sales, charges and fees:

- it can be cash and/or credit;
- it focuses on earned revenue;
- monies received in advance are not included as revenue items.

Account group 5: expenses

Expenses comprise the costs associated with earning the revenue:

- they focus on incurred expenses, even when not yet paid for;
- costs paid in advance are not included as an expense item.

The most important rule in transferring records to the above ledger accounts is that, for every debit entry, there must be a corresponding credit entry, and for every credit entry there must be a corresponding debit entry. In other words, for every left-side entry there must be an equivalent right-side entry. This means that the left-side totals must equal the right-side totals: hence the term double-entry bookkeeping. All financial recording can be summarized using the equation $A = L + P$ where P is $[C + R - E - D]$. That is, assets or items of value owned (A) are always equal to liabilities or amounts owed to others (L), plus proprietorship (P) or the owner's investment. Proprietorship, or owners' equity as it is often called, includes invested capital (C), revenue or amounts earned from trading (R), expenses or costs associated with earning revenue (E) and drawings that the owner may take out of the business (D). The equation can be rewritten as:

$$A = L + C + R - E - D.$$

This states that assets will increase when borrowings, revenue and investment in the business increase. It also says that assets will fall if expenses increase and capital is drawn out of the business. An injection of capital into the business will build up the asset base, while a fall in liabilities will also increase the asset base. Conversely, an excess of expenses over revenue will, all other things being equal, deliver a fall in assets.

It is one thing to understand the above equation, and to appreciate how different transactions impact on each of the five different groups of accounts. However, it is another thing to know if that account should be debited or credited. For example, what happens to the cash-in-the-bank account when a sponsor's cheque arrives on the desk? The answer is contained within the internal logic of the double-entry bookkeeping system, which provides a set of rules by which to process any transaction. These rules are listed in Table 7.3.

In using this table, two questions must be asked about each transaction that is being recorded. The first is to what category of accounts does the transaction belong? For instance, will it impact on a liability account, or will it impact on an asset account? The second question to ask is will it be a debit entry or a credit entry? These rules confirm that, whenever the transaction produces an increase in the level of assets and expenses, it is debited (i.e. placed on the left side of the ledger). And, when the transaction leads to an increase in liabilities, capital and revenue, it will have a credit (or right side of the ledger) entry.

TABLE 7.3 Financial recording rules

Account	Increase	Decrease
Asset	Debit	Credit
Liability	Credit	Debit
Capital	Credit	Debit
Revenue	Credit	Debit
Expense	Debit	Credit

SIMULATION EXERCISE 7.1

Small Town Tennis Club

These rules are used in recording transactions in the sample ledger for the fictitious Small Town Tennis Club, which has been constructed from a single general journal. These journal entries are listed in Table 7.4. They are the core documents for constructing the accounts for the club. This is where it all begins.

TABLE 7.4 Small Town Tennis Club – journal entries

Transactions – July

1	Deposit of $20,000 from member joining fee in business cheque account	11	Received payment for previous week's coaching clinic, to the value of $6,000
3	Bought computer and printer for $2,000 on credit	20	Paid for advertising in local paper for $400 in cash
4	Purchased office supplies (staplers, toner etc.) on credit for $500	25	Sold photocopier for $200 cash
5	Paid insurance for members of $10,000 in cash	29	Bought new photocopier for $2,500 on credit
7	Invoiced members for racket re-stringing to the value of $600	30	Paid utilities bills totalling $1,500 and rent of $2,500

These ten journal entries must now be posted to the ledgers using the double-entry bookkeeping rules listed above. As noted previously, the ledgers are constructed around each of the five basic account types, which are assets, liabilities, capital, revenue and expenses. It is also important to note that every transaction will have equal and offsetting entries in the ledger account. That is, they will not only be debited into one account, but also credited into another account. This is why the accounts will always balance.

Table 7.5 identifies the ways in which each transaction will be processed. In the first instance, member-joining fees (as distinct from annual membership fees) have been treated as an injection of capital into the club. This was done on the understanding that these fees could be reimbursed (and reissued, or off-sold to someone else if need be) if members wanted to withdraw their stakes in the club. By applying the double-entry bookkeeping recording rules, the capital account is credited (because it represents an increase), while the cash (asset) at bank account is debited (since the rules say this is done whenever an asset account increases). The office equipment and office supplies transactions both involve the purchase of assets on credit. Consequently, the office equipment (asset) account is debited in each case, but instead of crediting the cash at bank account, the accounts payable account is credited. This is because the items have been purchased on credit rather than cash.

TABLE 7.5 Small Town Tennis Club – summary of postings to ledger

Date		Particulars	Debit ($)	Credit ($)
July	1	Cash at bank (A – increases) Capital from member joining fee (C – increases) (member joining fees)	20,000	20,000
	3	Office equipment (A – increases) Accounts payable (L – increases) (purchased computer and printer on credit)	2,000	2,000
	4	Office supplies (A – increases) Accounts payable (L – increases) (purchased office supplies on credit)	500	500
	5	Insurance (E – increases) Cash at bank (A – decreases) (paid members' insurance)	10,000	10,000
	7	Accounts receivable (A – increases) Service revenue (R – increases) (invoiced members for racket re-stringing)	600	600
	11	Cash at bank (A – increases) Service revenue (R – increases) (payment received for coaching clinic)	6,000	6,000
	20	Advertising (E – increases) Cash at bank (A – decreases) (newspaper advertisement)	400	400
	25	Cash at bank (A – increases) Office equipment (A – decreases) (sale of photocopier)	200	200
	29	Office equipment (A – increases) Accounts payable (L – increases) (purchase of photocopier on credit)	2,500	2,500
	30	Utilities bills and rent (E – increases) Cash at bank (A – decreases) (utilities expenses)	4,000	4,000

When payment is finally made, the accounts payable account will be debited, while the cash account will be credited.

The racket re-string service constitutes earned revenue, even if payment is late. In this case the revenue account is credited, while the accounts receivable (asset) account is debited. Had the invoice been immediately paid, then the cash account would have been debited instead of accounts receivable. When all of the journal entries have been transferred to the ledger under the double-entry method, the account balances in Table 7.6 will result.

The next step is to create a trial balance, which is simply verification that equivalent debits and credits have been recorded in the accounts. Once this is done they form the basis for the construction of the financial statements. An example is shown in Table 7.7.

TABLE 7.6 Small Town Tennis Club – ledger

Date		Particulars	Debit ($)	Credit ($)	Balance ($)
		Assets			
July	1	Cash at bank (A – increases)	20,000		20,000
	5	Cash at bank (A – decreases)		10,000	10,000
	11	Cash at bank (A – increases)	6,000		16,000
	20	Cash at bank (A – decreases)		400	15,600
	25	Cash at bank (A – increases)	200		15,800
	30	Cash at bank (A – decreases)		4,000	11,800
	3	Office equipment (A – increases)	2,000		13,800
	4	Office supplies (A – increases)	500		14,300
	25	Office equipment (A – decreases)		200	14,100
	29	Office equipment (A – increases)	2,500		16,600
	7	Accounts receivable (A – increases)	600		17,200 Db
		Liabilities			
	3	Accounts payable (L – increases)		2,000	15,200
	4	Accounts payable (L – increases)		500	14,700
	29	Accounts payable (L – increases)		2,500	12,200
		Capital			
	1	Members' equity (joining fee) (C – increases)		20,000	–7,800 Cr
		Revenue			
	7	Re-stringing (R – increases)		600	–8,400
	11	Coaching clinic (R – increases)		6,000	–14,400 Cr
		Expenses			
	5	Insurance (E – increases)	10,000		–4,400
	20	Advertising (E – increases)	400		–4,000 Cr
	30	Utilities bills and rent (E – increases)	4,000		0
			46,200	46,200	

The trial balance

Trial balances are generally completed at the end of each month, and form the basis for financial statements. In this case some simple calculations can be made to establish the profit and losses incurred by the club, and in addition the balance of assets and liabilities.

TABLE 7.7 Small Town Tennis Club – trial balance (totals for July)

Account title	Debit ($)	Credit ($)
Assets		
Cash at bank	26,200	14,400
Office equipment	5,000	200
Accounts receivable	600	
Liabilities		
Accounts payable		5,000
Capital		
Members' equity (joining fee)		20,000
Revenue		
Re-stringing		600
Coaching clinic		6,000
Expenses		
Insurance	10,000	
Advertising	400	
Utilities bills and rent	4,000	
	46,200	46,200

So, once the trial balance has been completed we are left with a set of accounts that provides a picture of the Small Town Tennis Club's performance. The revenue account shows an aggregate figure of $6,600, while expenses are $14,400, thereby creating an operating deficit of $7,800. Over the same period the asset group of accounts has a balance of $17,200, comprising cash in bank $11,800 ($26,200 less $14,400), office equipment ($4,800) and accounts receivable ($600). Liabilities totalled $5,000 and invested capital owners' equity was $2,000. The accounting equation will therefore contain the following figures:

A (17,200) = L (5,000) + C (20,000) + R (6,600) – E (14,400).

In summary, the Small Town Tennis Club has made a loss on its operations so far, and its asset value has fallen from $20,000 (the initial injection of funds) to $17,200, its current balance. This is not a good trend, and if it continues into the future it will undermine the financial health of this small, but socially valuable, sport enterprise. It also becomes a very good reason to secure more revenue in order to improve its financial position and secure its operational future.

THE NEXT STEP

Once the accounts have been systematically compiled using an accrual accounting model, it is then possible to produce a set of financial statements that provide a clear picture of how the club, association or league is performing from a monetary perspective. The three key financial statements that need to be examined are (1) the profit and loss statement, (2) the balance sheet and (3) the cash flow statement. They will be discussed in more detail in the following chapter.

RECAP

A sporting enterprise that is not underpinned by a culture that values financial literacy, and does not have a structurally sound financial management system, is destined to fail. And, what is more, there is no good reason for not having a good working system in place. It is also essential that it be founded on the accrual system of accounting. Cash models are simple to follow, but do not deliver the best outcomes or provide the level of detail that is now required in any sport enterprise, no matter what its scope or scale. The other crucial point to note is that, while sport managers do not need to be trained accountants, they must have a sound working knowledge of accounting systems, and a detailed understanding of the language of accounting, to do their jobs properly. High levels of financial literacy are especially important when undertaking planning and strategy initiatives, and financial literacy begins with understanding the concept of accrual accounting, the principles of double-entry bookkeeping and how these principles underpin the construction of the accounts.

REVIEW QUESTIONS

A number of important questions follow on from these assertions.

1 Why is sound financial management so important to all sport organizations, no matter how large or small?

2 What are the key financial questions that all sport organizations need to ask in order to understand their overall financial well-being?

3 What financial records are the building blocks of all accounting systems?

4 What are the three core financial statements, and what do they aim to measure?

5 Distinguish between the cash method of accounting and the accrual method of accounting. Why is the accrual method a superior system of bookkeeping and accounting?

6 Describe the flow of a financial transaction from raw data to its absorption into a financial statement.

7 Explain the accounting equation and its underlying principles.

8 Identify the five core account types and their relationship to the accounting equation.

9 What is meant by the term 'double-entry bookkeeping', and how is it linked to the accounting equation?

10 Construct a table that explains how transactions will be recorded using the double-entry bookkeeping system.

11 Succinctly review the financial position of the Small Town Tennis Club.

12 What has the Small Town Tennis Club done well, and not so well?

13 How might the Small Town Tennis Club go about improving its financial performance?

FURTHER READING

For an easy-to-follow discussion of basic accounting systems and processes and the basics of double-entry bookkeeping, see Hoggett, J., Medlin, J., Edwards, L. and Tilling, M. (2012) *Financial Accounting*, 8th edition, Brisbane, Qld: John Wiley & Sons (Chapter 3: 'Recording transactions'). Another useful read on the theoretical foundations of accounting and the application of double-entry bookkeeping to account construction is Horngren, C., Harrison, W. and Oliver, M. (2011) *Accounting*, 9th edition, Upper Saddle River, NJ: Prentice Hall (Chapter 2: 'Recording business transactions').

An excellent sport-specific source is Wilson, R. (2011) *Managing Sport Finance*, London: Routledge (Chapter 3: 'Mechanics of financial accounting' and Chapter 5: 'From "T" accounts to financial statements'). Additional sports-specific discussion of the foundations of proper financial management in sport is contained in Fried, G., DeSchriver, T. and Mondello, M. (2013) *Sport Finance*, 3rd edition, Champaign, IL: Human Kinetics (Chapter 2: 'Basic financial concepts'). See also Fried, G., Shapiro, S. and Deschriver, T. (2003) *Sport Finance*, Champaign, IL: Human Kinetics (Chapter 2: 'Basic financial concepts').

A text that distils the basic concepts is Hart, L. (2006) *Accounting Demystified: A Self Teaching Guide*, New York: McGraw-Hill. A good starting point is Chapter 8 ('How to tell if something is a debit or a credit'). Chapter 9 ('A few simple transactions') puts the double-entry bookkeeping principles into practice.

USEFUL WEBSITES

• There are many websites that provide excellent learning experiences that cover the principles and practice of double-entry bookkeeping. One easy-to-follow site is **http://opentuition.com/fia/ma1/the-principles-of-double-entry-bookkeeping**.

- Another website that delivers sound advice about the principles of good accounting is **www.nios.ac.in/media/documents/VocInsServices/m1-5f.pdf**.
- A neat summary of the distinction between cash and accrual accounting is contained in **http://smallbusiness.chron.com/accounting-methods-cash-vs-accrual-3732.html**.
- A more detailed discussion of the accrual accounting model, and its application to the accounting process, is contained in **www.treasury.nt.gov.au/PMS/Publications/Budget Finance/TreasDir/TD-A1.1.pdf**.
- A succinct review of what financial statements look like is available in **http://accounting-simplified.com/financial/statements/types.html**.

CHAPTER 8

Making sense of the accounts

LEARNING OUTCOMES

At the end of this chapter readers will be able to:

- explain the composition of a balance sheet and discuss its key items
- understand the ways in which assets can be valued, and identify the problems that arise from a loss value through depreciation
- describe the structure of a profit and loss statement, being careful to distinguish between operating profits and losses and net profits and losses
- articulate the details of a cash flow statement, and the significance of its division into cash movement linked to operating, investment and financing activities.

CHAPTER SUMMARY

This chapter provides a detailed discussion of three key financial statements. The first is the balance sheet, which compares the various assets accumulated by the sport enterprise with the liabilities incurred in running its affairs. The vexing issue of how to best value assets, and what transactions can be reasonably included as assets, will be attended to at this point. The second is the profit and loss statement, where the difference between operating profits and losses will be contrasted with net profits and losses. The third document is the cash flow statement, where movements of cash in and out of the enterprise will be divided into operating, investment and financing. This will be followed by three simulation exercises that focus on the setting up and interpretation of accounts. These exercises will be used to highlight the key features of balance sheets, profit and loss statements and the cash flow statements, and what they tell us about the financial status of a sport enterprise. As with the previous chapter, model answers are supplied at the end of each simulation activity.

INTRODUCTION

As already noted, the effective management of any sport organization requires not only a sound knowledge of the principles of financial management, but also the support of a financial recording and reporting system that allows a quick and easy reading of the club's or association's financial health. It is now taken for granted that a professionally managed sport organization will produce three integrated annual financial reports. The first document is a statement of performance, or profit and loss, which reports on the revenues earned for the period, and the expenses incurred in generating the revenue. The second document is a statement of position, or balance sheet, which reports on the current level of assets, liabilities and equity. The third document is a statement of cash flows, which identifies the cash movements in and out of the organization. The cash flow statement is divided into activities related to day-to-day operations, activities that involve the sale and purchase of assets, and activities that involve the securing and borrowing of funds and their repayment. Each of the above three statements provides an important perspective on the financial operations of the organization, and they are discussed in more detail below.

THE BALANCE SHEET

We are now in a position to say more about the balance sheet and what it means. In Chapter 7 it was noted that the accounting equation is the foundation of the balance sheet. Assets are placed on the left-hand side of the balance sheet, while liabilities are placed on the right-hand side. Proprietorship or owners' equity is also located on the right-hand side. And, as also demonstrated in Chapter 7, it will always balance. In short, the balance sheet gives a clear picture of a sport organization's wealth by contrasting its assets (things it owns) with its liabilities (things it owes). The difference between assets and liabilities is known as the net worth of the business, and in the balance sheet the term 'net assets' is also used to identify the difference between assets and liabilities. The balance sheet can therefore be seen as a snapshot of the wealth of a sport club or association at a point in time.

The balance sheet also indicates how the assets of the organization have been funded. It can be done through equity (which is the capital investment of the owners), or from borrowed funds from some other organization or individual. However, not all assets are the same. They can be broken down into a number of categories. So too can liabilities. As a result, a balance sheet will be set up to provide a clear picture of the level of both current and non-current assets, and current and non-current liabilities. The level of owners' equity or shareholders' capital (or accumulated funds as it is usually called in non-profit organization financial statements) will also be identified in the balance sheet since it is effectively the difference between the two. This is because assets can be accumulated through either (1) the owner's capital, (2) reinvested profits or (3) borrowed funds.

Assets

As noted above, assets are all those things owned by an organization. To put it more technically, they constitute resources owned and controlled by an entity from which future benefits are expected to flow. The assets of a balance sheet are not only broken down into their various categories, but they are also listed according to their degree of liquidity, with the most liquid coming first and the less liquid coming later in the statement. The measure of an asset's liquidity is the ease with which it can be converted to cash, and all those assets that can easily be converted are listed under the 'current assets' heading. The most frequently cited current assets are cash in bank (which is stating the obvious, but it needs to be said nevertheless), accounts receivable or debtors (which, as we noted in Chapter 7, include those short-term invoices or bills for payment that have not yet been received), investments in the share market (which can be converted to cash through quick sale) and stocks of material and merchandise (which at a pinch can be sold for cash). Items such as prepaid expenses (that is, bills paid in advance) can also be included here. The level of current assets is an important indicator of the financial health of a sport organization, since it is the means by which bills are paid when they are due and creditors' demands for payment are met.

Assets are also listed as fixed or non-current. These assets include everything that cannot be easily and quickly converted to cash. Some stock and materials will be listed here when they do not have high turnover. The main items will be all those tangible or material assets that are essential for generating revenue, but are difficult to sell at an appropriate price in the short term. These items include office furniture and equipment (including all sorts of sports equipment), motor vehicles, buildings and land. Building improvements (e.g. a stadium upgrade) are also examples of fixed assets. The main categories of assets are listed in Table 8.1.

TABLE 8.1 Balance sheet – types of assets

Asset category	Degree of liquidity	Example
Cash in bank	High (current)	Trading account balance
Accounts receivable	Medium (current)	Monies owed by club members
Prepaid expenses	Medium (non-current)	Payment of next year's insurance
Company shares	Medium (current)	Ownership of shares
Inventory	Medium (current)	Stock of sports equipment
Office equipment	Low (non-current)	Computer system
Other equipment	Low (non-current)	Office furniture
Motor vehicles	Low (non-current)	Ownership of vehicle
Property	Low (non-current)	Ownership of office building
Building improvements	Low (non-current)	Stadium renewal

The balance sheet of a sporting organization can be complicated by a number of other factors. For example, assets can either increase in value over time (i.e. appreciate) or decrease in value over time (i.e. depreciate). On the one hand, property, stocks and shares, various scarce artefacts and random memorabilia are particularly prone to increase in value. On the other hand, there are other assets that can lose value quickly, including those things that incur constant use and wear and tear, or become obsolete, or both. Motor vehicles and computers are cases in point. Moreover, there are assets that, while not tangible, clearly add value to the organization, and should be accounted for. 'Goodwill', which accounts for the difference between the aggregate value of assets and the valuation others may place on the organization, is an example worth noting. Accountants have recognized these financial facts of life for many years, and have consequently devised strategies for managing these phenomena.

Depreciation

Depreciation is based on the principle that all fixed, non-current assets represent a store of service potential that the organization intends to use over the life of the asset. Assets therefore have a limited life as a result of their ongoing wear and tear and probable obsolescence. Accounting for depreciation is the process whereby the decline in the service potential of an asset, such as a motor vehicle, is progressively brought to account as a periodic charge against revenue. That is, the asset is devalued in relation to its purchase price or market value, and is offset against income. In order to allocate the cost of the asset to the period in which it is used, an estimate must be made of the asset's useful life. This will usually be less than its physical life. For example, in the case of a motor vehicle, it may be decided that after three years it will not be operating as efficiently and therefore will be worth less after this period, even though it is still running. If an asset has a residual, or resale, value then this amount will be subtracted from the asset cost to establish the actual amount to be depreciated.

The simplest method for depreciating an asset is the straight-line, or prime-cost, method. This method allocates an equal amount of depreciation to each full accounting period in the asset's useful life. The amount of depreciation for each period is determined by dividing the cost of the asset minus its residual value by the number of periods in the asset's useful life. Take, for example, a computer system that was purchased for $11,000. It is anticipated that the system will have a resale value of $1,000 after five years. Using the straight-line method of depreciation the annual depreciation will be $2,000. This figure is obtained by dividing the difference between the purchase price and the residual value ($10,000) by the five years of anticipated useful life. This annual depreciation will then be posted as an expense in the profit and loss statement for the following five years. This process of spreading the cost of an asset over a specific period of time is called amortization. The idea behind this process is that there needs to be a clear way of showing the relationship between the spread of benefits from an asset's use and the costs involved in creating those benefits.

Asset valuation

Asset values can also be changed to reflect current conditions and prices. Unless otherwise stated, assets are valued at their purchase price, which is known as historical cost. However, many assets, particularly land and buildings, can increase in value over time. Unless asset valuation is periodically done, the true values of assets can be seriously understated. This problem can be overcome by a revaluation of the assets by a certified valuer, with a note to this effect accompanying the annual statement of financial operations and standing.

Intangible assets

For sport clubs there is also the issue of how intangible assets should be treated, and how they can be valued. Intangible assets are by their very nature difficult to quantify, and their definition as non-monetary assets without physical substance merely confirms their ambiguity. A good starting point is to note that there are two types of intangible assets. They are, first, identifiable intangibles that include things such as trademarks, brand names, mastheads, franchises, licences and patents. Some of these intangibles, such as franchises, licences and patents, have a purchase price, and they can be amortized over their expected life. The second type of intangible assets is labelled as unidentifiable, the best example being goodwill. Goodwill arises from a combination of things such as superior management, customer and/or member loyalty and a favourable location. Goodwill is seen to possess value since it can produce future economic benefits that cannot be directly attributable to some other material asset. Goodwill is relevant to sport organizations, since the ability to attract fans often originates from often vague, but strong historical attachments between club image and fan identity. While few clubs have attempted to identify a goodwill value, it is often visible when a privately owned team is sold to a new owner. The difference between the sale price and the asset value of the team will in large part be attributable to the goodwill factor.

Players as assets

Professional sport clubs are also confronted by the issue of how players might be counted as assets, and, if it is possible, how they will be valued. This problem arises in professional sport leagues where teams are able to trade players through a transfer market. In the English Premier League, where large transfer fees are par for the course, this issue is dealt with by listing the transfer fee as an asset, and amortizing the fee over the contract life of the player. Take, for instance, Manchester United player Ronaldo, who transferred from Portugal in 2003. His transfer fee was just under GBP 12 million, and he signed with Manchester United for five years. Using the straight-line method of depreciation his fee would be amortized at around GBP 2.4 million a year, and charged as an expense for each of the five years of his contract. After two years he would therefore be valued at GBP 7.2 million (i.e. 12 less 4.8). At the end of his five-year contract his value would be technically zero. However, in practice his transfer price to Real Madrid in 2009 was around GBP 80 million. Thus, in keeping with his rise to stardom during his time at Manchester United, Ronaldo's market value ended up just under seven times his 'historical cost'. Manchester United's balance sheet was the winner here since the club was able to sell off the Ronaldo asset – so to speak – at a handsome profit. The value of a sample of Manchester United players during Ronaldo's stay at the club is listed in Table 8.2.

Under these arrangements for the amortization of player transfer fees, EPL clubs can therefore allocate a proportion of players' transfer fees as an annual expense, thereby reducing their taxable income. The bonus here is that, unlike other assets that lose value over time and are depreciated, many players will in fact have increased in value. However, the balance sheet will show them as having zero value at the end of their contracts. Under these conditions clubs' assets will be seriously undervalued.

TABLE 8.2 Manchester United Football Club – player valuations, 2005

Player	Contract period (years)	Transfer fee cost (GBP millions)	Annual expense charge (GBP millions)
Ferdinand	7	31	4.5
Howard	6	2.5	0.4
Smith	5	7	1.4
Rooney	6	25	6.1
Ronaldo	5	12	2.4

Source: Manchester United Football Club (2005: 13).

This situation does not present itself in sport leagues where player transfers can occur without a fee being paid to the club the player is exiting from. In America's NBA and Australia's NRL, players have no asset value, and therefore cannot be depreciated over time. They are just like any other business employee, which means they can leave when their contract has expired, or leave during their contract period subject to a negotiated termination arrangement without any compensation fee (a transfer fee, for instance) being paid to the former employer.

Liabilities

Simply put, liabilities are those things that an organization owes to others. To be more exact, they are the present obligations of an entity, which, when settled, involve the outflow of economic resources. Like assets, liabilities can be categorized into current and non-current. Current liabilities include monies that are owed to people in the immediate future for services and goods they have supplied. For example, a club may have purchased some sporting equipment on credit for which payment is due in thirty to sixty days. This is called accounts payable, or creditors. Other current liabilities include short-term borrowings, member income received in advance and taxes payable in the short term. Income received in advance is an interesting case because it is often intuitively viewed as revenue or an asset and not a liability. However, under the accrual accounting model it is clearly not relevant to the current flows of revenue and expenses. But as monies received it has to be accounted for. So, what happens is that it is debited to cash in bank and credited as something we owe to members in the future. That is, it is a liability that is listed as income received in advance.

Non-current liabilities include long-term borrowings, mortgage loans, deferred tax liabilities and long-term provisions for employees such as superannuation entitlements. The accumulation of liabilities is not in itself a problem, so long as the debt is used to build income-earning assets. However, if increasing debt is associated with losses rather than profits, then the gap between assets and liabilities will increase. In some AFL clubs the level of liabilities exceeds the value of their assets. For example, in 2005 the net worth of the Western Bulldogs and Carlton clubs was both negative and in excess of AUD 5 million in each instance. In 2011, it was revealed that the St Kilda club had accumulated more debt than assets and was thus also in difficult financial circumstances. These figures indicate a lengthy period where expenses constantly exceeded revenues, and assets were used to pay debt. In the long run these sorts of trends are unsustainable.

Balance sheets can say a lot about a sport organization's financial health. In the following chapter this will be discussed in more detail. However, balance sheets do not tell us much about a sport club's earnings, profits and losses over the course of a month, quarter or year. For this information we must turn to the profit and loss statement, or as it is often called in the non-profit area of sport, the income statement.

PROFITS AND LOSSES

It is not just a matter of examining a sport organization's assets and liabilities at a point in time in order to diagnose its financial health, it is also crucial to shift one's attention to the financial operation of sport clubs and associations over time. There are two types of financial statements that look at the movement of cash and earnings in and out of an organization. They are, first, the profit and loss statement and, second, the cash flow statement.

The first thing to be said about the profit and loss statement is that it can go under a number of names. It can also be called an income statement, which is the non-profit sector terminology, and is also referred to as a financial statement of performance. The point to remember about most sport organizations is that they do not focus on profits and losses, but rather surpluses and deficits. This is because they do not have shareholders, and therefore are not expected to deliver dividends. In any case, it does not alter the fact that these statements look at the revenue earned during a period (say three or twelve months) and compare it with the expenses incurred in generating the revenue for the same period. Profit and loss statements are straightforward to compile, and moderately easy to understand, but there are some tricky areas that need to be discussed.

The first point to make is that, while profit and loss statements contain many cash movements, they do not accurately represent the total cash movements in and out of the organization, since they are essentially about earned income and incurred expenses. As a result they will include many transactions that do not involve the movement of cash. As noted in Chapter 7, revenue can be earned, while the cash may come much later. However, under the accrual accounting method it is still a revenue item that needs to be identified in the profit and loss statement. For example, a sport consulting business may have completed a strategic planning exercise for a large national sport association, and invoiced it for $50,000. If, at the end of the accounting period, the invoice has not been paid, it will still be included in the profit and loss statement as income. The adjustment or offset in the accounts will be an equivalent (i.e. $50,000) increase (or debit) in the accounts receivable asset account. If the invoice had been immediately paid, the adjustment would have been made as an increase (or debit) of $50,000 to the cash in bank asset account.

Revenue, or income as it is frequently called, is typically divided into operating and non-operating items. Operating items include all those revenues such as member income, gate receipts and merchandise sales that provide the funds to support the day-to-day running of the club or association. Non-operating items include funds that are irregular, or even out of the ordinary. An asset sale, a special government grant or a large donation are examples of non-operating income. As indicated in Chapters 1 to 4, sport organization revenues have expanded dramatically over recent years, but for the non-professional clubs the main sources are still member fees, gate receipts, government grants, fundraising activities and sponsors. Fees from broadcasting rights are concentrated in the big professional sport leagues and mega-events.

Expenses should also be treated cautiously. The profit and loss statement should include all incurred expenses rather than just paid expenses. Buying something on credit or by cash is an expense. However, paying for something that will not be used until next year, for example, should not be listed as an expense for the period under consideration. It is an asset that goes under the line-item heading of a prepaid expense. For example, rental or insurance paid in advance involves a movement of cash out of the club or association, but does not constitute an expense incurred for the current period. From an accrual accounting perspective it is credited to cash account (money goes out) but will be debited as a prepaid expense (current assets increase) since it constitutes a benefit for later use.

Depreciation revisited

Depreciation is another expense issue that has to be dealt with. As indicated in the early part of this chapter, depreciation is an estimate of the wear and tear of working assets. In an office setting, computers are quickly depreciated for two reasons. First, they are heavily used and, second, they quickly become obsolete. Depreciation is therefore recognized as an expense and should be included in a profit and loss statement. Depreciation can be calculated in a number of ways, with, as already noted, the most simple being the straight-line method. If, for example, a motor vehicle is purchased for $30,000, and has an estimated life of five years and no residual value, then the depreciation expense for the following five years will be $6,000 per annum. Some sporting club finance managers make the mistake of listing the full cost of the motor vehicle in year 1 as an expense, but this is clearly misleading. It may be an appropriate thing to do under a cash accounting system, but is never part of the accrual accounting model. The correct way to treat this transaction is to list it as an asset, and then depreciate (i.e. amortize) it over its estimated lifetime. Interest paid and interest earned also appear on profit and loss statements. Interest paid will be classified as an expense while interest received will be classified as revenue.

Operating versus net profits

As already noted, when analysing profit and loss statements it is important to distinguish between operating profit (or surplus) and net profit (or surplus). The differences between these two terms comprise abnormal revenue and expenses, and extraordinary revenue and expenses. A transaction will be classified as abnormal if it is a regular occurrence, but in a specific case is significantly higher than normal. In the case of a sport club an abnormal item might be an accelerated depreciation of office equipment, or a supplementary government grant. A transaction will be classified as extraordinary if it is a significant transaction, and does not regularly occur. A sport club example includes a fine for breaching a salary cap regulation (this happens frequently in the Australian Football League and the National Rugby League) or the sale of an asset (this occurs in the English Premier League and most of the big European football competitions, where players can be traded under certain conditions as the equivalent of a tangible asset).

Operating profit does not include the abnormal and extraordinary items, and is confined to those transactions that are directly related to day-to-day activities that regularly recur over the standard accounting cycle. So, operating profit is the difference between operating income and operating expenses. Net profit is something else again, and will take into account all abnormal and extraordinary items. If the sport club happens to be part of a profit-making entity, then it may be required to pay tax on its profits. This item will be subtracted from operating profit to get to a net profit figure.

Depreciation is also frequently listed as a non-operating item and can also make a significant difference to the level of profit. An operating profit can be transformed into a net loss by the inclusion of depreciation as a non-operating expense. Sometimes claims are made that depreciation can distort the real profit of a sport organization, but in fact the opposite is the case. Depreciation is a legitimate expense since it takes into account that amount of assets used up to generate revenue. In the context of the above discussion a typical profit and loss or income statement is illustrated in Table 8.3.

TABLE 8.3 Profit and loss statement

Item	Amount ($)	Total ($)
Operating income		
Member fees	50,000	
Events	10,000	
Grants	3,000	
Total operating income		**90,000**
Operating expenses		
Administration	50,000	
Events	20,000	
Insurance	10,000	
Total operating expenses		**80,000**
Operating profit		10,000
Non-operating income		
Special government grant	10,000	
Non-operating expenses		
Depreciation	20,000	
Net profit		0

CASH FLOW

We can now move on to the cash flow statement. It should be apparent that profit and loss statements do not give a clear picture of the movement of cash in and out of a sport club or association. Cash flow statements aim to fill this gap by listing all movements of cash under three main headings. These headings are operating activities, investing activities and financing activities. The aim here is to get a picture of the net inflow and outflow of cash, and the extent to which a club or association is able to meet its cash payment obligations. This is an important issue, since without sufficient cash to pay bills when they fall due, there is the lingering possibility that creditors will take legal action to ensure payment. This may result in insolvency and bankruptcy.

The transactions that are included in the operating activity section include all those day-to-day activities that are required to keep the organization running. They include wages and salaries (cash out) and payment for supplies (cash out) on the one hand, and membership income (cash in) and government grants (cash in) on the other. Good financial management will aim to ensure that the cash coming from operating activities will exceed the cash going out, although a short-term net cash outflow may not be all that serious.

Investing activity transactions include all those things that involve the purchase and sale of assets. The sale of assets will be associated with cash inflow, while the purchase of assets will produce an outflow of cash. The purchase and sale of office equipment and property of various sorts will fall under the investing heading, and so too will the purchase and sale of stocks, shares and debentures. While the sale of assets can generate a quick supply of cash, it will also deplete the organization of income-earning resources, so a balance needs to be struck to ensure that crucial assets are not depleted. Conversely, the purchase of assets immediately absorbs cash, and it is therefore important to monitor the amount of cash being used for this purpose.

Financing activities involve all those things that involve the procurement of equity and borrowing of funds on the one hand, and the withdrawal of funds and repayment of borrowings on the other. An increase in cash holding can come from loans, bonds, mortgages, debentures and other borrowings, while a fall in cash holding will come from the repayment of loans and the redemption of debentures. A typical list of cash flow items is listed in Table 8.4.

A cash flow statement provides a clear and concise picture of how cash is used internally, and where it goes externally. It also signals the level of liquidity and the ease

TABLE 8.4 Cash flow statement template

Item	Cash in	Cash out
Operating activities		
Member fees	X	
Sponsor income	X	
Payment of salaries		X
Investing activities		
Sale of shares	X	
Purchase of computer		
Financing activities		
Long-term bank loan	X	
Repayment of loan		X

with which cash payments are supported by cash reserves. A chronic net cash outflow on operating activities is cause for concern, since it is likely to lead to asset sales or borrowings being used to finance the cash deficit. And, as was noted previously, this can lead to a fall in club or association net worth, and threaten its long-term viability.

SIMULATION EXERCISE 8.1

Global Sport Enterprises

The following fictitious case provides the material for the construction of a simple balance sheet. It starts with a series of transactions that have to be ordered and sorted. The final requirement is to construct a simple set of accounts that reveals how much was earned, and how successful the business has been. The case revolves around Marcel Mudflap, an entrepreneurial young man, who saw the opportunities that were emerging in the sport industry, and after completing a short course in *Visionary Decision-making* at the local technical education college, decided to set himself up as a sport management consultant and retailer. He had saved $20,000 from his job as a chef at his local hotel, and put it all into his newly established trading account under the business name of Global Sport Enterprises (GSE).

Marcel was aware that image was everything, and therefore set about setting up an office with the latest computer technology and office furniture. He spent $5,000 on a personal computer and colour laser printer, and another $4,000 on an elegant teak desk, an Italian-designed workbench and lounge chairs. Marcel paid cash for these items.

Marcel quickly obtained some work with the newly formed Shore-break Men's Synchronized Swimming Association (SMSSA) in which he was required to pro-mote its programmes in schools and sport clubs around the region. Marcel also attracted interest from the local bowls clubs, where many of the men wanted something more athletic and aesthetically pleasing. SMSSA paid him handsomely for his promotional services. The only problem was that he would not be getting any payment until early in the following year. The promotional work was priced at $10,000.

The constant travelling by bus began to irritate Marcel, so he decided to purchase a motor vehicle for the business. An Audi was the obvious choice, since it provided the status that Marcel was keen to project to his clients. However, he could only afford a small second-hand Ford Escort van. Marcel's bank manager was generous, and lent him $20,000 over five years to help finance the purchase of the van, which was ready to drive away. Marcel used $5,000 of his trading account funds to allow him to purchase the $25,000 van.

Marcel also decided to get into the merchandising field, and bought $2,000-worth of branded T-shirts. The T-shirt purchase was done on credit, and did not have to be paid for until the following year. That was the good news. The bad news was that Marcel was not able to sell any of the T-shirts. He had a quality garment, but no sales. Marcel also found out that the car needed maintenance to the tune of $5,000.

He did not have to pay cash for this work since his brother, who was a mechanic, gave him six months to pay. It was not a good time for Marcel.

However, Marcel's luck changed when he was offered a job organizing the Grand Prix Series for the Regional Darts Association. This was Marcel's most exciting task to date, and involved running events in the saloon bars of some of the city's best-known suburban hotels. This was a successful operation, since he was able to negotiate a sponsorship deal with a weight loss centre. He secured a healthy commission from the deal, and from this point on things got progressively better. Marcel went on to organize a triathlon for non-swimmers, and an indoor beach volleyball competition. Overall, Marcel earned revenues of $90,000 for the year from the darts, triathlon and beach volleyball programmes. He also incurred expenses of $30,000 in running the programmes. All the revenues were received as cash payments, while all expenses were paid for in cash at the time they were incurred.

Marcel decided that, in view of his ordinary year and his declining cash reserves, he would deposit most of the profits in the trading account, and therefore keep them in the business. At the same time, he creamed off $20,000 from the profit (in the form of drawings) for his personal use. Marcel has asked you to help him diagnose the financial health of GSE. He wants you to draft up a balance sheet in order to decide what his asset base is, and if his sport consulting business is better off at the end of his first year of operation than it was at the beginning.

The model answers are listed in Tables 8.5 to 8.11. They are organized around each of the five core account categories, where each transaction has the appropriate debit and credit entries.

TABLE 8.5 Model answer – Global Sport Enterprises asset accounts

Account name	Debit ($)	Item	Credit ($)	Item	Balance ($)
Cash	20,000	Investment	5,000	Computer	
	90,000	Consulting	4,000	Desk	
			5,000	Vehicle	
			30,000	Consulting	
			20,000	Drawings	46,000
Accounts receivable	10,000	Fees			10,000
Prepaid expenses	0				0
Office equipment/ supplies	5,000	Computer			
	4,000	Desk			9,000
Motor vehicle	25,000	Vehicle 1			25,000
Other assets	2,000	T-shirts			2,000
Total assets					**92,000**

TABLE 8.6 Model answer – Global Sport Enterprises liability accounts

Account name	Debit ($)	Item	Credit ($)	Item	Balance ($)
Accounts payable			2,000	T-shirts	
			5,000	Maintenance	7,000
Short-term loan			0		0
Long-term loan			20,000	Vehicle	20,000
Other liabilities			0		0
Total liabilities					**27,000**

TABLE 8.7 Model answer – Global Sport Enterprises revenue accounts

Account name	Debit ($)	Credit ($)	Balance ($)
Merchandise		0	0
Coaching		0	0
Consulting		90,000	90,000
Promotions		10,000	10,000
Total revenue			**100,000**

TABLE 8.8 Model answer – Global Sport Enterprises expense accounts

Account name	Debit ($)	Credit ($)	Balance ($)
Office supplies	0		0
Wages and salaries	0		0
Advertising	0		0
Consulting	30,000		30,000
Maintenance	5,000		5,000
Total expenses			**35,000**

TABLE 8.9 Model answer – Global Sport Enterprises capital accounts

Account name	Debit ($)	Credit ($)	Balance ($)
Investment		20,000	
Drawings	20,000		
Total capital			**0**

By applying the accounting equation to the above balances, the following relationships will result.

Assets ($92,000) equals liabilities ($27,000) plus revenue ($100,000) minus expenses ($35,000) plus capital ($20,000) minus drawings ($20,000). This can be expressed as:

$$A (92,000) = L (27,000) + R (100,000) - E (35,000) + C (20,000)$$
$$- D (20,000).$$

In other words, Marcel produced an operating profit of $65,000, which is the difference between the revenue ($100,000) and expenditure ($35,000). This can be shown as:

$$OP (65,000) = R (100,000) - E (35,000).$$

Coincidentally a net worth of $65,000 resulted. Net worth is the difference between the total assets ($92,000) and total liabilities ($27,000). This can be expressed as:

$$NW (65,000) = A (92,000) - L (27,000).$$

SIMULATION EXERCISE 8.2

Hot Shot Events

This fictitious case requires the construction of a profit and loss statement. It looks at earned revenue and incurred expenses, and makes a distinction between operating and net profit. It focuses on Claudia Cando, who has been managing her own event management business, Hot Shot Events (HSE) for five years, and reckoned that this year was pretty good for her.

Claudia's first event was a sport management seminar that she held at the new multimillion-dollar Convention Centre at the Blue Lakes campus of Twin Peaks University. The five speakers were paid $200 each, and the cost of hiring the Convention Centre ended up being $1,000 a day. It was a two-day conference. Claudia also had to arrange the catering, which cost another $2,000 per day. Other incidental costs amounted to $1,000. The conference was a raging success. One hundred people attended, and each paid $100 for the privilege of hearing Roger Federer's inspired oration on the character-building properties of tennis. Claudia was laughing all the way to the bank.

Her next event was the annual Blue Lakes community fun run and triathlon. She paid $20 an hour for casual staff, who put in a total of 100 hours for the day. Drink stations and various other participant support services cost another $2,000. She was relieved to know that 200 participants had paid $50 each to enter the event. However, it was not all good news, since the sponsor, Trustme Real Estate, withdrew at the last minute, and their $2,000 promise did not eventuate. She also had to pay the local ambulance service and a security company $5,000 for their combined services.

TABLE 8.10 Model answer – Hot Shot Events profit and loss statement

Item	Amount ($)	
Operating income		
Seminar admissions	10,000	
Agent fees	5,000	
Sponsorship	0	
Triathlon/fun run event entry fees	10,000	
Grants and subsidies	0	
Social functions	0	
Consulting fees	0	
Other income	0	
Total operating income		25,000
Operating expenditure		
Wages for general administration	6,000	
Wages for triathlon/fun run	2,000	
Seminar guest speakers' fees	1,000	
Seminar facility hire	2,000	
Safety and security charges	5,000	
Triathlon/fun run event support	2,000	
Seminar catering charges	4,000	
Indemnity insurance	0	
Incidentals	1,000	
Depreciation on office equipment	2,000	
Other expenses	0	
Total operating expenditure		25,000
Operating surplus/profit		0
Non-operating abnormal items	0	
Non-operating extraordinary items		
Government grant	4,000	
Damages	–4,000	
		0
Net surplus/profit		0

At the beginning of the year Claudia had also purchased a new computer system for $8,000. She was advised that the computer would have a useful life of four years and a resale value of zero. She was also advised to depreciate the computer using the straight-line method. Claudia also employed a contract office administrator who was paid an hourly rate of $20. The administrator's total working hours amounted to 300 over the year.

During the year Claudia received a one-off $4,000 grant from the government to assist the development of junior sport in the local district. She also got a letter from the Blue Lakes Convention Centre manager, advising that a $4,000 penalty was imposed for damages to the facility, which had a heritage classification. It had to be paid immediately. Around the same time Claudia also received an advance payment of $5,000 from the Desert Springs Underwater Hockey Association for a strategic planning job she was contracted to do next year. She was very happy to get this payment since she believed she had a bit of a cash flow problem.

Claudia continued to act as a player agent, and had a stable of basketballers, baseballers and footballers. She charged 1 per cent commission on all contracts, and during the year she negotiated contracts to the value of $500,000, which gave a return of $5,000. Towards the end of the year Claudia decided to pay the next financial year's professional indemnity insurance of $20,000. She had forgotten to take it out this year.

Claudia wants help in putting together a consolidated profit and loss statement using a number of line items. You have been invited to construct a profit and loss statement for HSE, making sure that, under the accrual accounting model, it includes only revenue earned and incurred expenses. Claudia also wants the statement to distinguish between operating profit and net profit. The model answers are summarized in Table 8.10. It compares earned income with earned expenditure, while also differentiating between operating and net profits.

The final result is a net profit of zero, which is the same as the operating profit. Although there are two extraordinary items, they offset each other. Depreciation is included under operating expenses, although in some sport association accounts it is listed as a non-operating item.

SIMULATION EXERCISE 8.3

Springfield Meadows Bocce Association

This fictitious case requires the completion of a cash flow statement. It involves the compilation of a statement that distinguishes between cash from operating activities, cash from investing activities and cash from finance activities. It centres on the task given to Margaret Monaghan, who is the finance director of the Springfield Meadows Bocce Association (SMBA).

Margaret has been advised that she needs to monitor the cash flows of SMBA on a monthly basis. Margaret has identified a number of transactions that appear to involve cash movements for the previous month. She needs your expert guidance in presenting a proper cash flow statement to the Board of Management. Margaret would like to identify a systematic set of net inflows and outflows. All cash transactions are listed below. Can you help?

Springfield Meadows Bocce Association – cash movements for month ending 31 December

1	Short-term borrowing from Citibank for office refurbishment	$10,000
2	Sale of shares in News Corporation	$5,000
3	Government operating grant received	$10,000
4	Payment to ACE Office Supplies for office equipment	$10,000
5	Annual sponsorship from Oceania Pasta Supplies	$50,000
6	Sale of used office furniture	$2,000
7	Late receipt of affiliation fees from clubs	$3,000
8	Promise by New Naples Traders Association for national championships	$10,000
9	Income from intensive strategic planning workshop for affiliated clubs	$5,000
10	Payment for next year's professional indemnity insurance	$10,000
11	Interest payment on Natbank loan to upgrade rink	$5,000
12	Free supply of promotional T-shirts from Department of Ethnic Affairs	value $3,000
13	Income received in advance for 2,001 gold-pass memberships	$2,000
14	Part repayment of medium-term loan from Natbank	$20,000
15	Payment of player expenses for international travel	$25,000
16	Proceeds from sale of historic painting titled *Bocce Game At Yarra Park*	$3,000
17	Payment to Know-It-All Sport Science Consulting Services for intensive team psychological counselling	$5,000
18	Purchase of shares in Barclay Bank	$10,000
19	Purchase of colour laser printer	$5,000
20	Interest received on interest-bearing deposits with Natbank	$2,000
21	Wage payments to casual staff	$15,000
22	Prize money for winning International Teams Trophy at Milan Masters event	$10,000
23	Additional registration fees received from Sussex Downs Branch	$18,000
24	Purchase of multimedia IT package to provide desktop publishing facility	$15,000

TABLE 8.11 Model answer – Springfield Meadows Bocce Association cash flow statement

	Cash in ($)	Cash out ($)	Net cash flow ($)
Cash flow from operating activities			
Grant	10,000		
Sponsor	50,000		
Fees	3,000		
Workshop	5,000		
Gold pass	2,000		
Interest received	2,000		
Prize money	10,000		
Sussex Downs	18,000		
Total cash in	**100,000**		
Insurance		10,000	
Interest paid		5,000	
Travel		25,000	
Sports science		5,000	
Wages		15,000	
Total cash out		**–60,000**	
Net cash flow from operating activities			**40,000**
Cash flow from investing activities			
Shares sale	5,000		
Furniture sale	2,000		
Painting sale	3,000		
Total cash in	**10,000**		
Equipment		10,000	
Share purchase (Barclay)		10,000	
Printer purchase		5,000	
Multimedia purchase		15,000	
Total cash out		**–40,000**	
Net cash flow from investing activities			**–30,000**
Cash flow from financing activities			
Citibank loan	10,000		
Total cash in	**10,000**		
Loan repayment (Natbank)		20,000	
Total cash out		**–20,000**	
Net cash flow from financing activities			**–10,000**
Net increase/decrease in cash held	**120,000**	**–120,000**	**0**

The model answers are compiled in Table 8.11. The statement is broken into (1) operating, (2) investing and (3) financing activities, and for each item the impact on cash inflow and cash outflow is designated.

This statement signals a healthy cash flow situation. In particular the operating activity net cash inflow of $40,000 indicates the capacity to maintain a highly liquid position: the strong cash flow in operating activities is able to cover the loan repayment.

RECAP

Any manager of a sport enterprise, no matter what its activities are, and no matter what its scale of operation, must have a sound working knowledge of the three core financial statements discussed above: a balance sheet, a profit and loss statement and a cash flow statement. Additionally, he or she should be able to explain their construction using the accrual accounting method and double-entry bookkeeping as the conceptual frames. While managers would not be expected to construct a set of accounts, it is imperative they have, first, a good working knowledge of how they are put together and, second, a very clear and detailed understanding of what each item in each of the accounts means. The other point to make is that these three account types have a high degree of interdependency and, as we will see in the next chapter, they are all very important when one is wanting to diagnose the financial health of a sport enterprise.

REVIEW QUESTIONS

The following questions address these points by inviting the reader to reflect on how each account type is constructed, what items they focus on, and what they tell us about a sport enterprise's financial affairs.

1 What does a balance sheet aim to show?

2 How are assets categorized in a balance sheet?

3 On what basis are assets revalued over time, and under what conditions might assets be revalued upwards?

4 Under what circumstances can players be legitimately viewed as assets?

5 What is the principle that underpins the concepts of depreciation and amortization, and how do they impact on the balance sheet figures?

6 What is the difference between tangible and intangible assets?

7 Identify some intangible assets that are particularly important for sport organizations.

8 Contrast current with non-current liabilities.

9 What does a profit and loss statement aim to show?

10 Give examples of how net profits can be different from operating profits where sport enterprises are concerned.

11 Where does depreciation fit within a profit and loss statement?

12 Explain why a profit and loss statement is a weak indicator of movements of cash.

13 What does a cash flow statement aim to show, and how is it constructed?

14 What are the three components of a cash flow statement?

15 Which component should generally deliver a positive net cash flow, and why?

FURTHER READING

For a succinct introduction to the structure and function of balance sheets, profit and loss statements and cash flow statements, see Hart, L. (2006) *Accounting Demystified: A Self Teaching Guide*, New York: McGraw-Hill (Chapter 2: 'Balance sheet', Chapter 3: 'Income statement', Chapter 4: 'Cash flow statement' and Chapter 5: 'How the financial statements are related').

For a more detailed and technical review of financial statements and what they say, see Hoggett, J., Edwards, L. and Medlin, J. (2006) *Accounting*, 6th edition, Brisbane, Qld: John Wiley & Sons (Chapter 25: 'Analysis and interpretation'). See also Atrill, P., McLaney, E., Harvey, D. and Jenner, M. (2006) *Accounting: An Introduction*, Melbourne, Vic.: Pearson Education Australia (Chapter 3: 'Measuring and reporting financial position', Chapter 4: 'Measuring and reporting financial performance' and Chapter 5: 'Measuring and reporting cash flows').

For a succinct discussion of financial statements in non-profit organizational settings, see Anthony, R. and Young, D. (2003) *Management Control in Non-profit Organizations*, 7th edition, New York: McGraw-Hill (Chapter 3: 'Published financial statements'). See also Institute of Chartered Accountants Australia (ICAA) (2013) *Enhancing Not-for-profit Annual and Financial Reporting*, Sydney, NSW: ICAA.

Specific materials on financial accounting in sport enterprises that demand to be read are multi-fold. The first is Wilson, R. (2011) *Managing Sport Finance*, London: Routledge (Chapter 7: 'Financial statements'). The second is Barker, M. (2013) 'Sports finance', in Beech, J. and Chadwick, S. (eds) *The Business of Sport Management*, 2nd edition, Harlow: Pearson, pp. 209–29. The third is O'Beirne, C. (2013) 'Managing small and not-for-profit sports organisations', in Beech, J. and Chadwick, S. (eds) *The Business of Sport Management*, 2nd edition, Harlow: Pearson, pp. 230–47. The fourth source is Winfree, J. and Rosentraub, M. (2012) *Sports Finance and Management: Real Estate, Entertainment, and the Remaking of Business*, Boca Raton, FL: CRC Press (Chapter 3: 'Financial statements, revenues and costs').

An additional sports-specific review of financial statements is contained in Gillentine, A. and Crow, R. (eds) (2005) *Foundations of Sport Management*, Morgantown, WV: Fitness Information Technology (Chapter 6: 'Sport finance'). Excellent material can be found in Fried, G., DeSchriver, T. and Mondello, M. (2013) *Sport Finance*, 3rd edition, Champaign, IL: Human Kinetics (Chapter 6: 'Financial statements'); and Brown, M., Rascher, D., Nagel, M. and McEvoy, C. (2010) *Financial Management in the Sport Industry*, Scottsdale, AZ: Holcomb Hathaway (Chapter 2: 'Financial statements and ratios').

USEFUL WEBSITES

- An excellent website for revisiting the key components of financial statements is **www.charteredaccountants.com.au/Students/Working-as-a-Chartered-Accountant/ Technical-vodcasts/Financial-statement-analysis/Financial-statement-analysis-video**.
- Succinct definitions of depreciation are provided at **http://financial-dictionary.the freedictionary.com/depreciation**.
- The technical distinction between amortization and depreciation is nicely summarized in **www.investopedia.com/ask/answers/06/amortizationvsdepreciation.asp**.
- For an update on player valuation visit **www.dailymail.co.uk/sport/football/article-2338149/Barcelona-best-adding-millions-players-price-tags–Premier-League-club-makes-assets.html**.
- The Football Observatory website contains an enormous amount of player details for Europe's elite football leagues. It also does a full valuation of players: **www.football-observatory.com/IMG/pdf/AR2013_exc-2.pdf**.
- A very illuminating, if slightly dated discussion of how players might be valued and depreciated in a set of accounts is contained in **www.bbk.ac.uk/management/ mscmres/publications/seanpublications/agameoftwohalves/Gof2H-chap7.shtml**.
- For introductory information on the calculation of financial ratios, see **www.ready ratios.com/reference/analysis/financial_statement_analysis.html**.
- Another succinct overview of ratio analysis, which leads nicely into Chapter 11, is available at **www.youtube.com/watch?v=TZZFBkbC2lA&src_vid=dw0MZVSgz9M& feature=iv&annotation_id=annotation_95427985**.

CHAPTER 9

Budgeting for financial control

LEARNING OUTCOMES

At the end of this chapter readers will be able to:

- remember what a budget is, and what it aims to do
- contrast an operating budget with a capital budget
- design an operating and/or cash budget for a sport enterprise that includes space for variance analysis
- use break-even analysis to assist the sport club budgeting process.

CHAPTER SUMMARY

This chapter discusses the ways in which budgeting systems can be used by sport enterprises to better manage their financial operations. It notes that budgets can cover both revenue and expenditure, but emphasizes the need to be ever vigilant when controlling expenditure. An initial distinction will be made between operating budgets and capital budgets, and how each of them can be constructed. Operating budgets will be divided into line item, programme and performance item, and their application to different sport situations will be discussed. Variance analysis will be explored as a means of monitoring both expenditure and income. The use of break-even analysis to manage costs will also be examined. A major theme threading its way through the chapter is the constant need to take a conservative approach to the budgeting process. This means revenue estimates should be underplayed, while expenditure estimates should be overplayed. The chapter will end with a brief analysis of capital budgeting and how it can be used to appraise the costing of sport venues and stadia. Finally, a major focus of this chapter is the proposition that budgeting is not only a good way of calculating the viability of projects and programmes, but is also a crucially important part of the planning and strategy formulation process.

THE BASICS OF BUDGETING

Budgeting is a crucial part of the financial management process. It is one thing to construct some simple accounts and diagnose the financial health of sport clubs, associations and leagues. It is another thing to make sure resources are available for allocation to the various parts of their operations. No matter how wealthy a sport organization is, its resource base will always be limited, and decisions have to be made about not only where the resources are allocated (facility maintenance, player salaries, coaching staff, equipment upgrade), but also how much each operational activity will receive. Moreover, budgets are finite, and the constraining factor will always be the amount of available funds.

Budgets are really financial plans that involve the allocation of funds to strategically important operations and activities. Budgets are essential for ensuring costs and expenses are contained, and do not exceed the planned revenue. Good budgets act as a constraint on spending, and also provide a clear picture of the anticipated sources of revenue. Budgets come in different shapes and forms, but they all share the desire to control spending patterns and make sure the spending is grounded in an appropriate level of funding and support.

BENEFITS OF BUDGETING

A good system of budgeting is crucially important for sport clubs and associations. As already noted the sports world has become increasingly complex, and the need to manage money effectively is stronger than ever. In addition, a well-planned budget is the basis for efficient management and ensuring viability over the long term. The benefits of budgeting are many. It can:

- help anticipate the future and thereby assist the strategic planning process;
- give a clear picture of resource needs and programme priorities;
- signal where there may be revenue shortfalls;
- allow management to better manage and monitor spending;
- communicate the club or association's financial plans to key stakeholders;
- enable precise measures of financial performance to be made.

TYPES OF BUDGETS

As already noted, budgets indicate the spending limits on different activities over particular periods. On the one hand, there is the operating budget (which is sometimes called a recurrent budget), and on the other hand there is the capital expenditure budget (which is sometimes called an investment budget). Whereas an operating budget refers to spending on the day-to-day operations of the sport club, association or league, a capital budget refers to spending on buildings, facilities and equipment, and other tangible assets.

Operating budgets

An operating budget is a statement of the anticipated levels of revenue for a period of time, and how the revenue will be spent. The figures are estimates only, since there will always be unforeseen circumstances that will change the financial parameters within which a club or association conducts its affairs. As a result, the financial projections that underpin the budget figures may not be realized due to changing economic and social conditions. For example, a sponsor may want to renegotiate its agreement, membership income may fall because of poor on-field performance, and coaching and support staff costs may blow out because of an increased demand for skilled specialists.

An operating budget aims to estimate accurately the likely level of revenue that a club or association will have to play with, and the anticipated expenses associated with the earning of that income. For every sport club and association it is crucial to ensure that revenue and expenses will balance and, at best, work towards the generation of a healthy surplus. The following example illustrates what an operating budget will look like, and what items might be included.

TABLE 9.1 Pleasant Valley Darts Club operating budget ($)

	March quarter	June quarter	September quarter	December quarter	Year total
Revenue					
Donations	500			1,000	1,500
Sponsor	6,000				6,000
Member fees	1,400	200	200	200	2,000
Gaming	1,400	1,300	1,100	700	4,500
Totals	**9,300**	**1,500**	**1,300**	**1,900**	**14,000**
Expenses					
General administration services	2,000	2,000	2,000	2,000	8,000
Coaching					0
Event administration		1,000	1,000		2,000
Travel		500	500	500	1,500
Dart board supplies	2,000				2,000
Totals	**4,000**	**3,500**	**3,500**	**2,500**	**13,500**

The budget shown in Table 9.1 immediately reveals a number of important things. First, it identifies the main items of revenue and spending. Clearly, in this fictitious case, the Pleasant Valley Darts Club (PVDC) is heavily dependent on the local sponsor, which just so happens to be the main hotel in town. It also shows that the day-to-day administration expenses are significant, although it would be good to have a breakdown of this item, since it might reveal specific activities such as marketing or office rental that need to be monitored. Second, it also shows when the revenue is earned and the expenses are being incurred. While this is a not a cash budget, it does indicate possible times of cash flow problems. However, this is unlikely to be problem here since most of the revenue is expected to arrive early in the year. The budget consequently allows the PVDC to monitor the balance between expense commitments and revenue collections for different parts of the financial planning period.

Operating budgets can also be organized in different ways. For example, an operating budget may be structured as a line-item budget, which is illustrated in Table 9.1. This involves breaking down spending and income into specific categories such as administration, travel, marketing and entertainment, and applying overall spending limits to each item. All of the different activities or programmes in the organization will work to these limits. The PVDC budget uses the line-item method in setting its forecast figures.

Programme budgets

An operating budget can also be organized as a programme budget. This involves allocating a designated amount of funds to each activity or programme. Each programme area is then allowed to spend on what they want, up to, but not beyond, the designated limit. For example, the PVDC may allocate funds to each of its junior, regional and veterans' league programmes along the lines shown in Table 9.2. Each programme manager can then decide how best to distribute the funds to each of its programme activities.

Programme budgets can be converted into performance budgets without too much difficulty. The strength of a performance budget is that it links the budget to the club or association's strategic plan. It forces the programme manager not only to work within the budget parameters, but also to ensure that the funds are directed to the achievement of relevant outcomes. In the case of the PVDC, a performance budget could take the shape shown in Table 9.3.

TABLE 9.2 Pleasant Valley Darts Club programme budget ($)

	Junior league programme	Regional league programme	Veterans' league programme
Budget	4,000	8,000	2,000

TABLE 9.3 Pleasant Valley Darts Club performance budget

	Junior league programme	Regional league programme	Veterans' league programme
	Goal To provide activities that attract young children to the club	**Goal** To provide activities that attract quality players through access to elite competition	**Goal** To provide activities that balance social and competition darts
	Anticipated outcome Increase in registered juniors	**Anticipated outcome** All teams finish in top half of league table	**Anticipated outcome** Viable competition
Budget ($)	4,000	8,000	2,000

VARIANCE ANALYSIS

Budgets can be used not only to estimate crucial financial indicators, but also to provide a mechanism for monitoring and controlling revenue collections and spending.

Once the budget cycle has started it is important to compare the budget figure with the actual figure. This can take the form of a monthly report that lists, first, the annual budget figure for revenue and expenses, second, the monthly equivalent (which is the annual figure divided by twelve) and, third, the actual monthly figure. These figures can then be used to calculate the variance between the budgeted figure and the actual figure. The variance can be used to identify areas on overspending on the one hand, or revenue shortfalls on the other.

Variance analysis is a simple but powerful technique for monitoring the financial progress of an organization. It can only be undertaken if a budget has been constructed. It is essentially an after-the-event exercise where the actual revenue and expense figures are compared and contrasted with the budgeted items. The variance can be either favourable or unfavourable. For example, if a fun run event recovered $3,000 from entry fees, when the budgeted figure was only $2,500, then the variance is favourable. That is, the entry fee revenue was greater than anticipated. Favourable variances are entered as a positive, while unfavourable variances are recorded as a negative figure. If the actual revenue was only $2,000, then the variance is unfavourable. That is, the revenue was less than anticipated. The same principle can be applied to expenses. If, for example, the actual fun run security expenses exceeded the budgeted figure, the outcome would be unfavourable, but if the security budget was not fully spent, then the outcome would be seen as favourable. In the case of PVDC, a quarterly comparison could be made for actual and budgeted revenue and actual and budgeted expenses, as shown in Table 9.4.

The variance analysis immediately picks up items of revenue that have not been reached, and items of expenditure that are higher than anticipated. This provides a signal to take remedial action to prevent a budget blow-out. In this particular case revenue collected is $700 below the budgeted figure, while expenditure to date is $1,400 above the budgeted amount. This means that revenue may have to be expanded in the short term, while expenditure might have to be closely monitored over the next two quarters.

CAPITAL BUDGETING

The capital budgeting process is different from the operating budget process. This is because decisions about capital involve significant investments that are intended to produce some level of financial return or public benefit. This return must be able to satisfy member or shareholder expectations, while also providing a surplus to meet any borrowing costs.

There are numerous tools for deciding what to invest in, and how much should be invested. Some are rubbery, while others are more methodologically exact. A useful rubbery method is the payback rule, which proposes that funds should only be provided to those projects where the initial outlay can be paid back in the shortest possible time. For example, if it is found that one project has a payback period of six years, and the other

TABLE 9.4 Pleasant Valley Darts Club variance analysis ($)

	Year total: budget	March quarter: budget	March quarter: actual	March quarter: variance	June quarter: budget	June quarter: actual	June quarter: variance	Year to date: budget	Year to date: actual	Year to date: variance
Revenue										
Donations	1,500	500	400	-100	0	100	100	500	500	0
Sponsor	6,000	6,000	3,000	-3,000	0	2,000	2,000	6,000	5,000	-1,000
Member fees	2,000	1,400	1,200	-200	200	800	600	1,600	2,000	400
Gaming	4,500	1,400	1,500	100	1,300	1,100	-200	2,700	2,600	-100
Total revenue	**14,000**	**9,300**	**6,100**	**-3,200**	**1,500**	**4,000**	**2,500**	**10,800**	**10,100**	**-700**
Expenses										
General administration services	8,000	2,000	2,100	-100	2,000	2,100	-100	4,000	4,200	-200
Coaching	0	0	0	0	0	1,000	-1,000	0	1,000	-1,000
Event administration	2,000	0	0	0	1,000	1,200	-200	1,000	1,200	-200
Travel	1,500	0	0	0	500	1,000	-500	500	1,000	-500
Dart board supplies	2,000	2,000	1,000	1,000	0	500	-500	2,000	1,500	500
Total expenditure	**13,500**	**4,000**	**3,100**	**900**	**3,500**	**5,800**	**-2,300**	**7,500**	**8,900**	**-1,400**

TABLE 9.5 Payback approach to capital budgeting

	Project 1: merchandise shop	Project 2: sports museum
Capital cost ($ millions)	3	2
Estimated annual return ($ thousands)	500	200
Payback period (years)	6	10

ten years, then the short payback investment will prevail. In the case shown in Table 9.5, Project 1 would be selected.

However, the payback rule is not able to say if the project might also be viable in the long run. All it does is to indicate that Project 1 is less risky. Moreover, it says nothing about the returns after the payback period has elapsed.

A slightly more robust tool is the accounting rate of return (ROR), which is an estimate of the ratio of the expected average annual profits from the investment to its capital cost. Therefore, an investment in a leisure centre of $10 million with an average annual profit return of $200,000 would produce an average ROR of 2 per cent. This could then be compared and contrasted with other projects to see where the largest return is.

The most systematic method for evaluating investment proposals is the discounted cash flow (DCF) method. As noted in Chapter 4, DFC takes into account the time value of money, which places greater weight on revenues and profits received in the early stages of the project, and less weight on revenues and profits received in the later stages of the project. That is, all expected returns are reduced to a present value, which is then used to evaluate the proposed investment (Brown *et al.* 2010: 194–5).

CASE STUDY 9.1

Mega-event budgeting – the Australian experience

The principles for designing an operating budget for a mega-sport event such as the Olympic or Commonwealth Games are no different from those for a community fun run. It is just that the mega-sport event is far more complex and logistically demanding. Take, for example, the Olympics. The Sydney Organizing Committee for the Olympic Games (SOCOG) released the Sydney 2000 Olympic Games Budget in early 1997. The Games Budget represents the forecast of revenues and expenditures associated with the organizing and staging of the Sydney 2000 Olympic Games. This, as we now know, is the operating budget.

The operating budget forecast a surplus of AUD 43 million, with revenue standing at AUD 2,333 million and spending estimated to be AUD 2,290. SOCOG also contributed AUD 370 million to the NSW Government for rental of venues, construction reimbursements and services, including security. The budget was the result of detailed operational planning and review, and was subsequently approved by the IOC (see Table 9.6).

TABLE 9.6 Sydney 2000 Olympic Games pre-event budget

	Games budget (AUD millions)
Revenues	
Sponsorship	829
Consumer products	61
Ticket sales	487
Television rights	955
Total revenues	**2,332**
Expenditures	
Accommodation, Olympic family and medical	83
Ceremonies	37
Consumer products and creative services	26
Executive office and legal	61
Financial, risk and project management	51
Human resources, communications and community relations	54
Logistics	44
Media: press and broadcasting	184
Sponsorship and general marketing	135
Sport	78
Technology, premises and administration	364
Ticketing	43
Torch relay, events and Olympic arts festivals	38
Transport and accreditation	53
Venue management and security	364
Venues and environment	284
Villages	198
Volunteers and uniforms	31
Contingencies	163
Total expenditures	**2,291**

Although the actual revenues and expenses subsequently exceeded the budgeted figures, the Games Budget provided a useful ballpark estimate of the sources and levels of revenue, and the scale of the main items of expenditure. In particular, it provided a clear picture of what revenues were required to cover the costs of mounting the Games. One of the weaknesses of these figures was that they only covered operating revenue and expenses, and did not include capital investment figures. That is, it is an operating budget only.

The AUD 1,100 million budget for the 2006 Melbourne Commonwealth Games made clear distinctions between capital and operating expenditures, but did not provide a detailed breakdown of core revenue and expenditure items. This led to public concern that some expense items, particularly those covering security, were not fully identified and accounted for.

CASE STUDY 9.2

Mega-event budgeting – the British experience

The London 2012 Olympic Games was by most measures a triumph for the London Organising Committee of the Olympic Games (LOCOG). It was also a triumph for the Olympic Movement as a whole. In virtually every sport there were spectacular performances, and nearly every visitor had a kind word to say about their Games experience. Apart from some skirmishes about the early shambolic distribution of tickets, the Games were exceedingly well run. There were no significant security breaches, and few significant drug-use scandals among the athletes. It was, for all intents and purposes, a smoothly conducted event that reflected well on the organizing capability of LOCOG.

However, these successes camouflaged some serious difficulties in managing the Games budget. In the initial stages of the bid document construction, LOCOG Chair, Sebastian Coe, cited a budget expense figure of GBP 2 billion, which would be sourced from broadcast rights, sponsor income, ticket sales and merchandising, in addition to government bonds and grants. He also noted that this amount was a realistic estimate and would not be subject to any serious blow-out. However, there were early signs that this was a highly optimistic figure when in a later (2005) version of the bid document it was estimated that the London Games would now cost around GBP 2.7 billion to run. This was roughly the equivalent of AUD 5 billion, and it should also be remembered that 1 billion equals 1,000 million. The Sydney 2000 Olympic Games cost about AUD 3.5 billion. In 2008, the London 2012 Games budget was again reviewed, and stakeholders were shocked to find that the new estimated cost of staging the Games was GBP 9.4 billion. There was further consternation when rumours spread that additional cost increases had since been accommodated into the budget, and that it now stood at just under GBP 12 billion. However, this figure was never confirmed, and once the Games had been completed, and the operational dust had settled, it was found that the all-up cost of running the Games had come in at just under GBP 9 billion.

The above narrative is brief, and hides the massively complex logistics of running a mega-sport event such as the Olympic Games. At the same time it highlights critical issues in the budgeting process. The first problem that emerges is the confusion between the funding of the infrastructure, and the funding of the operational side of the Games. In this instance the explanation for the cost blow-out was the escalating 'infrastructure' costs. This involved the cost overruns for a number of venue constructions, especially the main stadium, the velodrome and the swim centre. In addition, extra funds were needed to fully complete the big urban renewal projects, which included the development of the athletes' village and a comprehensive landscaping project that aimed to completely transform the aesthetics of the spaces around the Games precinct. Other large-cost items included a new transport system around the town of Stratford. It was also clear that LOCOG had under-estimated one of the most significant operational costs, which was security. The second problem is the tendency to underestimate the event costs, and overestimate the revenues. This is not helpful, but it is understandable. It is understandable because in justifying the hosting of an event the organizers must be able to defend the decision on both economic and social grounds. That is, it should not only give the participants a memorable experience, but also deliver it in such a way that the city or town hosting the event does not become burdened with significant deficits or debts. Strong budget processes will be able to detect these problems well in advance, and this can only be a good thing.

COSTING

When considering the costs of running a sport enterprise it is important to note that there are different ways of categorizing, managing and controlling them. A distinction can be made between fixed and variable costs, while controllable costs can be contrasted with uncontrollable costs. It is therefore important to manage the costs of delivering sport products and sporting services. A good starting point for controlling and managing costs is to contrast variable costs with fixed costs. Fixed costs are those that remain constant, and are independent of the level of activity, or numbers of spectators, clients or users. Fixed costs include things such as venue hire, equipment depreciation, most power and light costs, and core staff costs. Variable costs are those that change in direct relation to the number of spectators, clients and users. For example, more users mean more equipment supplies, more catering costs, more maintenance and additional staff. There are also costs that are called semi-fixed. These costs only change after a usage ceiling is met. A good example is the staffing costs in running a fitness or aerobics class. Security costs can also fit into this category. (See Figure 9.1.)

Once costs have been sorted and classified, then it is possible to undertake break-even analysis, which is a very effective way of working out just how many paying spectators, clients and users are required to cover all costs and ensure a viable operation. So, what is break-even analysis?

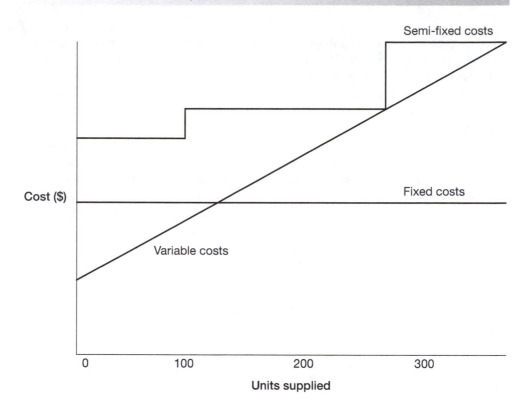

FIGURE 9.1 Variable, fixed and semi-fixed costs

BREAK-EVEN ANALYSIS

Break-even analysis (BEA) or, as it otherwise known, cost-volume-profit analysis, looks at how costs, revenues and profits change in relation to changes in sales, membership and attendance. BEA is a valuable budgeting tool, and helps in financial planning and decision-making. The break-even sales, membership and attendance point occurs where total revenue equals total costs. Below that point losses will be made, while above that point profits will result. BEA is particularly applicable to event management and sport service delivery. It answers the question: what attendance level or usage rate is needed to ensure a viable event or operation? It shows the changes in profits and losses that result from changing attendance or usage patterns, and changes in prices. As a result, it quickly shows if an event or operation is likely to be a commercial success.

There are a number of steps involved in identifying the break-even point. The first step involves dividing costs into fixed and variable. For example, for an event, fixed costs are those costs that remain constant as sales, membership and attendance levels change. They include the venue hire, rental, guest speakers, light and power, insurance and the cost associated with core or permanent staff. Variable costs will vary directly with changes in sales, membership and attendance levels. They include things such as the use of casual staff, equipment, consumables, giveaways and catering. The second step is to estimate anticipated revenues for every level of sales, membership and attendance. The third step is to compare and contrast total revenue and total cost for every sales, membership and attendance level. The following fictitious case gives a succinct picture of how BEA operates.

SIMULATION EXERCISE 9.1

Budgeting for a sport management conference

Janet Julian has been invited to do some budget figures for a sport management conference to be run next year. She has been asked to work out the minimum number of people attending to ensure a viable event. The first thing Janet does is to break down costs into fixed and variable. She finds out that the fixed costs include:

- light and power;
- core staff;
- venue hire;
- guest speakers.

She estimates that total fixed costs = $1,000. This is the cost of setting up the event, and remains constant whatever the attendance level. Janet does the same for variable costs, which is the additional cost incurred for every additional person who attends. She identifies three major variable costs items, which are:

- additional staff;
- printing, stationery and supplies;
- food and drink.

She has calculated that variable costs are $60 per person, which becomes the average variable cost for the event. She then has to do some figures for the revenue that comes from each person attending the conference. The total revenue estimates will be based on:

- the number of people attending;
- the registration fee per person.

Janet is considering a registration fee of $80 per person, which is the average admission charge. This $80 fee constitutes the additional revenue earned for every additional person who attends. Janet can then calculate the contribution margin, which is the difference between average revenue (the registration fee) and average variable cost. The contribution margin is therefore $80 − $60 = $20. This means that every additional person attending will generate a profit of $20.

The break-even attendance point = fixed costs ÷ contribution margin (where contribution margin = average revenue minus average variable cost). Consequently, the break-even point is $1,000 (fixed costs) divided by $20 (the contribution margin), which equals 50 attendees. In other words, if we assume that each person attending will be paying on average $80, then this will produce a profit of $20 per person. In order to cover the $1,000-worth of fixed costs, 50 people are required, thereby providing the $1,000 profit to offset the fixed costs.

If the attendance level falls below 50, then losses will occur, while for every attendee over the 50 cut-off, profits will increase. It should also be noted that any change in fixed costs, variable costs or admission prices will change the break-even point. If, for example, it is decided to cut the admission fee to $70, then the contribution margin will fall to $10. As a result, 100 people will need to attend to break even. A $90 registration fee would produce a contribution margin of $30 and as a result only 34 registrations would be required to break even. However, it would be imprudent to cut admission prices to $50, since this would produce a negative contribution of $10. In this case each additional person would increase the losses. Losses would consequently be minimized by having the lowest attendance possible. This would be an intolerable situation to create, unless of course the event was being subsidized to ensure the lowest possible registration fee.

SIMULATION EXERCISE 9.2

Budgeting for a community sport event

As noted previously, break-even analysis can provide a clear picture of the minimum required attendance levels for all sorts of events and programmes. In this fictitious case, Brian Brockhoff has been asked to run an indoor beach volleyball tournament for the local council using a local multipurpose recreation centre. Brian is new to indoor sport programmes, but has a few budgeting skills, one of which is the ability to undertake BEA for events and festivals. He is confident that the principles he learnt in the 'Arts' field can be easily applied to community sport activities. He has been given the financial data in Table 9.7 to work with.

Brian has to provide some recommendations to the local council as to the viability of running this event. He has been told that there is a 200-player ceiling on the tournament entries. Brian did a few sums and came up with the numbers in Table 9.8.

Brian remembered that the break-even attendance point was the number of participants required to cover all fixed costs. He noted the relatively large fixed costs, but also noted the handy contribution margin of $20. This meant that, for every person who attended the tournament, a profit of $20 would be secured. As a result, 250 players were needed to break even. Brian had two concerns at this point. First, getting 250 paid-up participants would be a big ask and, second, but even worse, the local council had put a 200-player ceiling on tournament entries. Brian thus had no other option in order to make the tournament financially workable. He had to increase entry fees. He noted that, if the tournament entry fee was increased to $110, the contribution margin would be $40 and consequently the break-even participation

TABLE 9.7 Volleyball tournament break-even analysis – line items

Item	($)
Tournament entry fee	90
Hall hire (fixed)	500
Security (fixed)	1,500
Administration staff (fixed)	1,000
Referee costs (per player)	5
Catering expenses (per player)	15
Insurance (public liability) (fixed)	1,400
Insurance (professional indemnity for referees) (fixed)	600
Medical and massage expenses (per player)	50

TABLE 9.8 Volleyball tournament break-even analysis – summary results

	($)
Total fixed costs	5,000
Average variable costs	70
Average revenue (price)	90
Contribution margin	20
Break-even player registrations	250

would now be around 138, which was both a more realistic participation level, and a figure that was well within the local council participation ceiling. He advised the council accordingly.

RECAP

Budgeting is an indispensable tool for managing a sport enterprise's finances. It is integral to the planning and strategy formulation processes. It provides a simple but highly effective means of both organizing a programme's funding arrangements and monitoring its implementation. Systematic budgeting is therefore at the base of every good managerial control process. However, there are different forms of budgets, with the two key types being a capital budget on the one hand, and an operating budget on the other. Operating budgets can also be organized differently and it is important to distinguish between line-item, programme and performance budgets. Managers need to be aware of not only their purpose, but also their internal logic, and their strengths and weaknesses.

REVIEW QUESTIONS

The following questions will assist readers to get a better feel for budgeting, and understand why it is such an important part of the management process in sport enterprises.

1 What is the purpose of a budget?

2 What benefits arise from the budget process?

3 Contrast an operating budget with a capital budget.

4 What is a line-item budget and how does it differ from a programme budget?

5 How can a programme budget be converted into a performance budget?

6 What is variance analysis, and how can it assist the budget process?

7 Describe the simplest form of capital budgeting, and explain how it assists in making decisions about investment and capital expenditure. What other forms of capital budgeting could be used in a sport setting?

8 What are costs, and how does one go about deciding which costs are fixed, and which costs are variable?

9 How might costs be segmented to better understand how costs can vary in response to changes in the supply of a sports good or service?

10 What is break-even analysis (BEA) all about, what does it aim to do and how is it related to the budgeting process?

11 Give an example of how a change in admission price levels for a sport event can affect the contribution margin, and how the contribution margin can, in turn, impact on the break-even level of attendance.

12 Having read the Brian Brockhoff volleyball tournament case, would you offer the same advice to the council as Brian, or would you do things differently?

13 From a budgeting perspective, is it appropriate for managers to be optimistic when it comes to estimating revenue, and flexible when it comes to calculating expenses? And, if your advice is no, then why is it not a good idea?

FURTHER READING

For a solid introduction to the budgeting process, see Hoggett, J., Edwards, L. and Medlin, J. (2006) *Accounting*, 6th edition, Brisbane, Qld: John Wiley & Sons (Chapter 11: 'Cost-volume profit analysis' and Chapter 12: 'Budgeting for planning and control'). A detailed analysis of costing and budgeting processes, with an instructive review of BEA, is contained in Anthony, R. and Young, D. (2003) *Management Control in Non-profit Organizations*, 7th edition, New York: McGraw-Hill (Chapter 6: 'Measurement and use of differential costs' and Chapter 10: 'Budgeting').

An illuminating discussion of budgeting and costing in a sport setting occurs in Wilson, R. (2011) *Managing Sport Finance*, London: Routledge (Chapter 10: 'Cost in sport' and Chapter 12: 'Budgeting appraisal'). A similarly detailed account of the budgeting process in sport enterprises is contained in Shibli, S. and Wilson, R. (2012) 'Budgeting and budgetary control in sport', in Trenberth, L. and Hassan, D. (eds) *Managing Sport Business: An Introduction*, London: Routledge, pp. 185–208. An additionally good account of budgeting and its strategic importance is provided by Brown, M., Rascher, D., Nagel, M. and McEvoy, C. (2010) *Financial Management in the Sport Industry*, Scottsdale, AZ: Holcomb Hathaway (Chapter 6: 'Budgeting'). For an instructive introduction to break-even analysis see Barker, M. (2013) 'Sports finance', in Beech, J. and Chadwick, S. (eds) *The Business of Sport Management*, 2nd edition, Harlow: Pearson, pp. 209–29.

An additional and succinct introduction to sport-related budgeting processes and practices is contained in Whitehouse, J. and Tilley, C. (1992) *Finance and Leisure*, Harlow: Longman (especially Chapter 8: 'Budgets and budgetary control' and Chapter 9: 'Concept of cost'). A useful discussion of budgeting in the American sport setting is contained in Fried, G., DeSchriver, T. and Mondello, M. (2013) *Sport Finance*, 3rd edition, Champaign, IL: Human Kinetics (Chapter 3: 'Budgeting'); and Fried, G., Shapiro, S. and Deschriver, T. (2003) *Sport Finance*, Champaign, IL: Human Kinetics (Chapter 7, which focuses on financial planning). Another Americanized sport-related discussion of budgeting is provided by Horine, L. and Stotlar, D. (2004) *Administration of Physical Education and Sport Programs*, 5th Edition, New York: McGraw-Hill (Chapter 6: 'Financial management'). A useful complementary discussion on budgeting in a sports setting is contained in Sawyer, T., Hypes, M. and Hypes, J. (2004) *Financing the Sport Enterprise*, Urbana, IL: Sagamore (Chapter 4: 'Budgeting').

USEFUL WEBSITES

- An excellent introduction to the budgeting process, and how it can be used to better manage the affairs of non-profit organizations, of which sport is a significant part, is available in **http://culture.alberta.ca/bdp/bulletins/BudgetingforN-f-POrgs09-print.pdf**.
- The following website provides a brief introduction to the 'basics' of budgeting. It has a neat section on the distinction between fixed and variable costs: **www.nonprofitaccountingbasics.org/reporting-operations/budgeting-terms-concepts**.
- The following website contains a clear and concise slide show on the budgeting process and how it can be applied to different costing and pricing situations: **www.slideshare.net/AMSolutions/budgeting-101-12574460**.
- An operating budget for a swim club is reproduced in **www.usaswimming.org/_Rainbow/Documents/8e0687f5-c1ed-4797-a099-7d7b8693fa23/1%20Sample%20Budget.pdf**.
- A detailed account of where budgets fit in the planning of sport events is given in **www.ipswich.qld.gov.au/documents/health/event_management_workbook.pdf**.
- The ways in which break-even analysis can be used to budget for a sport-related event is neatly illustrated at **www.leoisaac.com/evt/evt012.htm**.

CHAPTER 10

Price setting

LEARNING OUTCOMES

At the end of this chapter readers will be able to:

- articulate the crucial importance of pricing in optimizing club, agency, association and sport league revenues
- explain the different approaches to price setting in sport, which include cost-plus pricing, demand-based pricing, competition-based pricing, discriminatory pricing, premium pricing and equity pricing
- explain the concept of price elasticity, and apply it to a variety of real-world sport-related settings
- identify those situations where it may be appropriate to price sports goods or services below cost through the use of subsidies and recurrent grants.

CHAPTER SUMMARY

This chapter examines the pricing of sport services and products from both a theoretical and practical perspective. Pricing is an important issue to address for sport managers since it directly impacts on sales and revenue. It is also a double-edged sword, so to speak. This is because price increases can, while increasing unit revenue, also dampen demand. Conversely, while lower prices can stimulate demand they also reduce revenue per unit. With these concerns in mind, a number of different pricing models will be discussed, including cost-plus pricing, demand-based pricing, competition-based pricing, discriminatory pricing, premium pricing and equity pricing. Special attention will be given to elasticity pricing, since assumptions about elasticity provide strong reasons to drive up prices on the one hand, or reduce them as much as possible on the other. Each pricing method will be applied to sport leagues, sport events and community sport activities to assess their impact on demand, revenue and profits. The pricing of professional sport events will also be discussed.

IS THERE A RIGHT PRICE?

Pricing is an important financial issue for sport enterprises. Setting the right price can increase revenue, but it is not easy to establish just what the right price should be. If prices are too high, then the demand for the good or service will be dampened, while a price that is too low will fail to secure any consumer surplus. Take, for example, the 2003 Rugby World Cup (RWC) in Sydney. The tournament was a success from many perspectives, as will be indicated in Chapter 15. However, the pricing strategy was problematic. A number of optimistic assumptions were made about the number of international tourists who would visit Australia in 2003, but a subsequent terrorist alert cut the level of international tourism, and as a result the demand for tickets was lower than anticipated. The high-priced tickets (from AUD 80 to AUD 100) were especially slow to sell. In hindsight, it may have been better to provide more discounted seat prices to both international visitors and local fans. In addition, lower prices could have been set for the early games, with prices increasing as the tournament entered the semi-finals stage. The fact of the matter is that, for mega-sport events such as the RWC, it is difficult to set prices that maximize revenue since there will always be intervening incidents and events that shift the demand conditions for the events. The price-setting job is made even more difficult if there is an inclusivity policy, where prices should never be set so high that they scare off people on low incomes.

Pricing is not only linked to demand, it is also linked to cost. The ticket prices for the opening ceremony of the 2006 Commonwealth Games in Melbourne ranged from AUD 40 to AUD 500. Part of the explanation for the high prices is the scarcity of seats (the 92,000 maximum seating capacity of the MCG combined with extremely high levels of demand). The other explanation is the very high cost of staging the opening ceremony, which was estimated to be around AUD 20 million. As a point of comparison, the opening ceremony at Sydney 2000 was nearer AUD 30 million, with ticket prices ranging from AUD 20 to AUD 850. So, the question arises as to what constitutes effective pricing, and what specific strategies might be used to ensure both appropriate levels of revenue and the recovery of costs, while at the same time enabling broad community access.

HIGH OR LOW PRICES?

Setting prices for sport activities can be quite complicated. It is often difficult to balance the need to cover costs and make profits with the desire to give people access and not have prohibitively high entry fees and prices. At the same time, in the sports industry there are a number of guiding principles that can be used to defend specific pricing policies and strategies. While commercial sport pricing usually aims to extract as much money from fans as demand conditions allow, there are many instances when there is a need to adopt pricing policies that provide access to all categories of participants and supporters. This is why discounted entry fees are arranged for people who are disabled, on low incomes or unemployed. In the area of community sport and leisure there is often an even more pressing need to price sporting services to ensure broad access. However, prices cannot be so low that the facilities are sustained only through massive local taxpayer subsidies. There are many arguments both for and against the setting of admission fees that cover the full costs of participation on the one hand, or account for only a small part of the fee on the other.

Full cost recovery

There are a number of reasons for setting prices that recover the costs of providing the service. They apply equally to spectator sports where a multitude of fans are keen to see the sporting heroes on the field of play, and community sport where the focus is on enabling people to participate in a range of sporting activities. Specifically, a number of benefits arise from full cost recovery pricing.

First, it encourages commercial investment in sport-related activities: private developers will be encouraged to put resources into sport facilities and sport events if they see an appropriate price incentive and can more easily replicate the successes of existing sport service providers. As a result the range and level of sport opportunities will be improved. Second, it provides funds for the ongoing development of sport facilities and services. Many facilities and programmes could not be provided if fees were not charged. This applies not only to commercial operations, but also to those non-commercial facilities and programmes that have high overhead costs or are provided by organizations with limited budgets. Third, it permits some costly, but socially beneficial, activities to be subsidized. Facilities that can generate a profit allow the operator to deliver low-demand, but socially desirable, facilities and programmes that could otherwise not be provided. For instance, the surplus from full cost recovery pricing in high-demand areas such as aerobics and fitness training can be used to fund discounted specialist services such as massages for the disabled and remedial physiotherapy. Finally, it provides funds for service improvements. In particular, it enables continual equipment upgrade, and permits the employment of more and better-trained staff.

Pricing below cost

However, there are persuasive arguments against having a blanket policy that says all fees and charges should be based on full cost recovery. Although in reality there must be some way of paying the cost of delivering sport activity experiences (i.e. someone has to pay), there may be occasions when a fee or charge well below the cost of providing the service will be appropriate. The first point to be made is that high fees and charges create privileged access where the use of the facility or access of the service is dependent upon the income of the user. Where the right of use is assumed by a narrow base of participants, it discourages other individual and community group use. In the most severe case, existing users may see themselves as lessees with the right to reject initiatives to diversify the programme or lower the cost of participation. This is why community-based swim centres usually price their services below cost. It signals to the community that the facility is not only open to all, but is also a priority activity that has a valuable social benefit (in this case a fit and healthy local community). Second, high fees and charges can exclude the disadvantaged. The higher price may come with a few add-on services, but it also penalizes the young, the unemployed, the socially disadvantaged and the elderly. And it is these groups who gain most from participating in a properly supported physical activity programme. Finally, fees and charges based on a strict cost recovery model often lack a rationale or proper costing process. As Chapter 9 indicated, budgeting for specific pro-grammes and activities is fraught with difficulty, and there is always a margin for error that can produce underestimates of revenue and overestimates of costs.

PRICING STRATEGIES

As indicated previously, pricing sport products can be a challenging exercise. Since most sport organizations are not for profit it is not essential to set prices that maximize profits. Some sport organizations have a charter to provide their services to as many people as possible, not to ensure price is not a barrier to participation. At the same time, price is both an important marketing tool, and the means by which revenue is raised. There is therefore a balance to be achieved, with community access and accessibility at one end of the pricing policy continuum, and the need to raise as much revenue as possible at the other end of the continuum. In practice there is a multitude of ways to price a sport product, some of which are geared to providing access and equity, some of which are centred on ensuring a competitive edge over rivals and others that are aimed at maximizing revenues. In short, there are a number of principles and strategies that can be used when pricing sport products. They are listed below.

Cost-plus pricing

In the vast majority of cases it will be necessary to set a price that not only covers the cost of providing the sport activity or competition, but also includes a margin that contributes to the overall profitability of the club, association, event or league. In the commercial business sector different formulae are used to decide what level of markup will be installed. For example, large department stores will often set prices that are two times higher than the purchase cost of the merchandise to ensure that all selling costs are covered, leaving a relatively modest unit profit. For professional services or consulting businesses, the rule of thumb is to bill clients at an hourly rate that is two to three times the hourly rate charged to the individual consulting team. The payment is subsequently broken down into three segments. The first segment aims to cover the business's overheads and fixed costs, the second covers the consultants' salaries, while the final segment becomes the profit margin. For example, a consulting team of three might charge the national governing body for volleyball $600 an hour for their services. From this $600 'pool', $200 will be allocated to team expenses, $200 to the team consultancy fee, and $200 in profits to the agency contracted to do the job.

In a sport programme delivery setting the same approach can be adopted. For example, a costing study may have shown that the average cost of delivering a swim programme to users is around $15 a person, comprising $4 for the cost of using the facility, $2 for maintenance costs and $9 for staff costs. A swim charge of $17 will therefore not only cover all the costs of delivering the service, but also give a $2 profit margin per user. So, for every person who uses the facility a $2 profit will be made.

Equity pricing

Equity pricing is effectively the opposite of cost-plus pricing, since the aim here is to set a price that does not impede people on low incomes, or from socially disadvantaged communities, in accessing the product or service. As noted in the earlier section of this chapter, equity pricing will most probably involve setting a price below the average cost of delivering the service. Equity pricing can only be sustained if there is a grant or subsidy to cover the funding shortfall. Equity pricing is often used in community sport, and is frequently used in local sport to enable access and opportunity to the whole neighbourhood. Equity pricing is less frequently used in commercial sport, where the need to break even is more important and where special funding support is not available.

Demand-based pricing

In some instances, prices are set around what the market will bear. There are many examples of this in sport, particularly where spectators are involved. For most sport events there is a fixed supply. That is, there is a fixed number of seats that cannot be changed in the short run. If, however, it is anticipated that demand will increase strongly because the event has a star performer, or it is crucial to the league standing, then it makes sense to increase the price in the belief that the stadium will still draw a capacity attendance because of the sharp increase in the demand for seats. This always occurs for grand finals and championship contests, and any case where the contest matters. So, it is not unexpected that an Ashes test match between Australia and England will have a higher demand and hence higher admission prices than a friendly game between New Zealand and the Netherlands.

Demand-based pricing, or variable pricing as it is sometimes called, is based on two assumptions about the relationship between supply and demand. The first assumption is that, where demand is high, it is reasonable to increase price in the knowledge that the level of usage or support will remain at roughly the same level. The second assumption is that, when demand is low, it is time to lower price in order to stimulate the level of participant use and spectator support.

There are a number of situations where the demand for sport products will be high, and prices can be increased. In the case of spectator sport, demand will be highest at the weekend rather than a weeknight, where there are a number of star players involved (the Federer, Woods and Ronaldo factors are at work here), where two high-performing teams are playing, and when the premiership race is tightly contested. Alternatively, prices should be lowered where these factors are not present. Demand will be particularly weak when two low-performing teams with few stars are playing in a weekday match that does not matter much. Variable pricing is not common in professional sport leagues, where admission prices are fixed at the beginning of the season. It is used extensively though in community sport and leisure service provision. For example, in gymnasia and fitness centres the casual rate is always higher in peak periods (e.g. late afternoon and early evening) and lower in off-peak periods (e.g. mid-morning). The various situations where high demand can accommodate higher prices, and low demand lower prices, are listed in Table 10.1.

TABLE 10.1 High- and low-demand conditions in sport and leisure	
High-demand situation	*Low-demand situation*
Weekend	Mid-week
Late afternoon	Mid-morning
Monday evening	Friday evening

Elasticity pricing

Elasticity pricing, like demand-based pricing, is based on the changing relationships between demand and supply. However, unlike demand-based pricing, it aims to set a price on the basis of estimations of how sensitive demand is likely to be to a change in price. There are two possibilities to consider here.

First, demand can be sensitive to price change. For example, studies may have found that, when the price of fitness centre annual membership fell by 10 per cent (from $200 to $180), the demand for memberships increased by 20 per cent (from 300 to 360). This means that, whereas total member receipts were $60,000 (300 × $200) at the higher price, it was $64,800 (360 × $180) at the lower price. In this instance demand is described as elastic, which means it is better to charge lower prices, since total receipts or revenue will increase as a result (see Table 10.2).

TABLE 10.2 Relationship between elastic demand, prices and revenue			
Elastic demand	Demand is sensitive to price change	Price increase generates a fall in revenue	Price fall generates an increase in revenue

Alternatively, demand can be insensitive to price change. If, for example, another study found that demand for fitness centre memberships fell by a miniscule 3 per cent (from 300 to 291) in response to a price increase of 10 per cent (from $200 to $220), then demand would be price inelastic. That is, demand was relatively insensitive to a change in price. In this case the increase in memberships leads to an increase in total member receipts or revenue. Whereas the lower price generated revenues of $60,000, the higher price generated revenues of just over $64,000. In this case it therefore makes commercial sense to increase membership fees (see Table 10.3).

TABLE 10.3 Relationship between inelastic demand, prices and revenue			
Inelastic demand	Demand is insensitive to price change	Price increase generates an increase in revenue	Price fall generates a fall in revenue

The same principle applies to ticket pricing for professional sport leagues. However, the evidence is ambiguous when it comes to deciding if the demand for stadium seats is price elastic or price inelastic. The intuitive response is to say that demand is price inelastic because, as noted in Chapter 1, sport fans have strong emotional attachments to teams. Research has also indicated a high degree of inelasticity for some American sport league games (Boyd and Boyd 1998: 70). However, this is only partly true since not all fans are so passionate that they will attend despite any increase in admission prices. Many fans will attend if they expect good value for money, and may have a price threshold beyond which they are not prepared to go. In addition, price sensitivity may change with income levels. Fans on high incomes, for instance, may be insensitive to price, while low-income earners may be far more price sensitive to different sport experiences.

Prestige pricing

When buyers want a special experience, their sensitivity to product features generally overrides their sensitivity to price. Owning an exclusive and high-status product gives some people not only confidence in their purchase, but also security in their own sense of self. Highly priced products are more exclusive to own, and hence become more desirable to those who seek out status and prestige. Prestige goods can be used to authenticate success or economic power, and are sometimes called positional goods. This is because their prestige value is contingent upon them being relatively scarce, and available only to a select few.

Prestige pricing is particularly prevalent in the provision of sport stadium seats. Private boxes and luxury suites are highly priced and therefore only accessible to an exclusive few. This makes it very attractive to the fan who wants prestige and status in addition to a quality game experience. The provision of exclusive membership packages serves the same function. The high price comes with additional service benefits such as gourmet meals, luxury seats and free drinks, but the main benefit is the belief that the membership package is only available to a select few.

Quality-assurance pricing

In many instances price can be used to reinforce a brand image of quality as exemplified in the slogan 'quality comes at a price'. In this case the higher price is indicative of a superior product, and a low price indicative of a lower-quality product. In other words, buyers believe that you get what you pay for, and therefore will pay more with the expectation of getting more. Simply put, a high price can enhance the perceived quality of a product when compared to substitutes. For example, when battery-run electronic clocks and watches first appeared on the market their low initial price was seen as indicative of low quality. Sales soared when prices were raised to levels comparable to their mechanical substitutes. The problem created by the initial low price was that consumers did not believe they were getting more than they were used to paying for, largely because the cost and quality innovations were radical and not visibly apparent. Price can therefore be used to signal that extra effort has been made to produce a superior product that will perform to the buyer's satisfaction.

Quality-assurance pricing is particularly relevant to sport. Mega-sport events use a quality-assurance model when they set prices for their tournaments. In Australia, an international sport fixture in any code of football will always attract a premium price. While a local inter-club game, even when involving two high-quality professional teams, will have a price between AUD 52 and AUD 60, a game involving the national team will attract an admission price of AUD 100 to AUD 500. In 2006, the Australian world-football team played Greece at the MCG, and on the expectation of a quality game featuring Australia's best players, tickets were marked from AUD 50 to AUD 600. The game was a sell-out. A similar situation arose at the 2006 Commonwealth Games, when the opening ceremony confirmed the expectation that it would be a quality experience by setting ticket prices in the AUD 40 to AUD 500 range. Similar pricing arrangements were put in place when Manchester United FC came to Australia in 2013.

Discriminatory pricing

Discriminatory pricing, or differential pricing as it is sometimes called, involves charging different prices to different market segments and product users. The underlying assumption behind this approach is that different groups of people have quite different capacities to pay, and that the greater the capacity to pay, the higher the price to be charged. Capacity to pay is in turn linked to the income levels of consumers. As a result, this model of pricing concludes that professional workers such as company directors, lawyers, doctors and academics will be able to pay higher prices than teachers, clerks and nurses for a similar good or service. At the other end of the socioeconomic spectrum, the unemployed and students will have a very low capacity to pay, and will thus be repelled by high prices for anything but essential products such as food, drink and rent.

Discriminatory pricing operates at two levels. First, it aims to maximize revenue by adopting a high-price threshold for high-income earners where demand is not choked, but receipts are maximized. Second, it targets low-income earners with the bait of low prices to ensure a higher level of demand. By segmenting the market on the basis of capacity to pay, it is anticipated that total revenue will be optimized, and certainly higher than if a single price was charged to everyone.

This is a common feature of sport pricing at both the participant and spectator level. Low prices are charged for the unemployed and people on disability pensions, while a discount is also provided to students. A higher price is charged for adults, while a special price is charged for family groups. The family price is usually a middle-ground price that provides an average family member charge that is somewhere between the adult entry and the student entry.

Competition pricing

In this instance prices are placed in line with competitors. This is done to first ensure that prices are not so high that potential purchasers will shift their spending to competitors' products. The second reason is to ensure that a price is not so low that, while it attracts new purchasers, it fails to secure any available consumer surplus.

This device is frequently used in sport. At the community level one of the first things a sport and fitness centre does is compile a list of competitor prices as a means of setting a benchmark price for its services. While this can quickly establish a pricing band (which sets a minimum and maximum fee or charge), it can also squeeze the potential for profits by not taking the cost structure of competitors into account. For example, if a swim centre finds that the average entry fee for its competitors is $8, it may want to set a competitive entry fee of $9. This seems reasonable, but it might find that, while the average operating costs of its competitors are around $7, its own operating costs are $10. If it also aims to break even on its operations, a $9 entry fee will not be sustainable.

Penetration pricing

Penetration pricing occurs when a price is initially discounted, and then set below cost. The aim is to build market share and earn profits from future repeat sales. A business can offer a penetration price in several ways. At the extreme, for example, a company selling new pharmaceuticals will often introduce them at a zero price through free sampling. Computer software is also often given away to opinion leaders. Penetration pricing can be a very effective pricing strategy for the following reasons:

- it results in faster adoption and market penetration, which can take the competition by surprise;
- it creates an early-adopter goodwill, which results in more word-of-mouth adoptions;
- it creates cost-reduction and cost-control pressures and this creates the condition for productivity improvements and high levels of efficiency;
- it discourages the entry of competitors by signalling to others that it has sustainable, cost-competitive advantage.

Penetration pricing has the potential for use in some sport situations, and in particular where a new sport league has been introduced, or a new gymnasium programme is offered. Penetration pricing can also be usefully employed in attracting new members to community sport clubs and leisure centres, where the level of service and facility quality is similar between competing organizations. In this case the probability of creating a value-for-money experience is high and word of mouth can elicit a second swell of interest, even if prices are increased for this group of users.

Price skimming

Price skimming is the opposite of penetration pricing, since it sets a relatively high level to attract a threshold of buyers who value the product most highly. Its aim is to set a price above its competitors so as to ensure a high surplus for a limited demand. Like premium pricing, it requires a loyal market where quality is valued over price. It is also best used when supply is limited. In sport it can be applied to luxury stadium seating and exclusive gymnasium facilities. It can be combined with premium pricing to capture high-income consumers who put high value on positional goods such as an opening ceremony at a mega-sport event.

CASE STUDY 10.1

Pricing strategies in American professional sport leagues

The centrality of ticketing

Despite the growth of sporting sponsorship and broadcasting rights fees, game tickets sales are still an important source of revenue for professional sport leagues and clubs. Although this source of revenue has fallen in relative terms (in the 1970s it comprised between 50 and 70 per cent of club revenues), it is still in the top four revenue streams for most large sport clubs and leagues.

The other point to note is that, while ticket prices have risen for all of America's professional sport leagues, the rates of change are different for each of the sport leagues. For the eighteen-year period between 1991 and 2011, the NFL had the most significant increase in average ticket prices. It increased from USD 40 to just under USD 80. MLB commenced from a much lower base of $15, but it too exhibited a consistent increase in ticket prices, having settled at just under $30 by 2009. NBA and NHL ticket prices fluctuated over time, which resulted in lower overall price rises over the same eighteen-year period. NBA ticket average prices increased from $35 to $50, while NHL average ticket prices remained relatively constant at around the $50 mark (Winfree and Rosentraub 2012: 348–52).

Pricing is a crucial component of a professional sport league's revenue collection for two reasons. First, it establishes the contribution that each paying fan will make to league and club finances and, second, it also impacts on the demand for tickets. Research has shown that, in USA professional sport leagues, fans cite the cost of attending games as the single most important factor influencing their preparedness to attend. Whereas only 14 per cent of fans said that a change in team performance would impact upon their decision to buy a ticket, 57 per cent said that increasing ticket prices would influence their pattern of attendance (Howard and Crompton 2004: 39). This begs the question as to how ticket prices are determined in professional sport leagues. On the basis of the earlier analysis of pricing it would be logical to adopt pricing strategies that, in the first instance, cover costs, second, compare favourably with the price of rival leagues and competitors and, third, create demand conditions.

Influences on ticket prices

In another study of ticket pricing in the NFL it was found that team performance was the single most important factor. In other words, when teams were winning more than they were losing, ticket sellers wanted to increase ticket prices. Behind this view is the assumption that a winning team would attract more fans who would be prepared to pay more – a premium if you like – for a winning experience. Other important factors that drove ticket prices up included the need to secure more revenue, general economic conditions and the level of fan identification. The least important factors were the expected television coverage, access to the game, weather

TABLE 10.4 Factors influencing ticket pricing in the NFL		
Description	Most important (%)	Not important (%)
Team performance	43	11
Revenue needs	37	11
Average price	32	21
Economic factors	21	21
Market price toleration	21	16
Fan identification	16	16
Public relations	16	11
Capacity of facility	11	21
Competing entertainment	11	37
Condition of facility	11	64
Average income	6	43
Population	0	64
Schedule	0	85
Television media coverage	0	85
Accessibility	0	90
Star players	0	95
Weather conditions	0	100
Racial composition	0	100

Source: Reese and Mittelstaedt (2001).

conditions and the presence of star players. A list of the factors and their relative importance are shown in Table 10.4.

However, the research should not be taken as confirmation that sports pricing is rational and systematic, or based on firm costing principles. In fact, when it comes to ticket pricing, some critics believe that sport managers operate 'by the seat of their pants' (Howard and Crompton 2004: 356). According to some sport economists, the pricing of tickets in the USA is nothing more than 'best informed guesses' (Quirk and Fort 1992: 144). The rough rule of thumb for most sport event organizers is to set prices that, first, generate an appropriate cash flow, second, compare favourably with related sport events and, finally, take into account any threshold price that fans would baulk at paying. In other words, they charge the 'going rate'. The going rate is a safe and conservative approach, but there is no guarantee that this approach will deliver enough revenue to cover costs. Tickets may alternatively be priced to ensure they cover all event or operating costs. In some instances it may be necessary to set a price that aims to recover both the capital repayment cost as well as operating costs. At the other extreme, ticket prices may be set below the operating cost to stimulate club membership, regenerate fan interest and give admission access to the socially disadvantaged.

This raises the question of whether or not ticket prices are too high or too low in American professional sport leagues. This is a difficult issue to resolve, although at first glance it is difficult to defend a USD 2,000 ticket for a premium seats, but this has often occurred at MLB and NBA games, with the Los Angeles Lakers and New York Yankees being the most frequent offenders, so to speak. However, the evidence suggests that prices are lower than demand conditions might suggest. There is always lurking in the background an incentive to increase prices to the limit because fans are usually not very sensitive to price. That is, a higher price will not dampen demand all that much. On the other hand some commentators believe that most sport leagues have resisted the temptation to increase prices at every turn, which suggests that ticket prices are not excessive or exploitative (Winfree and Rosentraub 2012: 354).

CASE STUDY 10.2

The problem of escalating admission prices in English and Australian professional sport leagues

As noted previously, price performs a number of essential functions for sport organizations. First, it is the basis of every revenue stream. Sponsorships, league and club merchandise and media rights all have a price, and at the most fundamental level, membership and game admission both come at a price. Second, it is a tool for extracting revenue from different corporate, member and fan segments. Sport marketers have developed sophisticated techniques for dividing up the sport experience into a variety of categories, and pricing each category on the basis of the different benefits that are provided. Club memberships and sport stadium seating are good cases in point. Third, price can be used as a policy tool by setting high fees or charges for one group of members or fans, and using the surplus to fund a low or indeed below-cost fee for low-income earners or some other disadvantaged group.

For the fan, price is simply part of the cost of obtaining a sport experience. It can be a source of attraction insofar as it represents a bargain, or just value for money. Conversely, it may have the effect of excluding some fans and privileging others. So, what can we say about the pricing of sport events in Australia and the UK, and the changes that have occurred over recent years? And how might we explain these changes? In the first place, the price of attending elite sport events has escalated over recent times. There are two inflationary forces at work here. The first is administrative salaries and player payments. In the AFL, for example, the average player salary has increased from AUD 50,000 in 1990 to AUD 150,000 in 2005 to 200,000 in 2012. In the NRL a similar explosion of player wages occurred. The second factor is stadium construction and maintenance costs. During the 1900s, major stadium redevelopment took place in the USA, Europe and Australia, with the construction costs frequently exceeding AUD 400 million (Foster *et al.* 2006).

According to Howard and Crompton (2004), investment in sport stadia and arenas has increased exponentially over the last ten to fifteen years. Furthermore, the actual cost of constructing the facility can sometimes be less than 50 per cent of the total project costs. In one stadium development costing more than USD 470 million, land purchase and site preparation cost USD 100 million, relocating transport infrastructure cost another USD 65 million, and the establishment of parking facilities cost another USD 10 million (Howard and Crompton 2004: 52). While these additional costs are necessary, they put additional pressures on the game admission prices.

There is also an additional factor that needs to be addressed. This complicating factor is the revenue that leagues and clubs obtain from the corporate world. TV rights, merchandising income and sponsorship fees now provide a dominant contribution to their revenue base. This non-admission charge revenue source can not only add to profits, but can also be used to subsidize admission charges and membership fees. The AFL claims that the full cost of maintaining the national competition is around AUD 50 per person attending. However, the sponsorship and other corporate funding enables the AFL to currently charge no more than AUD 30 per person attending on a walk-up basis. In addition, Table 10.5 shows a relatively modest increase in standard AFL ticket prices between 1990 and 2003. It is thus difficult to prove that AFL ticket prices are exploitatively high.

TABLE 10.5 AFL base admission charges to home and away games (AUD)			
1990	*1995*	*2000*	*2003*
10	13	14	20

Despite the size of the corporate subsidy, the pressure on ticket prices has been severe. As a result, the general level of admission prices for professional sport leagues has risen substantially over the last ten years. When this is combined with the replacement of terrace-based grounds with all-seat stadia, there was pressure to seek out affluent fans who were prepared to pay something extra for a quality experience. In other words, a new type of fan was targeted at the expense of the old. The traditional working-class fan has been marginalized, while the more affluent professional middle-class supporter has been more strongly targeted (King 1998). In the USA this trend in professional sport has been identified as a process of 'white-collarization'. Table 10.6 shows the scale of the change in ticket prices between 1991 and 2003.

A similar trend occurred in English professional sport in general and in the English Premier League (EPL) in particular. In 2006, a standard seat at Chelsea's Stamford Bridge stadium cost from GBP 45 to GBP 50. By contrast, a seat in 1995 cost GBP 10. The pressure to increase ticket prices in the EPL was compounded by the Glazer

TABLE 10.6 Costs of attending major league sporting events for a family of four (USD)		
League	1991	2003
MLB	77	145
NBA	139	255
NFL	153	290
NHL	133	240

Source: Howard and Crompton (2004).

family buy-out of Manchester United in 2005. In order to help cover GBP 650 million in loans acquired to purchase the club, plans were made to increase ticket prices by over 50 per cent over the next five years. The movement in EPL ticket prices over the last fifteen years is illustrated in Table 10.7.

TABLE 10.7 EPL standard ticket price trends, 1990 to 2005 (GBP)			
1990	1995	2000	2005
10	16	25	35

The quality experience that professional sport in Britain now provides its fans has come at a cost. The all-seat stadium that offers superior sightlines, greater comfort, a weatherproof playing surface, extensive food and drink, protection from the rain and even the occasional retractable roof, has ensured a quality spectator experience. However, it also comes with a stiff ticket price. Many low-income supporters have been priced out of regular attendance, and into their place have sauntered middle-class, white-collar families. Television is now the medium by which most fans watch their favourite professional sport teams. Live attendance is now all about capacity to pay, and paying for the privilege.

In the short term, a pricing strategy that customizes the needs of fans around the capacity to pay will boost revenue. In the long term, the benefits may be undermined by two factors. First, ticket prices may exceed the price threshold of many fans. Second, many fickle theatre-goers may decide to direct their discretionary spending to some newly fashionable leisure experience. This begs the question as to whether loyalty and passion have been subordinated to preparedness to pay as the primary link between fans and professional sport leagues. And, if they have, will professional sport maintain its mass appeal?

RECAP

For any sport enterprise, no matter how large or how small, the prices of its services (its intangible products) and its goods (its tangible products) are key determinants of its subsequent revenues. Pricing, though, is a very sensitive issue. This is because high prices can not only expand revenue per unit, but also reduce the number of units sold. Low prices can stimulate demand, which is good, but they can also squeeze revenue per unit, which is not a good thing. Part of the solution to this problem has been to segment markets and charge different prices to different segments, with the prices reflecting each segment's capacity to pay. So, what can be done, or what should be done? The following questions focus on this point.

REVIEW QUESTIONS

Pricing is a vexing issue in sport because of the conflicting demands it imposes on the suppliers of sport products on the one hand, and the users of sport products on the other. It thus produces many questions that are often difficult to satisfactorily answer.

1 Why is pricing so important to the financial viability of sport organizations?

2 What is meant by full cost recovery pricing?

3 Contrast full cost recovery pricing with pricing below cost. Under what circumstances would it be possible and proper to price below cost for a sport service? Where does equity pricing fit into this context?

4 Give examples of cost-plus pricing in sport.

5 How does demand-based pricing work in sport?

6 Give examples of sport products that might have a low price elasticity of demand, and those sport products that might have a high price elasticity of demand.

7 How does prestige pricing work in sport, at both the low and high ends of the market? And how can quality-assurance pricing be linked to prestige pricing?

8 How does discriminatory pricing work in sport? Give examples from community sport and recreation and professional sport leagues.

9 Contrast penetration pricing with price skimming. Under what conditions would one approach be used over the other?

10 How important is competition pricing in sport?

11 What are the pressures on ticket prices in professional sport?

12 Is there room for flexible pricing in sport, where prices for tickets to the same game are changed in accordance with demand as the game day approaches?

13 Is there any evidence that higher ticket prices for professional sport league games are threatening attendance levels?

FURTHER READING

An extensive analysis of different pricing regimes, including full cost pricing, market-based pricing, subsidized pricing and free pricing, is provided by Anthony, R. and Young, D. (2003) *Management Control in Non-profit Organizations*, 7th edition, New York: McGraw-Hill (Chapter 7: 'Pricing decisions'). For a concise introduction to the pricing of services (including sport-related services), see Hoffman, K. and Bateson, J. (2001) *Essentials of Services Marketing*, 2nd edition, Mason, OH: South-Western. Chapter 7 ('The pricing of services') is especially instructive since it includes a discussion of the distinction between cost, price and value.

In Foster, G., Greyser, S. and Walsh, B. (2006) *The Business of Sports*, Mason, OH: Thomson, there is a succinct analysis of how ticket prices for USA professional sport leagues are packaged and tiered. See, for example, section 7, which addresses local revenue enhancement and ticket pricing. An excellent follow-up examination of ticket prices in American professional sport leagues is contained in Winfree, J. and Rosentraub, M. (2012) *Sports Finance and Management: Real Estate, Entertainment, and the Remaking of Business*, Boca Raton, FL: CRC Press (Chapter 10: 'Pricing strategies').

A useful introduction to the pricing of sport products is contained in Mullin, B., Hardy, S. and Sutton, W. (2001) *Sport Marketing*, 2nd edition, Champaign, IL: Human Kinetics (Chapter 9: 'Pricing strategies'). For an extensive analysis of the economics of pricing in the sport and leisure sector see Tribe, J. (2004) *The Economics of Recreation, Leisure and Tourism*, 3rd edition, Oxford: Elsevier. In Howard, D. and Crompton, J. (2004) *Financing Sport*, 2nd edition, Morgantown, WV: Fitness Information Technology, there is an extensive analysis of pricing and ticketing in USA professional sport leagues. See Chapter 9 for a solid discussion on ticket sales and operations.

USEFUL WEBSITES

- A clear and comprehensive account of pricing strategies is contained in **www.netmba.com/marketing/pricing**.
- A relatively lengthy, but highly informative, slide show on pricing is contained in **www.youtube.com/watch?v=H8aZr-Ula1w**.
- The following website contains a more esoteric analysis of pricing strategy. There is an interesting section on pricing power, which is all about independent price setting: **http://sloanreview.mit.edu/article/is-it-time-to-rethink-your-pricing-strategy**.
- The following website looks at the concept of dynamic pricing (DP) and its application to sport events. DP is all about making prices flexible and fluid rather than fixed: **www.forbes.com/sites/prishe/2012/01/06/dynamic-pricing-the-future-of-ticket-pricing-in-sports**.
- *The Economist* has also written a piece on flexible ticket pricing in sport: **www.economist.com/blogs/gametheory/2012/01/sports-ticketing**.
- There is a tidy discussion of variability in ticket pricing at **www.investopedia.com/financial-edge/1012/why-the-prices-of-sports-tickets-vary-so-much-.aspx**.

ANALYSIS

Critical capabilities

CHAPTER 11

Interrogating the accounts

LEARNING OUTCOMES

At the end of this chapter readers will be able to:

- explain why it is so important to have a method for accurately and succinctly assessing the financial performance of sport enterprises
- understand the importance of using multiple data sets to assist in this process
- explain what is meant by the term 'ratio analysis'
- calculate ratios for profitability, liquidity, long-term indebtedness, efficiency and net worth.

CHAPTER SUMMARY

This chapter provides a detailed discussion of the ways in which the financial performance of sport enterprises can be analysed using the financial statements. It makes the crucial point that more than one performance indicator is needed to get a clear and unambiguous under-standing of how well a club, association or league is trending from a financial perspective. It thus follows that the balance sheet, profit and loss statement and cash flow statement must all be interrogated, both separately and conjointly. The remainder of the chapter focuses on specific measures for gauging an enterprise's financial well-being and future prospects. Special attention is paid to the use of 'ratio analysis', which involves the use of at least two sets of data to calculate a specific performance indicator. The main indicators addressed are profitability, liquidity, long-term indebtedness, efficiency and net worth. Customized measures to suit the special requirements of different sport organizations are also discussed.

THE STRATEGIC IMPORTANCE OF MEASURING FINANCIAL PERFORMANCE

The ability to measure financial performance is fundamental to the proper management of sport enterprises. Two equally important approaches need to be taken, though. The first is a 'rating' approach, where the financial health of an enterprise is compared to some historical benchmark. The second is a 'ranking' approach, where the financial performance of one enterprise is compared to the performance of other enterprises that deliver similar products. So, for instance, a semi-professional netball club may have earned 10 per cent more revenue per year for the last five years, and increased its operating surplus for each of these years. By historical standards this would represent a highly successful outcome. However, when compared to other similar clubs, its performance may have been sub-standard, since they may have increased their revenues by 15 per cent per annum over the last five years. Thus, everything is relative.

With these two principles in the backs of our minds, it becomes crystal clear that one needs to do far more than just compile a few accounts, keep an eye on how much credit a sport club or association has built up, and monitor revenue and expenses from time to time. It is also essential to calculate precise measures of a sport club's financial perform-ance over time. This second task requires exposure to a number of tools for measuring profitability, short-term financial stability, long-term financial stability and, finally, the club's or association's level of net worth or wealth. A discussion of these four approaches to financial analysis will follow.

As noted above, in order to make sense of financial information it is necessary to establish some sort of reference point or benchmark. At first glance the revelation that a club has secured $20 million in annual revenue may seem to be a good result. However, it may be only 5 per cent more than the revenue earned five years ago when the economy was depressed. In addition, annual expenses have increased by 10 per cent over the same time period, thereby cutting into club surpluses. Moreover, it is found that a majority of clubs in the same sport league are earning in excess of $25 million, with two clubs earning more than $30 million. This immediately places the club's or association's financial performance into a specific context. It is consequently important to measure a club's financial position using reference points and benchmarks that give a stronger sense of relative financial well-being.

There are three reference points that need to be identified before any effective analysis can take place. The first is a sport club's previous performance. In this instance the question to ask is what happened last year, five years ago or even ten years ago. This is called horizontal analysis, but is also referred to as longitudinal or trend analysis. Trend analysis can highlight significant increases or falls in broad items such as annual revenue and total expenses, or even more specific items such as sponsorship income, merchandise sales, player payments and advertising expenses. The second reference point is a base figure in the accounts such as total assets or total revenue. In this instance it is possible to examine one figure in relation to another. So, instead of just identifying a profit or surplus, it will be possible to view it in relation to some other item. A profit of $2 million, for example, can be viewed as a proportion of total revenue of $50 million to give a profit ratio of 4 per cent. If your asset base is $25 million, the return on assets calculation will be 2 over 25, which is 8 per cent. The final reference point is the performance of clubs similar to yours. In this instance the question to ask is: did we do better or worse than the club in the next suburb or local competition, or indeed a similar club in another region or country? For example, a county or state cricket association may have just posted a record level of annual revenue, made a handsome surplus and smugly concluded that it had done very well. However, if all other county or state governing bodies had exceeded its bottom line results, then its comparative performance would be viewed as dismal.

Each of the above three reference points can be used to strengthen the analysis by providing comparative data, and encouraging a more contextual examination of the figures. However, whatever approach is taken, it is crucial to understand the variety of measures that can be used to assess both broad and specific financial issues within a sport club or association. This involves undertaking some form of ratio analysis that has as its focus profitability, short-term financial stability, long-term financial stability and, finally, the club's or association's level of wealth or net worth.

MEASURES OF PROFITABILITY

Profit (or surplus) is superficially easy to measure since it is straightforward to calculate the difference between aggregate income and aggregate expenditure. However, we also need to clearly distinguish between operating profit and net profit. There can sometimes be a substantial difference between the two since, as was noted in the previous chapter, depreciation, abnormal and extraordinary items on both the income and expenditure side need to be taken into account. Moreover, the relationship between revenue (aggregate income), expenses (aggregate expenditure) and profits can be examined from a number of perspectives.

Return on revenue

First, we can look at profit in relation to revenue, earnings or income. For example, if aggregate income for the year was $4 million and expenditure was $3.6 million the profit or surplus is $0.4 million. If profit is expressed as a percentage of income it comes out at 10 per cent. So, the return on revenue is 10 per cent. For a not-for-profit organization such as a sporting club this would be a good result, since profit-making is not its prime goal and, in any case, additional earnings are retained by the club. A club can end up with a high or small ratio, a high or improved ratio being an indicator of good performance.

It is also possible to compare expenditure to income with a view to producing an expenditure to income ratio. Using the above example, the ratio is calculated by dividing the $3.6 million expenditure into the $4 million revenue. The ratio is 1.1 and can be expressed as 1:1.1. That is, for every dollar of expenditure the club earned 1.1 dollars of income. A ratio less than 1 would be unsatisfactory, since losses will be made, while a figure in excess of 1 would indicate the capacity to operate profitably (see Table 11.1).

TABLE 11.1 Example of profit ratio

Profit ($)	Revenue ($)	Profit ratio (profit/revenue)
20,000	500,000	0.4 (4%)

Return on assets

We can also link income or profits to assets. In this case we are finding out how productively we use our assets to generate revenue to ensure the sustainability of our operations. For example, one club may have tangible asset backing of $2 million, and generate revenue of $500,000. The revenue return on assets is consequently 25 per cent. Another club may have earned $1 million, but on a much higher tangible asset base of $5 million. In this case the revenue return on assets is 20 per cent, which may suggest a poorer use of its revenue-generating capacity. Again, all other things being equal, the higher the ratio, the better the performance.

The same calculations can be made for profits and assets. In this case either the operating or net profit can be compared to the assets of the club or association. If the operating profit is $20,000 and the value of the tangible assets is $5 million, then the profit return on assets is $200,000 divided by the $5 million, which is 0.4 or 4 per cent (see Table 11.2).

TABLE 11.2 Example of return on assets ratio

Profit ($ millions)	Tangible assets ($ millions)	Return on assets (profit/assets)
0.5	10	0.4 (4%)

MEASURING SHORT-TERM FINANCIAL STABILITY

We also need a measure of how well we can service our short-term debts when they fall due. For example, sport clubs will usually build up their 'accounts payable' item by buying things on credit. There is no problem with this so long as the club has the funds to pay these short-term debts at the appropriate time. And, of course, they have to be paid for in cash. If a sport club or association regularly fails to pay its bills, then when they are due creditors can take legal action to force them to pay, and this can lead to insolvency and bankruptcy whereby the club or association must sell off all its assets and stop operating. Consequently, all sport clubs and associations need a way of monitoring their capacity to pay bills when required. The key issue here is to have enough cash, or assets that can be easily and quickly converted to cash, to cover all short-term debt.

Working capital

The best indicator of a sport club's ability to pay its short-term debt is its working capital, or level of liquidity, which is the difference between current assets and current liabilities. Current assets include items such as cash (which is axiomatic), accounts receivable (which includes those transactions where payment is imminent), inventory (which is merchandise for sale) and stocks and shares that can be converted to cash in a matter of days. Current liabilities include mainly those transactions for which payment to a creditor is due in thirty to ninety days, and are called 'accounts payable'. The ideal situation is to have current assets exceed current liabilities. This indicates the capacity to cover all short-term debt. For example, one club may have current assets of $1.9 million and current liabilities of $2.2 million, while another club may have current assets of $1.5 million and current liabilities of $1.2 million. In the case of the first club its working capital is –$0.3 million, which would be cause for concern. In the case of the second club, the working capital is +$0.3 million, which provides a solid buffer from which to comfortably pay its short-term debts when they become due. These raw figures can also be converted to a ratio by dividing current assets by current liabilities. In the above case the first club has a working capital ratio (or current ratio, as it is often called) of 0.86, or 0.86:1. This means that for every dollar of current liabilities the club has only 86 cents of current assets, which is not a satisfactory position to maintain for any length of time. Conversely, the second club has a working capital/current ratio of 1.25 or 1.25:1. This means that for every dollar of current liabilities the club has $1.25 in current assets, and it can therefore comfortably pay its short-term debts when they are due (see Table 11.3 for another example).

TABLE 11.3 Example of working capital (current) ratio

Current assets ($ millions)	Current liabilities ($ millions)	Current ratio (current assets/ current liabilities)
3	3.2	0.94 (0.9:1)

CASH FLOW

The cash flow statement can also be used to identify the strength of a club's or association's cash reserves. A useful tool here is the cash flow adequacy ratio, which assesses the capacity of an organization to provide sufficient net cash inflow from its operating activities to cover its repayment of long-term borrowings and any assets it acquired. It can also include dividends paid, but for most sport clubs this will not be relevant. For example, a club may have generated a net cash flow from operating activities of $900,000, but at the same time repaid $600,000 of long-term debt, purchased property for $450,000 and installed a computer system worth $50,000. The cash flow adequacy ratio is calculated by adding up the loan repayment and asset purchases ($1.1 million), and dividing this into net cash flow from operating activities ($900,000). This will produce a ratio of 0.82, or 0.82:1. That is, for every dollar of aggregated loan repayment and asset purchases it is only supported by 82 cents of cash from its operating activities. This may not be a problem for one or two years, but would signal the need to better manage investing and financing activities. This trend would clearly need to be reversed over the longer term to ensure appropriate levels of net cash inflow (see Table 11.4).

TABLE 11.4 Example of cash flow adequacy ratio

Loan and asset payments ($)	Net cash from operating activities ($)	Cash flow adequacy ratio (cash from operations/ loans and assets purchased)
90,000	70,000	0.72 (0.72:1)

MEASURES OF OPERATING EFFICIENCY

It is also important to have some way of identifying how well club, association or league revenues and resources are being managed, and how effectively they are being used. In professional sport there is an assumed link between total revenue received and successes delivered (this issue is discussed in detail in Chapters 2 and 3). In other words, the greater the revenue-generating capacity of a club or association, the greater the likelihood of on-field success. This is particularly evident in the English Premier League, where the five richest clubs (Manchester United, Chelsea, Liverpool, Arsenal and Manchester City) inevitably occupy one of the top six positions in the league table. However, the correlation is not perfect and there are many instances of relatively wealthy clubs who underachieve on the one hand, and poor clubs who – in boxing parlance – punch above their weight on the other.

Revenue efficiency ratio

One important indicator of a club's efficient use of revenues and resources is its ability to generate revenue from its supporter and fan base. While it is important to cultivate a broad supporter base, it is equally important to create a level of fan loyalty, whereby they contribute consistently to the club's revenue stream. Whereas one club may have a large fan catchment (i.e. it has a large surrounding population, or possesses a strong brand image that attracts people from all over the place), many of their fans may be only marginally attached to the club, and attend games and take out memberships only when the club is playing well, or the weather is fine.

For instance, a club might have a revenue base of $50 million and an average home attendance of 25,000. This relationship between total revenue and average home attendance is called 'revenue efficiency', and measures the ability of the club to attract financial support from it fans. The ratio is calculated by dividing average home attendance into total revenue, and measuring the revenue received for each fan who attends a home game. In the above example, the revenue efficiency ratio is 50 million divided by 25,000, which is 200,000 or 200,000:1. That is, for every fan who attends each week, the club generates $200,000 in revenue. Without any benchmark it may seem a reasonable outcome. However, another club with a much smaller support base, and consequently a much lower average game attendance of 15,000, may have an annual revenue of $45 million. In this case the revenue efficiency will be 300,000:1. The club is consequently able to extract an average of $300,000 from each fan who attends on a weekly basis. So, even though the second club has a lower revenue base, it is able to better utilize its fan base.

TABLE 11.5 Example of revenue efficiency ratio

Total annual revenue ($ millions)	Average home attendance	Revenue efficiency ratio (annual revenue/ average home attendance)
2	25,000	80 (80:1)

This could be the result of a stronger merchandising programme, more effective member servicing, or a more passionate and committed relationship between fans and their club (see Table 11.5 for another example).

Wage efficiency ratio

Another indicator of a club's efficient use of revenues and resources is its ability to win games without incurring huge wage bills. As indicated earlier, there is, generally speaking, a positive correlation between revenues earned and games won. This proposition is close to being axiomatic, since clubs with large revenue streams can obviously lure the best players with the bait of more money. However, there are also many instances where rich clubs who can afford to buy the best players do not do so at the level they expect, while less wealthy clubs can often compete successfully on much smaller budgets. Let us assume, for example, that Club 1 has an annual wage bill covering players, coaches and support staff of $15 million and last season it won fifteen out of twenty games. Club 2, on the other hand, won eighteen games, but had an annual wage budget of $22 million. To calculate a wage efficiency ratio – or the cost–win ratio, as it is alternatively known as – total wage costs are divided by league wins. The wage efficiency (cost–win) ratio for Club 1 is 1 million (or 1 million:1). That is, it cost an average $1 million in wages to win each game. Conversely, even though it won more games, Club 2 had a higher wage efficiency ratio. It was therefore less efficient than Club 1 since it needed $1.2 million on average to win each game (see Table 11.6 for another example).

TABLE 11.6 Example of wage efficiency ratio

Total wage bill ($ millions)	Games won	Wage efficiency ratio (total wages/games won)
5	20	250,000 (250,000:1)

MEASURING LONG-TERM FINANCIAL STABILITY

We also want to get a clear picture of how much long-term debt a sport club has built up. It does not automatically follow that a large amount of borrowed money is going to be a problem, but it does present a potential for later difficulties if profit levels fall, and it becomes difficult to pay back both the loan (that is the principal) and the interest on it. The Melbourne Cricket Club, one of Australia's largest sport organizations, is a good example of this as can be noted in its balance sheet. However, the Moonee Valley Racing Club, another large sport organization, has virtually no long-term debt, which reflects little long-term borrowing of money over ten to thirty years.

We can use the financial leverage ratio or the debt to equity ratio to measure the relative levels of long-term indebtedness. Both measures are comparing the amount of borrowed money in the business with the amount of invested funds from either the owners in the form of their own capital, or profits that have been ploughed back into the business. For example, the North Riding Horse Racing Club finds that it has $2 million

TABLE 11.7 Example of debt to equity ratio

Debt ($ millions)	Equity ($ millions)	Debt to equity ratio
5	10	0.5 (0.5:1)

of debt (both current and long-term) and $500,000 in equity or accumulated member funds. Its debt to equity ratio is therefore $2 million divided by $500,000, which is 4 or 4:1. That is, for every dollar of equity the club has $4 of debt. This indicates a high level of debt dependency (see Table 11.7 for another example).

It is also appropriate to contrast the total assets with total long-term liabilities. This identifies the proportion of the total funds in the club or business that comes from long-term borrowings and bank loans. The bigger the proportion, the greater the risk.

MEASURING WEALTH

Finally, we need to have some way of deciding if a sport club is any more or less wealthy than it was five or ten years ago. A sport organization that has become less wealthy over the years would be cause for concern. A quick look at the Australian and British Olympic Committees suggests that they might just be in this situation, since they will accumulate assets for the early part of the four-year Olympic cycle only to liquidate a large slab of them in the later part of the cycle in order to fund athletes' participation at the Games. Alternatively, it would be hard to see Tennis Australia or the All England Tennis Club being worse off now than they were in 1996, given the overwhelming success of the Grand Slam tennis championships.

Despite the intricacies involved in estimating the value of sport enterprises, which were discussed in Chapter 4, measuring wealth is relatively easy when using data from a financial statement. It is merely a matter of comparing total assets with total liabilities. The difference is the net-asset base of the organization, which in fact is usually designated at the bottom of the balance sheet. This is also referred to as the net worth, which is also equal to the level of accumulated surplus or members' funds, which is the non-profit sector name for shareholders' funds.

CASE STUDY 11.1

Melbourne Cricket Club

The Melbourne Cricket Club (MCC) is one of Australia's oldest sporting clubs. It is also one of the wealthiest. It has the advantage of managing the Melbourne Cricket Ground (MCG), one of the world's great sporting icons. Its great financial strength is its capacity to attract thousands of members who are prepared to pay a hefty annual fee (around AUD 600) to secure the right to attend sporting events and use the club's extensive hospitality and facilities. It is also the home of cricket and

Australian football. At the same time it has borrowed heavily over the past twenty or so years to upgrade the stadium. This begs the question as to just how financially healthy the MCC is.

Table 11.8 summarizes its key financial indicators over a fifteen-year period. The table begins in 1990, when the MCC began its major redevelopment, and ends in 2005, when stage two of the redevelopment was completed in time for the 2006 Commonwealth Games. The stadium underwent a complete overhaul during this period.

TABLE 11.8 Melbourne Cricket Club financial indicators, 1990 to 2005 (AUD millions)

Indicator	1990	1997	2002	2005
Operating income	14.1	41.6	62.3	69.4
Members' fees	7.9	16.8	22.6	30.5
Events	1.7	7.6	16.2	12.5
Sponsors and marketing	3.5	9.5	17.8	17.5
Operating expenses	10.3	30.1	57.9	61.3
Administration	2.2	6.4	18.1	16.5
Arena operations/ maintenance	3.7	5.1	10.4	11.3
Interest paid	1.8	13.4	10.7	7.9
Operating profit	**3.8**	**11.5**	**4.4**	**8.1**
Depreciation/amortization	−1.6	−9.7	Included in administration expenses	Included in administration expenses
Non-operating activities	−1.4	16.1#	8.3	64.1*
Net profit	**1.6**	**19.5**	**12.7**	**72.2**
Total assets	**35.9**	**185.8**	**178.2**	**494.3**
Cash	5.9	14.1	4.5	32.2
Current	6.9	16.9	14.5	50.0
Investments	1.1	1.9	0	0
Property and improvements	35.9	185.7	133.7	273.4
Total liabilities	**22.7**	**154.7**	**150.7**	**305.7**
Current	9.8	20.2	23.5	37.9
Non-current	12.9	134.5	127.2	267.8
Net assets (member funds)	**13.2**	**31.1**	**27.5**	**188.6**
Repaid borrowings	0.4	5.9	31.3	1.2

Notes: # Government loan to MCC written off. * comprises government funds for MCG/ Commonwealth Games redevelopment.

Source: Melbourne Cricket Club (2006).

The indicators show that the MCC increased its scale of operations significantly over these fifteen years. Operating income increased from AUD 14 million to AUD 69 million, and expenses were constrained to ensure the generation of continuing surpluses. The great strength of the MCC has been its membership income, which increased from AUD 8 million to nearly AUD 31 million. On the expense side, one of the most revenue-absorbing items was interest paid, which in 1997 comprised nearly 30 per cent of operating income. This resulted from the MCC's heavy borrowings, which were used to fund its stadium redevelopment. This heavy dependency on debt was reflected in its high debt to equity ratio, which was 5:1 in 2002.

The MCG has always been one of the world's great sport stadiums, and while its redevelopment was underpinned by debt finance, it gave the stadium enormous revenue-generation capacity. Its long-term sustainability continues to be strong since it continues to attract quality sport events throughout the year. In 2013, it generated AUD 142 million of revenue, which delivered an operating profit of just under AUD 19 million. Total assets were valued at AUD 537 million, while total liabilities were around AUD 315 million. The only soft spot in 2013 was the cash flow statement. Despite a positive cash inflow from operations, the overall cash flows were negative at AUD 14 million. This was due to investments of AUD 47 million and the repayment of borrowings of AUD 14 million.

CASE STUDY 11.2

Wage efficiency ratios in professional sport leagues

English Premier League

As previously noted, the English Premier League (EPL) is close to being the world's most popular sport league. It is massively popular, but it is also massively unequal. For the last twenty years the competition has been dominated by Manchester United, Chelsea, Arsenal, Liverpool and, in more recent times, Manchester City. And, as the resource-based view of the firm proposes, organizations with superior resources at their disposal will nearly always outperform those organizations with a more limited resource base. Studies of the EPL show this to be the case for the most part, since, as Gerrard (2012) showed, Manchester United, Chelsea, Arsenal and Liverpool not only filled the top four positions in the 2008 season, but also had the largest revenue streams, with total incomes of GBP 121 million, GBP 172 million, GBP 101 million and GBP 90 million respectively.

However, these figures do not tell the full picture, since within the middle band of clubs there were significant discrepancies. In some cases clubs with substantial resources were unable to achieve a high finish, while in other cases clubs with relatively meagre resources were able to achieve significant successes. These discrepancies are nicely illustrated through the calculation of a wage efficiency ratio, or, as we will now call it, a cost–win ratio. This is simply the measure of the relationship between the club's total wage bill and the number of premiership points accumulated over the season. So, the higher the wage per premiership point earned (the cost–win ratio), the lower the club's efficiency ranking. Thus, a club with a total wage bill of $30 million and a premiership point tally of 40 ($750,000 per point earned) will have a lower efficiency ranking than a club with a total wage bill of $25 million and a premiership point tally of 38 ($658,000 per point earned).

The first thing to note is that all of the top four finishing clubs had relatively high cost–win ratios. What this means is that, while these clubs were able to utilize their massive stocks of resources to secure talented players, pay them very well, and thus achieve success, it was not done efficiently, and probably involved a wasteful use of some resource, be it extravagant payment to run-of-the-mill players, expensive training camps or the indiscriminate employment of specialist coaching staff. The cost–win ratios for Manchester United, Chelsea, Arsenal and Liverpool were GBP 1.3 million per league point accrued over the season, GBP 2 million, GBP 1.2 million and GBP 1.1 million respectively. The only club with a higher cost–win ratio was Derby County with GBP 2.4:1. Its wages budget for the year was a paltry GBP 26 million, but its league performance was an even more miserable 11 points. In short, every premiership point cost the club GBP 2.4 million. Blackburn Rovers had the best cost–win ratio with GBP 684,000, closely followed by Everton with GBP 685,000. The other under-performing club was Newcastle United FC. Its budget allocation for wages for the 2008 season was a very strong GBP 79 million, making it the fifth best-paying club in the competition. However, it could only accumulate 43 premiership points, which gave it a cost–win ratio of GBP 1.9 million per premiership point earned. Only Derby County and, surprisingly, Chelsea were more inefficient. The Chelsea case is instructive since it demonstrates that, in the end, an obscenely large amount of money, even if it is poorly managed and imprudently spent, will deliver some measure of success.

Australia's football leagues

The Australian Football League (AFL) is Australia's premier professional sport league. It attracts more fans and has the most lucrative broadcast rights fees. It is also heavily regulated through a commission that imposes a salary cap and redistributes revenue to give clubs a guaranteed minimum income. At the same time, some clubs receive salary cap bonuses, while other clubs do not use up the full amount of their caps. In addition, there are no controls over payments to coaching, medical and support staff. As a result the total player and coaching and support wage bills vary between clubs.

And, just like the EPL, some clubs have historically received a very poor return from their wage funds. For example, in 2005 the Sydney Swans had the highest wages bill, which came in at AUD 14.5 million. North Melbourne Kangaroos, however, had the lowest wage bill, which was AUD 9.8 million. When the wage bills are compared with the end-of-year league standings there are many interesting differences. The club with the highest cost–win ratio at this time was the Collingwood Football Club. Whereas its wage bill of AUD 12.9 million was in the top quartile, it finished second bottom on the league ladder. Its cost–win ratio was AUD 645,000, which means that for every league standing point it paid out AUD 645,000 in wage costs. The club with the best (that is, lowest) cost–win ratio was the Adelaide Crows, who only paid out AUD 171,000 for each premiership point. Details of this are expanded in Table 11.9.

TABLE 11.9 AFL wage efficiency ratios, 2005

Club	League points 2005	Total football department wage costs (AUD millions)	Player payments (AUD millions)	Wage efficiency ratio:1
Adelaide Crows	68	11.6	7.5	171
West Coast Eagles	68	12.6	8.0	186
St Kilda Saints	56	10.4	7.4	186
North Melbourne Kangaroos	52	9.8	6.9	188
Melbourne Demons	48	10.7	7.1	223
Geelong Cats	48	11.0	7.2	230
Western Bulldogs	44	10.6	7.5	240
Sydney Swans	60	14.5	9.5	242
Fremantle Dockers	44	11.1	7.4	251
Port Adelaide Power	46	11.7	7.8	254
Richmond Tigers	40	10.3	7.6	256
Brisbane Lions	40	13.2	8.6	330
Essendon Bombers	32	12.1	7.9	379
Hawthorn Hawks	20	11.3	8.0	566
Carlton Blues	18	10.9	7.8	609
Collingwood Magpies	20	12.9	7.9	644

Source: Denham (2006).

The EPL and AFL experiences both show that throwing money at players, and spending one's way to success, makes strategic sense if the sole goal is winning at any cost. However, for most sport clubs this is an unrealistic aspiration. It is also an extremely poor use of resources, and cannot usually be sustained for any length of time. Michael Lewis (2003), in his best-selling book *Moneyball: The Art of Winning an Unfair Game,* told the story of the Oakland As, which was a middle-of-the-range club in Major League Baseball. It did exactly what an efficiency expert would advise. That is, if you have limited resources, but you want to improve your league standing, you need to work out ways of securing resources that are not only undervalued, but can be worked on to deliver the maximum amount of 'added value'. Through clever recruitment and superior player development programmes the club was able to maintain a top three league position during the 2001 and 2002 seasons while working within the third lowest operating budget in the league. It was an astonishing achievement.

CASE STUDY 11.3

International Cricket Council and International Rugby Board

The international governing bodies for sport, otherwise known as International Sporting Organizations (ISOs), depend for their financial viability on the revenues they can secure from major sport events. Two of the most highly credentialled ISOs are the International Cricket Council (ICC) and the International Rugby Board (IRB).

The ICC, which has ninety-six member countries, runs two major competitions, the World Cup and the Champions Trophy. The Champions Trophy was run in 2005, and its success is reflected in the sharp increase in its operating income for that year. The ICC's financial indicators for 2004 and 2005 are listed in Table 11.10.

TABLE 11.10 Financial indicators for the International Cricket Council (USD millions)

	2005	2004
Operating income	49.4	11.9
Event income	37.9	2.0
Member subscriptions	11.1	9.7
Operating expenses	29.8	19.4
Cricket development	7.2	8.2
Total assets	77.6	86.8
Cash assets	44.5	69.5
Total liabilities	61.0	79.9
Current liabilities	30.7	75.5

By 2011, the ICCs finances were, by any measure, strong and growing exponentially. The revenue from ICC events, which included the World Cup, was USD 321 million. With running costs coming in at USD 122 million, it delivered an operational profit of USD 199 million. After all of its additional activities had been accounted for, its net surplus for the year was just under USD 204 million. It had additionally accumulated USD 160 million in assets, and incurred liabilities of

USD 126 million, USD 77 million of which were monies owed to its member nations. The ICC is in an extremely healthy financial position.

The International Rugby Board (IRB), which has 115 member nations, operates a similar financial cycle. The World Cup was conducted in 2003 in Australia, and by any measure was highly successful. In 2004, with no global competition, revenues contracted. Its financial indicators for this period are listed in Table 11.11.

TABLE 11.11 Financial indicators for the International Rugby Board (GBP millions)

	2004	2003
Operating income	19.5	72.2
Broadcasting	17.1	25.2
Sponsorship	0.2	12.1
Licensing	2.1	34.0
Operating expenses	14.5	29.0
Total assets	**80.3**	**82.3**
Total liabilities	**3.9**	**4.9**
Current liabilities	63.6	66.8
Cash assets	51.7	42.8

In 2011, the IRB had, like the ICC, built up a very strong financial base, with the World Cup delivering most of its revenue. Its revenue for the year was GBP 219 million, and it incurred GBP 117 million in expenses, leaving an operating profit of GBP 102 million. On the balance sheet front, it had accumulated GBP 190 million of assets and built up GBP 35 million of liabilities, leaving a net worth of GBP 155 million. This was an impressive set of figures.

When measuring the comparative financial performances of the ICC and IRB, it is important to convert the figures to a common currency. In 2006, the average exchange rate was GBP 1 to AUD 2.5, while in 2012 it was approximately 1:2. The 2012 GBP–USD conversion rate was similar. Both organizations have strong revenue streams, but bearing in mind the exchange rate, the IRB figures are significantly stronger. The IRB also has few liabilities and a higher level of net assets.

RECAP

In planning for the future, setting strategies and designating goals, the financial implications should always be front and centre. The same applies when assessing performance levels – no matter what sporting enterprise is being examined, its financial performance should always be the priority. In those instances where it is taken casually, and there are no good quantitative measures in place, it can often produce catastrophic outcomes. Furthermore, it is not enough to rely on a single measure. There need to be multiple measures that include revenues and costs, operating surpluses, liquidity levels, levels of debt, cash flows in relation to borrowings, interest paid and investments, and, finally, the relative movements of total assets and total liabilities.

REVIEW QUESTIONS

The following questions highlight the crucial importance of using ratio analysis to undertake an evaluation of a sport enterprise's financial operations.

1 Identify three reference points that can be used to build a model of financial analysis for a sport organization.

2 Identify three ways you can go about measuring profitability in a sport organization.

3 Nominate the strengths and weaknesses of each method.

4 What does the level of working capital reveal about a sport organization's short-term financial health?

5 How can the level of working capital be converted to a ratio?

6 How might the cash flow statement be used to reveal the level of liquidity of a sport organization?

7 Identify and explain two measures of operating efficiency.

8 Is there any evidence to suggest that there are significant operating efficiency differences between clubs in the same sport league? If so, give examples.

9 How might you go about measuring the extent to which a sport organization depends on debt to fund it operations?

10 After examining the financial indicators of the Melbourne Cricket Club, how would you rate its financial performance over the last 25 years? What are its financial strengths and weaknesses?

11 What do comparative tables of wage efficiency (cost–win) ratios tell you about how well sport clubs convert their player wage bills into on-field success?

12 In the light of the data provided, which EPL clubs have the best and worst cost–win ratios?

13 Which AFL clubs have the best and worst cost–win ratios?

14 Compare and contrast the financial performance of the IRB and the ICC over recent times.

15 How do you explain the annual fluctuations in operating income for these two international sporting bodies?

---

16 Which of these two sporting bodies has the strongest profile from a financial perspective? Give reasons for your answer.

FURTHER READING

For a broad-based generic review of financial ratios and what they mean, see Atrill, P., McLaney, E., Harvey, D. and Jenner, M. (2006) *Accounting: An Introduction*, 3rd edition, Melbourne, Vic.: Pearson Education Australia (Chapter 6: 'Analysis and interpretation'). A basic, but comprehensive, analysis of the use and abuse of financial ratios is provided in Hart, L. (2006) *Accounting Demystified: A Self Teaching Guide*, New York: McGraw Hill (Chapter 13: 'Cautions', Chapter 14: 'Prep-work', Chapter 15: 'Profit ratios', Chapter 16: 'Liquidity', Chapter 17: 'Cash ratios' and Chapter 18: 'Financial ratios'). For a succinct account of how ratio analysis can be applied to the financial statements of non-profit organizations, see Anthony, R. and Young, D. (2003) *Management Control in Non-profit Organizations*, 7th edition, New York: McGraw-Hill (Chapter 4: 'Analysing financial statements').

A detailed exposition of the use of ratio analysis to interrogate the financial performance of sporting enterprises is contained in Wilson, R. (2011) *Managing Sport Finance*, London: Routledge. In Chapter 8 Wilson sets up the analysis by first looking at the concept of the annual report, and then discussing the pivotal space given to the presentation of financial statements. This provides the context for an in-depth study of ratio analysis in a sport setting (Chapter 9).

For an up-to-date discussion of recent cases and issues in sport, see Winfree, J. and Rosentraub, M. (2012) *Sports Finance and Management: Real Estate, Entertainment, and the Remaking of Business*, Boca Raton, FL: CRC Press (Chapter 3: 'Financial statements, revenues and costs'). There are also many good examples and vignettes in Brown, M., Rascher, D., Nagel, M. and McEvoy, C. (2010) *Financial Management in the Sport Industry*, Scottsdale, AZ: Holcomb Hathaway. Chapter 2, which covers financial statements and ratios, is especially useful.

Additionally, an excellent sport-specific guide to financial performance evaluation is contained in Gerrard, W. (2004) 'Sport finance', in Beech, J. and Chadwick, S. (eds) *The Business of Sport Management*, Harlow: Pearson, pp. 154–90. At the end of this chapter there is an extensive case study of the financial meltdown of Leeds United Football Club in 2002.

In Brown, A. and Walsh, A. (1999) *Not For Sale: Manchester United, Murdoch and the Defeat of BSkyB*, Edinburgh: Mainstream, there is an impressive analysis of the rise and rise of Manchester United Football Club, and how it became the wealthiest sport club in the world. An update of the commercial and cultural dominance of MUFC is contained in Gerrard, W. (2004) 'Why does Manchester United keep winning?', in Andrews, D. (ed.) *Manchester United: A Thematic Study*, Abingdon: Routledge, pp. 65–86. This chapter is particularly instructive in explaining how MUFC has been able to sustain its competitive advantage for so long. According to Gerrard, it was all about the club's capacity to build its playing talent, fan goodwill and organizational effectiveness. For an extensive analysis of the value and profitability of the Liverpool Football Club, go to Foster, G., Greyser, P. and Walsh, B. (2006) *The Business of Sports: Texts and Cases on Strategy and Management*, Mason, OH: Thomson ('Case 10.2: Liverpool Football Club: what is its current market value?').

The ways in which 'Olympic sport' clubs and associations go about measuring their economic and financial success, and how they are balanced against social and cultural measures, are examined in Chappelet, J. and Bayle, E. (2005) *Strategic and Performance Management of Olympic Sport Organizations*, Champaign, IL: Human Kinetics. Readers are directed to Chapter 5, which discusses the parameters of performance management, and Chapter 6, which goes into more detail on how sport enterprise performance might be measured.

USEFUL WEBSITES

- The article on this website provides a detailed account of why it is so important to tailor performance indicators to the organization's purpose and 'mission statement': **http://ro.uow.edu.au/cgi/viewcontent.cgi?article=1320&context=commpapers**.
- The following website contains an excellent analysis of cash flow and liquidity statements, and how they can be used to measure financial performance: **http:// scholarworks.umass.edu/cgi/viewcontent.cgi?article=1018&context=jhfm**.
- This website contains a succinct discussion of the ways in which financial performance indicators can be customized to best fit the operations of not-for-profit agencies. They are particularly useful for the evaluation of sport clubs, associations and leagues: **http://nonprofitfinancefund.org/blog/top-indicators-nonprofit-financial-health**.
- This website contains a slide show on the finances of club sport in New Zealand: **www.shu.ac.uk/research/downloads/Cordery2MaySHUPresentation.pdf**.
- The following website houses the 2012/13 *Annual Report* for the Melbourne Cricket Club (MCC). The financial statements are listed on pp.14–19: **www.mcc.org.au/~/media/Files/2012_13%20annual%20report.pdf**.
- The 2012 financial statement for the IRB is housed at **www.irb.com/mm/document/newsmedia/mediazone/02/06/75/10/sdevelopc413061111100.pdf**.
- The ICC's financial statements for 2001–13 are housed at **www.icc-cricket.com/about/112/publications/annual-report**.
- And, to get a feel for the numbers for Barcelona FC and Real Madrid, two of the world's wealthiest sport clubs, go to **http://swissramble.blogspot.com.au/2012/04/truth-about-debt-at-barcelona-and-real.html**.

CHAPTER 12

Dealing with financial mismanagement

LEARNING OUTCOMES

At the end of this chapter readers will be able to:

- understand the factors (both contextual and internal) that cause sport enterprises to experience financial instability
- explain why an increase in revenue and/or assets can often be insufficient to deliver sport enterprises a healthy bank balance over time
- identify examples of financial mismanagement using a range of financial reports and documents
- recommend what remedial action needs to be taken once an unfavourable diagnosis of a sport club's financial affairs has been reported.

CHAPTER SUMMARY

This chapter examines a sample of cases in which serious financial problems emerged and threatened the sustainability of a number of clubs and associations. Four cases are discussed: the Coventry Football Club, the Borussia Dortmund Football Club, the Glasgow Rangers Football Club and the Women's National Basketball Association. While each case is distinctive, they all demonstrate the importance of careful planning and disciplined spending. Three themes run through each case. The first is that optimistic expectations about revenue streams initially set the scene for the budgeting process, but the reality is that they are more often than not unrealized. The second is that, unless the expenditure budget is properly monitored, it will inevitably blow out under the pressures to deliver superior services and to remain competitive. The third is that managers seem to think they can borrow without incurring any significant cost or future burden. This is clearly not the case. The WNBA case is additionally illustrative, since it shows that the financial sustainability of sport enterprises also has a gendered component to it, and this must be taken into account when planning a sport's future development.

INTRODUCTION

Paradoxes abound in the world of sport. As we have already noted, as sport becomes popular and more commercialized, and as it takes on a more business-like approach to its operations, it can lose the support of those people who place a high value on sport's traditions and its links to local communities. A good example from Australian sport is the redevelopment of the Adelaide cricket ground. The Adelaide Oval, as it is more commonly known, was regarded as one of the most picturesque sporting venues in the world. This was because of its 150-year-old grandstands, its heavily grassed and perfectly sloped viewing spaces, its heritage scoreboard and the views spectators had of the superb surrounding parkland. It was an aesthetic masterpiece. This all changed with its refurbishment as a major international-standard stadium. It opened in 2014 complete with three multi-tiered, 'state of the art' stands with sight lines that were unimaginable under the old model. The old members' pavilion had been subsumed into a hypermodern facility, a large proportion of the grassy slopes had been removed, and the views of the surrounding parklands had been erased. But the changes had also increased the seating capacity, and actually made the seating comfortable as well. It delivered spectacular viewing positions, it provided civilized hospitality services, and it provided the sort of toilet facilities that are now just taken for granted in any modern entertainment venue.

The other paradox is a financial one. As noted above many times over, sport has gone through a commercial revolution. It has secured a funding base that could only have been dreamed about fifty years ago. The earlier chapters have provided example upon example of how and why this has occurred, but suffice to say it has delivered spectators not only highly accessible experiences, but also memorable ones as well. The scale of international sport's commercial impact is exemplified in a 2012 *Forbes* magazine study of the ten richest sporting events in the world. In constructing the list, Forbes' feature writer, Monte Burke, focused solely on the prize money (in USD) paid out to the winner of the event or tournament. Using this simple indicator, he compiled the following list:

- UEFA Champions League – $77 million;
- UEFA European Football Championship – $33 million;
- FIFA World Cup – $31 million;
- NFL Super Bowl – $16 million;
- MLB World Series – $15 million;
- Dubai Horse Racing World Cup Night – $10 million;
- UEFA Europa League – $9 million;
- ICC Cricket World Cup – $4 million.

Monte also included the World Series of Poker, with prize money of USD 9 million. However, from this book's perspective it fails to meet the conditions for being designated as a sport. It might be high on strategy and bluff, but it has always been low on physical prowess.

All of this prize money represents income to a sport enterprise somewhere in the world. And, moreover, these funds are just a small sample of what is on offer. As Chapter 2 highlights, there is now a multitude of sources from which sport enterprises can extract the revenue to fund their operations. But, in a world where sport has never been so flush with funds, there are hundreds of cases every year where sport enterprises have not only been unable to balance their books, but have also increased their debt to absurdly risky levels. This is the other paradox of contemporary sport.

The cases discussed below showcase this paradox. However, over and above the paradox, there is a serious management issue to address here. How is it, in an age where so many university programmes are educating students about what it is to be a prudent accountant, and when so many sport enterprise managers are building up their financial management expertise, that this state of affairs can be allowed to happen so often, and can be allowed to deliver so much damage to stakeholders? The following cases show what can cause these financial disasters. They also hint at what can be done not only to minimize the fallout, but also, even better, to ensure it does not happen in the first place.

CASE STUDY 12.1

Coventry City Football Club

The place

Coventry City Football Club (CCFC) is the club that represents the city of Coventry, which is located in the West Midlands region of England. Coventry began as a manufacturing centre in the eighteenth century, focusing on clothing and textiles. It became a major bicycle producer in the late nineteenth century, and by the beginning of the twentieth century the bicycle trade was booming, and Coventry had developed the largest bicycle industry in the world. It employed nearly 40,000 workers in more than 250 manufacturing locations. However, by the 1930s motor vehicles had taken over as the main manufacturing industry, with Daimler, Rover and the Rootes Group being the three dominant producers. Coventry suffered severe bombing during the Second World War but recovered strongly. However, it did not adjust well to the forces of globalization and free trade during the 1980s, which led to high unemployment. Over the last twenty-five years it has undertaken an urban regeneration programme, and now has a strong service sector. Its population is now just over 300,000.

The football club

CCFC goes back a long way. The club was founded in 1883 by Willie Stanley, an employee of the Singer Cycle Company, which was one of the largest in the region. The club was known as Singers FC until 1898, when the name was changed to Coventry City. A year later it relocated to its Highfield Road site, which became its home for the next 114 years.

For the first fifty years of the twentieth century its progress was solid but uneventful. Coventry was better known for its motor vehicle industry than its football team, but this all changed in 1961 with the arrival of Jimmy Hill as manager. This sparked a revolution at the club. A new sky blue uniform was unveiled, the nickname was changed to the Sky Blues, trains were scheduled for fans to travel to away games, and pre-match entertainment became commonplace. In 1963, after an impressive FA Cup run, CCFC lost in the quarter-finals to Manchester United, but in the following season CCFC were champions of Division 3, boasting a season average crowd of 26,000. The Highfield Road stadium was also rebuilt around this time, and the club was primed for more success.

In the 1966–7 season, CCFC went unbeaten for twenty-five games, and the campaign reached an exhilarating finale when CCFC defeated its arch rivals, Wolverhampton Wanderers, in front of a record home crowd of 51,000. CCFC thus clinched the Division 2 championship, and secured a place in the First Division, which was the equivalent of today's Premier League. Coventry stayed in the top flight of English football from 1967 to 2001 – thirty-four years – without being relegated. At the time of its 2001 relegation only Arsenal, Everton and Liverpool could boast longer tenures in England's 'premier' competition.

The problem

CCFC's greatest achievement came in the 1987 FA Cup Final against Tottenham Hotspur, which it won. The euphoria was palpable, but thereafter things began to slide. There were moments of hope, but they were mainly false. Crowds of 30,000 were common, ground improvements were made and a few star players were signed on. In 1999, CCFC pulled off a major coup by signing the talented Republic of Ireland international, Robbie Keane, for GBP 6 million – a club record fee. But, as it turned out, this was the beginning of a massive decline for CCFC. Keane's departure to Inter Milan, a powerful Italian team, left the club in disarray, and in 2001 it was relegated to the lower division. The club was also in dire financial straits, having accumulated a GBP 60 million debt, despite having received GBP 13 million for Keane's Inter Milan transfer. The club, however, was still prepared to pay GBP 5 million for Lee Hughes from West Bromwich Albion around the same time. Huge cost-cutting was consequently required to prevent the club from going into administration, and this was subsequently achieved in part through the sale of many high-earning players. The debt was reduced, but it was still a horrific GBP 23 million in 2004. The club had been living beyond its means for a long time and, as was later revealed, the club had been propped up by the reckless borrowing of funds.

A bright – if tiny – light shone on the Sky Blues in late 2003 when the City Council gave the green light for a new rejuvenation project that would house the club's new 32,000-seat stadium. It acquired a naming rights sponsor in the form of Ricoh, but the rental agreement proved to be another liability it just could not afford. It struggled to pay the GBP 1 million annual rent to Coventry City Council, which co-owned the facility. By the end of the 2007 season it was clear that something was seriously wrong with the financial affairs of CCFC. Its turnover for the year was a serviceable GBP 7.7 million, but its wage bill was more than GBP 8 million. Its operations were completely unsustainable.

And, what is more, the crisis worsened in the off-season, when the club was facing administration and potential liquidation. A London-based investment group, SISU, stepped in and took ownership of the club. With the club at this point losing over GBP 500,000 a month, Coventry supporters would have been forgiven for thinking that SISU would be the club's saviour, but it proved to be the antithesis of this. It turned out that SISU was not an effective caretaker, and all it could do was sell off some of the club's key squad members for bargain basement fees. The pool of player talent dropped considerably, but it did little to improve the club's financial health. SISU was also reported to have injected GBP 40 million into the club since it took over in 2008, but it did nothing to stop the rush into ruin.

At the end of 2012, the off-the-field situation continued to be precarious. The club was forced to look for a temporary home in which to play their home games from 2013–14 following unsuccessful talks with the Ricoh Arena management. It culminated in an announcement that SISU – who still owned the club despite its failure to stop the haemorrhaging – would fund the construction of a new stadium, which would hand the club access to all match-day revenue streams. This plan was a long way off, though, so it was decided to seek a ground-share arrangement with the League Two side Northampton Town for three years while a new stadium was being built. The first of those fixtures saw the Sky Blues host Bristol City in their League One clash in August 2013.

So, by 2013 the club had been relegated to League One. It had a shoestring squad, it was riddled by crippling debt, it was a tenant in another club's stadium, and it had gone through ten managers in the eleven years prior to 2013. Surely things could not get any worse.

From an outsider's point of view, though, things would suggest that CCFC, while clearly not up to EPL standard, should still be at least a top-level championship side. This is because it secured a 'state of the art' new stadium in 2005, it is a club with a very strong football tradition, and it is relatively well known across Europe. And, most importantly, it is the only major football club in a city of 300,000 people, which gives it a significant supporter base to work from. Things are in place for CCFC to be a success, and for a while it was. So what went wrong, and how did the club slide so quickly into a financial quicksand? The following numbers, all in GBP, give a feel for the scale of the problem CCFC has faced over the last few years. They do not provide a pretty picture, and they also show successive administrations in a very poor light:

- Cash in bank fell from 592,000 to 103,000 in 2011.
- Current liabilities increased from 20 million in 2007 to 57 million in 2011.
- Current assets fell from 1.8 million in 2007 to 418,000 in 2011.
- Long-term liabilities fell from 13 million in 2007 to zero in 2011.
- Total liabilities increased from 33 million in 2007 to 57 million in 2011.
- Total assets fell from 4 million in 2007 to 2 million in 2011.
- Total revenues increased from 8 million in 2007 to 10 million in 2011.
- For every year between 2007 and 2011 every pound of revenue was swallowed up by wage and salary demands.
- Operating losses of 6–8 million were incurred for each year between 2007 and 2011.

This case illustrates many things – and not all good – about the management of football in Britain. It does not reflect well on the financial management skills of CCFC, and it highlights the often irrational desire to be successful at any price, but it provides no financial safety net if things go wrong. It also seems as though things were hidden from the Board or, even worse, that no one knew just how serious the club's financial problems were. This case is an exemplar of how not to manage a sport enterprise.

CASE STUDY 12.2

Borussia Dortmund Football Club

The place

Dortmund is an affluent city situated in the heartland of Germany. Germany itself is an advanced industrial nation of 80 million inhabitants with an international reputation for quality manufacturing. It is also a sport-loving nation that has achieved many successes on the international stage. Football is the national sport, and Germany is rarely out of the top five global ratings.

Dortmund, like nearly every other city in Germany, has a rich and evocative history; it is located in the centre of Westphalia and has a population of nearly 600,000. This makes it the seventh largest city in Germany. Like most other industrial cities in Europe, Dortmund has experienced significant structural change, but it is now a modern city with a strong service sector, especially in information technology.

The football club

Borussia Dortmund is a member of Germany's main professional football competition, which is called the Bundesliga. It is one of few Bundesliga clubs registered as a public company, and as a result its shares are traded on the stock exchange. The club has a chequered history, having experienced both the soul-destroying horrors of dismal failure, and the blissful joy of high-level successes. By the time the 2004–5 season had commenced, Borussia Dortmund was on its last legs and experiencing the worst time in its 100-year history. It had accumulated nearly EUR 120 million of debt and was on the brink of bankruptcy. Its very existence was under threat. However, it miraculously turned itself around, and went on to win the Bundesliga championship twice, and in 2012 played arch rival, Bayern Munich FC, in the European Champions League final, which it lost. And, what is more, soon after the defeat it posted a record net profit of EUR 34.3 million. So, how did this club, with so much debt seven years previously, and so much management dysfunction, go on to become such a strong, competitive and financially sound club? There is clearly an instructive story to be told here.

The problem

In late 2004, with Bayern Munich on the march towards yet another Bundesliga title, Borussia Dortmund found itself on the verge of bankruptcy, with huge debts being amassed as a result of extravagant payments for new player contracts. This optimistic but high-risk strategy was executed in the hope of extending a successful period stretching back to the mid-1990s. Having won the 1997 Champions League title, the club was floated on the Frankfurt Stock Exchange in October 2000, but the cash poured out quicker than it flowed in. A drop in share values occurred, and was followed in the 2003–4 season with failure to qualify for the UEFA Champions League. With earnings tumbling and debt spiralling upwards, the club could no longer pay its bills.

Such was Borussia Dortmund's financial desperation in 2004 that Bayern Munich, Germany's biggest club, delivered the club a crucial loan of EUR 2 million with an open-ended payback requirement. However, this was not enough to save Borussia Dortmund, because the club's total debt had risen to more than EUR 200 million. The threat of bankruptcy was real, and its liquidation would have seen it drop out of the Bundesliga and enter into the relative obscurity of low-level football.

When President Gerd Niebaum resigned in late October 2004, the club was riddled with debt. Niebaum's successor, Reinhard Rauball, faced the unenviable task of turning the club around. Rauball had sorted out some club problems previously, but this was something else. So, in early 2005, the club's officials set about persuading the club's key stakeholders – its 6,000 shareholders, the banks it owed money to, the German Football League, the club's fans and sundry supporters – that the club had a future. Its share price plummeted by 80 per cent, the club's creditors effectively controlled its operations, the players took a 20 per cent pay cut, administration expenses were slashed and, most importantly of all as it turned out, the club sold off many of its highly paid players to other clubs.

With bankruptcy avoided by the thinnest of margins, the club did a 180-degree strategic turn by jettisoning its debt-driven approach to success, and instead took a youth-development approach. Things were turbulent in the short run, and successes came slowly. The club struggled for form, had three different managers between 2006 and 2008, and could finish no better than thirteenth in the league. The club's finances stabilized though, and so too did its coaching team with the appointment of Jurgen Klopp, who had helped Mainz 05 to promotion to the Bundesliga in 2004.

Klopp's impact was immediate. He secured a sixth-place finish in his first season in 2008, he got the club to fifth in 2009 and, amazingly, claimed the first of back-to-back league titles in 2010–11, with another win in the 2011–12 season. The turnaround was completed in 2013 when Borussia Dortmund announced a record profit of EUR 53 million and a total turnover of EUR 305 million for the 2012–13 season – well above the previous year's figure of EUR 215 million. And this all happened in the space of eight years. And, as the CEO noted, the club had finally been able to 'synchronize sporting and financial successes'.

But, how did this extraordinary turnabout happen so quickly and, apparently, so effortlessly? The answer seems to be found, in the first instance, in the player transfer market. Not only were players strategically sold off in the early part of the rebuilding period, but it continued right through to 2013. In 2012, the club offloaded Ivan Perisic to Wolfsburg, and in early 2013 it shunted Mario Gotze to Bayern Munich. These transfers earned the club EUR 37 million, and this cash injection more than covered any expenditure shortfalls and debt repayment obligations. This 'transfer-driven' strategy appeared to work, but as the figures below suggest, all in EUR, the club is not completely 'out of the woods' just yet:

- Between 2005 and 2010 annual revenues increased from 77 million to 107 million.
- Ticket sales increased from 18 million to 23 million during that period.
- Income from television broadcast rights increased from 15 million to 21 million over the same period.
- In 2005 total operating expenses were 117 million.
- In 2010 total operating expenses were 110 million.
- Total employment costs rose from 75 million to 100 million in 2012.
- Around 76 million of this 100 million was spent on the team, that is, the playing squad.
- In 2006 the club took out a fifteen-year 79 million loan with the Morgan Stanley Finance Group.
- Part of this loan was used to assist in buying back the club's stadium, thus avoiding annual rent.
- The remainder of the loan was used to reduce its overall debt levels and free up funds to allocate to player development.
- For the 2012–13 period the club collected revenues of 305 million.
- This was an increase of 84 million from the previous year.
- Net profit for the year was 51 million compared to 28 million for the previous year.
- As at 2013 Dortmund had 57 million tied up in liabilities.
- It had 80 million in accounts receivable, which is a very healthy current asset position.
- But . . . it is not clear as to how much debt it has accumulated since 2006. This could still be a soft spot, financially speaking.
- We do know, though, that in 2013 the club had 15 million more in liabilities than it did in 2012.
- But, it would be fair to say, Borussia Dortmund is, unlike eight years ago, now able to pay its debts as they become due.
- Overall, the club may not be 'debt free', but it seems to be 'debt manageable'.

This case demonstrates that clubs can trade their way out of a financial crisis if certain things are done at the appropriate time. For this to happen, though, it is crucial that information be disclosed when it becomes available rather than when management decides to make it public. It is also important to understand what amount of cash is required to pay debts when they fall due. It is also important to liquidate assets – which includes players – to protect one's financial credibility. It also requires a different strategic option to be considered, which in this case is about using young, inexperienced, but 'low-cost' talent to achieve results in the longer term, rather than importing mature but expensive players with a view to getting a 'quick fix' in the short term.

CASE STUDY 12.3

Glasgow Rangers Football Club

The place

Originally a small salmon-fishing village at a crossing point on the River Clyde in the Scottish lowlands, Glasgow went on to become a major trading centre during the seventeenth and eighteenth centuries. Due to its location in the west of the country, Glasgow was well positioned to send shipping to the West Indies and America, and by the eighteenth century many merchants had acquired great wealth by importing sugar, rum and tobacco. The existence of vast deposits of coal and iron ore in the Glasgow area shaped the next two centuries of Glasgow's history, and with the coming of the Industrial Revolution, and the technical genius of inventors such as James Watt, the railway locomotive and shipbuilding industries flourished. Locomotives were exported throughout the world, the 'Clyde-Built' slogan became synonymous with quality and reliability, and the launch of the three 'Queen' luxury passenger liners signified the pinnacle of Glasgow's shipbuilding achievement. Glasgow became a very wealthy city during this period, although it also had a large underclass.

But like so many other 'heavy industry' cities hit by global competition during the second half of the twentieth century, the Clyde-side region no longer employs large populations of people in the rail locomotive or shipbuilding trades. Today Glasgow is a major tourist destination. It has some of the best nineteenth-century architecture in the world and is a focal point for literature, museums and the arts. Glasgow's population continues to grow slowly, and it now houses just under 600,000 people.

The football club

Glasgow Rangers FC was founded in 1872 and went on to become one of Europe's best-known football clubs. It was also highly successful, having won fifty-four league titles, which is more than any other team in the world. Rangers was also a massively parochial club, and prided itself on being a club for Protestant Christians. It consequently established an often hostile rivalry with its intra-city rival Celtic FC, which just happened to be Catholic Christian. They have dominated the Scottish football scene for more than a hundred years.

Rangers became the first British club to reach the final of a UEFA competition in 1961 when they made it to the European Cup Winners' Cup Final. They finally won it in 1972 having twice been finalists. In the meantime, they also went through some hard times. Tragedy struck in 1971 when, during a New Year's home game at the club's Ibrox stadium against Celtic, the 'crush' barriers collapsed as thousands of fans left the stadium. During the stampede that followed sixty-six people were killed. This tragic event came to be called the Ibrox disaster, and subsequent to a number of inquiries, the stadium underwent a complete overhaul and redevelopment. Throughout the 1970s and 1980s Rangers and Celtic dominated the Scottish Football League. In 1998, the latter was reconfigured as the Scottish Premier League (SPL) in an attempt to model itself on the English Premier League (EPL). Over the next thirteen years Rangers and Celtic continued their domination by winning every championship between them. No other club got a look-in, but this came as no surprise since professional football in Scotland had never been known for its competitive balance.

Overall, though, the Rangers–Celtic rivalry was the foundation of the SPL's popularity, and 'local derbies' were always viewed as marquee events. This rivalry was also responsible for an outsized share of the league's overall television viewership. There have been twelve clubs in the league, but only two clubs really mattered in terms of television viewership and attendance. The two clubs together provided 60 per cent of the SPL's fan base, 80 per cent of all gate receipts for league matches and more than 90 per cent of all television viewership. In other words, the other ten teams in the SPL were only responsible for 10 per cent of the total viewers when you remove Rangers and Celtic from the equation. The average viewership of SPL games was 150,000, but the average viewership for Rangers versus Celtic was 900,000. There was no other professional sport league in the world where two teams dominated the competition so comprehensively and for so long.

The problem

Despite all its successes, its massive fan base, its frequent sell-out games and its blanket media presence, Rangers FC declared itself bankrupt in early 2012. Additionally, Scotland's football clubs voted to relegate it to the country's bottom division, and disallowed it from re-entering the SPL until the 2015–16 season. So, how did this happen, and what does it say about the management of Glasgow Rangers' financial affairs during the first ten years of the new millennium?

At one level the answer was simple and straightforward, since it was quickly found that Rangers had consistently spent more on players than they could afford in order to keep pace with Celtic. In the eleven years to 2010, the club lost an average of GBP 13 million a season. It managed to stay in business by borrowing money and by doing well enough in the SPL to qualify for the Champions League in Europe, which offered generous payouts to participants. In recent years, however, Rangers suffered three disruptions to this tenuous equilibrium. First, in 2008–9 they were upset in the Champions League qualifiers by FBK Kaunas, a modest Lithuanian team. That cut their revenues by GBP 10 million. The following season, they recovered on the pitch to win the SPL, but by then Britain's economic recession had taken its toll on their attendance and revenue stream.

While there are many contributing factors that led to the club's collapse, the evidence points to a smug self-confidence – or hubris – as the underlying cause. The club believed it was too successful, and too well known, to fold. But there were a number of signs that suggested all was not well. Television revenues for clubs in the SPL were becoming increasingly smaller as a percentage of turnover, and season ticket sales had also declined from around 44,000 in 2005 to 37,500 in 2010.

It was as if Rangers were, metaphorically speaking, rearranging the deckchairs on the Titanic. Clearly, Rangers believed their Titanic was incapable of sinking, and simply too big to fail. By failing to acknowledge the global shifts and winds of change, and ignoring the obvious problems with their balance sheet, Rangers continued to pay more than they could afford to players, managers and executives. In 2010, they were feeding GBP 26 million into wage commitments, but were only earning GBP 35 million of revenue. Even by American professional sport league standards this was absurdly high. In the NFL, for example, the total wage bill would never exceed 60 per cent of total revenues. In the case of Rangers, employee benefits and perks were also excessive, and consequently created an unsustainable set of obligations for a club that was seeing revenues stagnate and expenses continuing to grow. Rangers' attendance fell by just under 9 per cent between the 2008–9 and 2010–11 seasons, and while this was not altogether due to club mismanagement – since the recession in the British economy had played a role in damping down demand – Rangers' management team did little to halt the slide.

The final blow – the straw that broke the camel's back, if you like – was the unravelling of a risky scheme intended to reduce the club's tax liability. It was disclosed that, from 2001 to 2010, the team had rerouted just over GBP 48 million owed to players and staff through trust accounts held at a company in the British dependency of Jersey, a small island that doubles as a tax haven for many international businesses.

Under the British government's tax laws these types of payment had traditionally been treated as loans. This meant they were not taxable until employees had actually withdrawn the money from the trust. However, a change in the interpretation of the laws meant that, since these transfers were in fact incorporated into player contracts, they were viewed as salaries and thus taxable on a regular basis. Therefore, it was decided that half of the payments should be taxable, especially when they involved high-income workers such as football players. As a result, Rangers FC was forced to pay GBP 21 million of back taxes. The club did not have anywhere near this amount of money in the form of cash, and was also burdened with significant holdings of debt. Everything thus conspired to push the club into bankruptcy.

The demise of such a powerful football club as Rangers FC is difficult to comprehend. But when you examine its recent history you find that, like the Coventry case, Rangers were not prepared to face their financial problems, or to take quick and decisive action that might cut their losses and lower their debt. Once again, blinkered views about what constitutes prudent financial management, and a complete inability to tailor their costs to fit their revenues, led to a club's undoing.

CASE STUDY 12.4

American Women's National Basketball Association

The place

The Women's National Basketball Association, or WNBA as it is more colloquially known, is a national competition situated in the home of professional sport leagues, the United States of America. The USA is the cultural home of women's basketball, and the national team regularly wins the world and Olympics titles.

The league

During the latter part of the twentieth century there was constant chatter among the American basketball fraternity that a national women's league should be introduced. There were good reasons for this initiative. Not only was women's basketball played across the nation, but it was also especially popular among college students. There were many national advertisers and sponsors waiting in the wings, so to speak, and there was an optimistic belief that a professional women's basketball competition would attract both viable attendances and a solid television audience.

So, in early 1996, after a lot of deliberation and careful planning, the National Basketball Association (NBA) Board of Governors approved the concept of a women's professional basketball league, the WNBA. There had been some earlier abortive attempts to get a women's league off the ground, but they had failed due to poor organization and a lack of a strong cash flow. This initiative was different because it had the support of the NBA and its huge resource base, and it therefore followed that the WNBA had a good chance of paying its way to a successful future.

Things got off to a flying start when, even before any players had signed playing contracts, the league established its broadcast partnerships with three major television networks, NBC, ESPN and Lifetime. This not only meant a guaranteed stream of revenue, but it also meant that games could be televised live. The league was also given an interesting twist when it was decided that the WNBA season would be played during the summer. Additionally, it secured the Spalding sport equipment supplier as national advertiser, who designed the orange and oatmeal-coloured WNBA signature ball. The league also heavily marketed its catchy slogan, 'We Got Next', prior to the season commencing.

Eight teams were announced for the inaugural season, and were organized into two conferences or divisions. The Eastern Conference consisted of the Charlotte Sting, Cleveland Rockers, Houston Comets and New York Liberty, while the Western Conference was comprised of the Los Angeles Sparks, Phoenix Mercury, Sacramento Monarchs and Utah Starzz. Teams were allocated designated players, and a so-called 'elite draft' was used to recruit foreign players.

The problem

The season commenced in the summer of 1997. In the early part of the league's development there were few problems and many successes. As noted above, the league was backed, both symbolically and financially, by the NBA. It also had a unique organizational and legal structure, since every team was effectively owned by the league. In this 'single entity' competition, clubs were not franchises, but rather operating divisions of the league. This meant the central body had control over wage levels and recruitment, and therefore substantial control over costs, which in the first instance seemed a very good thing.

The league also captured the imagination of television viewers in the first instance. During a successful inaugural season, more than 50 million viewers watched WNBA games on the three networks. The WNBA also delivered a unique audience profile for an elite sporting competition. In the case of at-arena attendance, the gender break-down was about 70 per cent female and 30 per cent male. The TV audience was around 50 per cent female and 50 per cent male, with a stronger percentage of non-adult viewers than is normally the case. In short, a lot of young, mostly middle-class women supported the league.

Following on from the successful inaugural season, the WNBA expanded from eight teams to sixteen. The Detroit Shock and Washington Mystics joined the league in 1998, the Minnesota Lynx and Orlando Miracle in 1999, and the Indiana Fever, Miami Sol, Portland Fire and Seattle Storm in 2000. The 2002 season was highly successful, and signalled to the sports-going public that professional sport leagues for women were not only viable, but were also destined to become an integral part of the north-American sporting landscape. There were 176 women playing professional basketball in 256 regular-season WNBA games. In the inaugural 1997 season only twenty-eight games were played. The future of the league looked assured.

However, the gloss faded, and the optimism was blunted over the following ten years.

The WNBA went through difficult times, and by 2013 – the seventeenth year of the competition – there were only twelve teams in the league. So what went wrong, both strategically and financially? Strategically, it appears that the league may have expanded too rapidly, and exposed itself to a build-up of costs. Financially, the evidence now indicates that, despite its initial progress, and despite the committed support from millions of women who desperately wanted the competition to succeed, it was never going to be financially viable. Looking back it becomes clear that operating revenues rarely covered operating costs, and most clubs were running losses.

As one commentator claimed, the WNBA had, over the course of its first seventeen years, 'never made a dime', which in accounting parlance means it could never deliver an operating profit for its owners, the NBA. In other words, the WNBA has survived – from a financial perspective – only because of the subsidies provided by the NBA. This may be a harsh and even an unfair thing to say, and additionally plays into the hands of sporting traditionalists who see real professional sports as a 'men only' affair. But it may also be the only reasonable conclusion to be drawn from the facts. However, what are the so-called facts, and who do we believe anyway? To assist in the analysis of this case, the following points are made:

- The WNBA started out with eight teams, and grew to sixteen before several franchises folded. It now fields twelve teams. Six teams – Indiana, New York, Minnesota, Phoenix, San Antonio and Washington – are owned by NBA franchises. The WNBA teams share training facilities and arenas.

- Just how bad, then, are the WNBA's finances? Apparently the league's first-ever 'cash flow positive' team was the Connecticut Sun in 2010. NBA commissioner David Stern regularly conceded that the NBA has subsidized the WNBA in recent years by up to USD 4 million a season.
- Sponsorships have been an important revenue stream for the league, boosted by the league's successful marketing campaign geared towards branding the league showcase for healthy values. Team sponsorship revenue increased by around 10 per cent from 2005 to 2010. The WNBA also secured a strong commercial relationship with Boost Mobile (BM), and the BM logo was placed on eleven of the league's twelve shirts. The league recently added Anheuser-Busch as a major sponsor.
- Average attendance over recent years has fallen by more than 4 per cent. Average game attendance for the league is now around 7,700.
- In 2011, the WNBA signed new partnerships with Jamba Juice, Coca-Cola and Pirate's Booty snack food.
- The WNBA often averages a 0.2 cable rating (around 263,000) on ESPN2. By any measure this is a minuscule audience for a nationally telecast American television programme.

The above information provides some insight into the structural and financial problems facing the WNBA, but does not provide any significant financial data that can illuminate the overall problem, or identify or even expose the key cost burdens and revenue shortfalls. We can only imagine what is going on, but it is clear that the problem is not a cost one. To put it more precisely, the problem is not an inflated player salary one. According to the league's collective bargaining agreement (CBA), the 2012 team salary cap was just under USD 900,000. When allocated over the player roster it comes in at around USD 70,000 per player per season. This, by any professional sport league measure, is meagre. In contrast, the salary cap for the men's league is USD 25 million. Most male basketball players claim an annual salary of USD 3–4 million. The gap is obscene from a gender equality perspective, but this is the reality of professional sport. It is all about capacity to pay, which suggests that the revenue base of the WNBA has been frighteningly low for the entirety of its existence. This is a serious problem, and it appears that, unless there are dramatic changes ahead, the league may not be around, at least in its present form, in 2020.

This case has many facets to it. It is about women's sport, it is about the role played by subsidies, and it is also about the lack of transparency that operates in many sports around the world. In this instance we just do not know what is going on from a financial perspective, and this is not a good thing. The other interesting thing about this case is that it has been played out in a setting that, at first glance, lends itself to accommodating a women's professional sport league. The USA has a population of more than 330 million, it is one of the world's wealthiest nations, women are for the most part liberated from the oppression of hyper-masculine men with hyper-masculine belief systems, and, additionally, sport is a national obsession. It should, by any account, be the perfect setting for a sport league of this type to flourish, both culturally and financially. But something has gone horribly wrong somewhere.

RECAP

Despite the commercialization and professionalization of sport, there have been many pockets of serious maladministration. In particular, there appear to have been some serious problems in properly managing club and association finances. There is some ignorance, and not wanting to know what is happening from a financial perspective, there is a volatile mix of hyperbole and fantasy that creates unrealizable expectations, and there is also a lot of maladministration. This is troublesome, and suggests that not only are finances being poorly managed, but that they are also being managed in often very covert ways. It all supports the case for much higher levels of professional conduct when it comes to managing sport enterprises.

REVIEW QUESTIONS

The following questions follow up on the above cases and will assist the reader to better understand how the crises emerged in the first place, and how they were subsequently responded to.

1 What are the key indicators of poor financial management and weak financial performance? Be careful to distinguish between debt-related indicators and profit-related indicators.

2 Discuss the Coventry City case by first reviewing the lead up to its massive financial meltdown.

3 Succinctly explain the scale of its financial problems.

4 What does it tell us about the club's management systems?

5 How would you rate the performance of the management team?

6 What did the club do wrong and is there a way out?

7 What financial problems did Borussia Dortmund have in the mid-2000s?

8 How did the club come back from the brink of financial disaster?

9 Are there lessons to be learnt for other clubs faced by similar problems?

10 How do you explain the financial collapse of the Glasgow Rangers Football Club? Who would you blame and why?

11 What needs to done to bring Rangers back to the Scottish Premier League as a viable entity?

12 Are the SPL finances better off without Rangers?

13 What were the strengths of the WNBA when the league commenced?

14 Were uncontrolled expenses the source of the problem? If not, then why not?

15 To what extent was the success of the WNBA undermined by shrinking revenue streams? If so, then what was the soft revenue stream?

16 Just how precarious is the WNBA from a financial perspective?

17 What is the future for the WNBA?

FURTHER READING

The information for the four cases discussed above (Coventry FC, Borussia Dortmund FC, Glasgow Rangers FC and the Women's National Basketball Association) were taken from the (1) *The Daily Telegraph* and *The Guardian*, (2) *The Economist*, (3) *Forbes* and *The Wall Street Journal* in the USA, and (4) club websites. For the Glasgow Rangers case additional information was obtained from Bahain, P. (2012) *Downfall: How Rangers FC Self-Destructed*, Edinburgh: Frontline Noir.

Other sources used in writing this chapter were (1) Deloitte Sports Business Group (2013) *Football Money League*, London: Deloitte; (2) Barajas, A. and Rodriguez, P. (2010) 'Spanish football club finances', *International Journal of Sport Finance*, 5: 52–66; (3) Szymanski, S. (2010) 'The financial crisis and English football', *International Journal of Sport Finance*, 5: 28–40; (4) DeJonghe, T. and Vandeweghe, H. (2006) 'Belgian football', *Journal of Sports Economics*, 7(1): 105–13; (5) Dietl, H. and Franck, E. (2007) 'Governance failure and financial crisis in German football', *Journal of Sports Economics*, 8(6): 662–9; and (6) Andreff, W. (2007) 'French football: a financial crisis rooted in weak governance', *Journal of Sports Economics*, 8(6): 652–61.

Other valuable references include (1) Lago, U., Simmons, R. and Szymanski, S. (2010) 'The financial crisis in European football', in Szymanski, S. (ed.) *Football Economics and Policy*, Basingstoke: Palgrave Macmillan, pp. 151–61; (2) Buraimo, B., Simmons, R. and Szymanski, S. (2010) 'English football', in Szymanski, S. (ed.) *Football Economics and Policy*, Basingstoke: Palgrave Macmillan, pp. 162–81; and (3) Babatunde, B. and Simmons, R. (2008) 'The profitability of sports teams: international perspectives', in Humphreys, B. and Howard, D. (eds) *The Business of Sports, Volume 1: Perspectives on the Sports Industry*, Westport, CT: Praeger, pp. 33–58.

USEFUL WEBSITES

- The following website neatly summarizes the parlous state of Coventry City FC at the beginning of the 2013–14 football season: **www.mirror.co.uk/sport/football/news/crisis-club-coventry-hit-fresh-2119315**.

- Two especially useful websites that give additional information on the Glasgow Rangers FC financial meltdown are:

    - **www.economist.com/blogs/gametheory/2012/07/glasgow-rangers%E2%80%99-bankruptcy**
    - **www.forbes.com/sites/sportsmoney/2012/10/08/what-can-we-learn-from-the-financial-meltdown-of-glasgow-rangers-fc**.

- For two additional discussions on the financial problems faced by European football in general during the 2008–13 period, see:
  - www.ft.com/cms/s/0/a13db70c-05d7-11e3-8ed5-00144feab7de.html #axzz2paYOpxaZ
  - www.dailyrecord.co.uk/sport/football/football-news/european-footballs-debt-mountain-has-grown-1585888.

- A few of the financial problems faced by Spanish football in 2013 are reviewed in www.aljazeera.com/sport/football/2013/12/european-union-investigates-spanish-clubs-20131218113215679491.html.

- Some extra material on the WNBA's long-time financial problems is given in the following three websites:
  - www.salon.com/2009/02/06/wnba_2
  - http://tib.cjcs.com/8556/wnba-roster-beyond-2012
  - www.sportsbusinessdaily.com/Daily/Issues/2012/09/26/Research-and-Ratings/WNBA-gate.aspx.

CHAPTER 13

Ensuring financial transparency

LEARNING OUTCOMES

At the end of this chapter readers will be able to:

- understand the concepts of transparency and accountability, and their applicability to the financial management of sport enterprises
- explain why so many sport enterprise managers do not disclose financial information to the public
- identify the problems that can arise from a failure to disclose important financial information to key stakeholders
- make recommendations on the policies and rules that could be put in place to ensure greater financial transparency and more management accountability in sport enterprises.

CHAPTER SUMMARY

This chapter examines the problems that come from the failure of many sport enterprises to (1) meet minimum accounting standards, (2) disclose financial information in a transparent way and (3) use their funds – especially when they come from taxpayers – to deliver social good that goes beyond the narrow parameters of profits and competitive success. A number of cases are used to illustrate these issues: the Pittsburg Pirates Baseball Club, the financial meltdown of Spanish football, the UEFA 'fair play' template, and the IOC's good governance programme. These cases not only divulge the social costs that come from extreme secrecy and narrowly defined goals, but they also invite readers of this book to address club strategies that will deliver initiatives that place transparency, full disclosure and social utility front and centre.

IS SPORT PROFITABLE?

From an outsider's perspective it seems that sport is divided into two segments. The first contains the big professional sport clubs, which generate massive amounts of revenue from things such as gate admissions, media rights fees, sponsorship and merchandising. The second contains the local community sport clubs that depend on member fees, donations and fundraising functions to generate the income to deliver basic services. The first is building corporate-like profits day by day, while the second is on a financial knife edge, and barely capable of doing its job. This view is far too simplistic, and is for the most part not true. The fact of the matter is that hundreds of professional sport clubs are in financial disarray despite their ability to accumulate significant amounts of revenue.

IS SPORT TRANSPARENT?

In addition, we find that many clubs, associations and leagues are very secretive when it comes to publicly discussing their financial status. Moreover, and as the cases examined in this chapter demonstrate, their concern for secrecy increases exponentially when they find themselves in financial trouble. Conversely, the public's demand for full disclosure increases at the same exponential rate. This obsession for secrecy occurs not only in privately owned sport enterprises, but also in those organizations that are theoretically owned by their members, and depend on government assistance to fund some of their programmes. This desire for secrecy – which is often reinterpreted by club officials as a legitimate need for confidentiality – is defended on the grounds that, to publicize individual player salaries, the wages of coaches and senior officials, and the amounts spent on sport science and specialized training, will expose their performance-improvement strategies to their rivals, and thus deny them a possible competitive edge. However, the critics of financial secrecy argue that anything that denies the sporting public – the stakeholders to be more precise – access to information that allows them to monitor their relationship with their clubs, and assess their preparedness to continue the relationship into the future, is a dereliction of the professional duties of club officials. This is because it allows a club's officials to pretend that a solution – be it a winning streak, an improved sponsorship deal, a windfall grant from the governing body, or a massive increase in membership – is just around the corner, when any impartial commentator would view it as completely fanciful. As a result, a failure to disclose sensitive information does nothing to alleviate the problem that is being hidden, and if anything is likely to compound it. Additionally, there is always the risk that a failure to disclose vital financial information may be little more than a brazen attempt to conceal corrupt behaviour.

There is now a growing interest in the issues of accountability and transparency in the governance and management of sport, and the rules and policies that might be put in place to make clubs, leagues and associations more transparent in the way they deal with financial issues, and more accountable when addressing strategic initiatives and their financial implications. The discussion that follows will add a bit of muscle to the transparency bone by first examining cases where a public demand for transparency has been ignored and then exploring policies that might force sport enterprises to be more honest and forthcoming when it comes to engaging in public conversations about their financial affairs.

This brings up the issue of how clubs go about undermining the demands for transparency and the need for public disclosure of sport clubs' financial operations. There are many instances of sport enterprises hiding their true financial positions through a combination of secrecy and fabricating the accounts in order to secure the best possible outcome. Schalke 04, a leading club in the Bundesliga, Germany's premier football competition, is a case in point. In 2003, the club had come close to becoming insolvent, but instead of exposing its predicament to the public gaze, decided to reorganize its financial statements. As a first step in camouflaging its escalating losses and expanding debt, the club decided to sell off its ageing home stadium back to its former owner, the city of Gelsenkirchen. The sale price was a tokenistic EUR 1, but the Schalke 04 management team decided to revalue it at just under EUR 16 million. But the conjuring trick did not stop there because the club then incorporated this EUR 16 million non-cash item into its profit and loss statement as additional income. Then, in a not-too-subtle sleight of hand, it immediately reduced the club's net loss for the year from EUR 20 million to EUR 4 million. FC Kaiserslautern also manipulated its profit and loss statements to secure a better financial outcome. In the early 2000s it hid a number of additional salary payments to some of its star players, and as a result was able to reduce its annual player expenses item by around EUR 20 million.

CASE STUDY 13.1

Pittsburgh Pirates Baseball Club

The place

The Pittsburgh Pirates Baseball Club (PPBC) is a long-standing sport enterprise that represents the city of Pittsburgh, which is located adjacent to the Ohio River in the state of Pennsylvania. During most of the eighteenth century it was a prime agricultural district, but by the mid-1800s it had assembled a wide range of industrial activities that included steamboat production and glass manufacture. It also housed many large textile mills, and in the 1860s Pittsburgh was the world's largest refiner of petroleum products. It then became a major producer of steel products, which continued right through to the 1970s. However, because of the forces of globalization and the rise of East Asia as a cheap producer of high-quality steel, Pittsburgh suffered badly, and employment in its steelworks fell from 90,000 in 1980 to 44,000 in 1985. Its population also fell. For most of the 1960s it was around 700,000, but it had fallen to just under 500,000 by the early 1990s. However, during the 1990s and early 2000s, Pittsburgh reinvented itself by transitioning from heavy manufacturing to high technology industries that focused their sights on medical research, computer systems and robotics technologies, as well as the arts and culture.

The baseball club

PPBC joined the National League in 1887, and the 'Pirates' nickname was attached to the club in the early 1890s after they were accused of 'poaching' a player who was already contracted to play with another club. At the turn of the twentieth century the newly formed American League raided National League teams for talent, but never got around to luring away the better Pirate players. By keeping their roster intact the Pirates became a pre-eminent franchise in the National League, and opened the twentieth century by winning three consecutive pennants. From 1928 to 1945 the franchise was middle ranking, but things got worse during the 1946–57 period when it managed only one season where it had more wins than losses. However, the 1970s was a golden age, and the Pirates dominated the newly formed National League Eastern Division, winning it five out of the six years between 1970 and 1975, and again in 1979.

After lean years in the 1980s, the Pirates produced a special talent in Barry Bonds, who went on to break a whole raft of home-run records. The Pirates won three consecutive division titles in 1990, 1991 and 1992, with Bonds leading the way. However, the club failed to advance to the World Series in any of those seasons, and in 1993 took a severe nosedive from which it has yet to recover. The club was unable to win more games than it lost for the whole of the 1992–2010 period.

The problem

It appears that over the last ten to fifteen years the club has entered a period of 'controlled frugality', where costs were curtailed and player salaries were rarely excessive. While many commentators agree that this strategy delivered a positive bottom line on the club's financial statements, they also suggest that it also (1) drove away talent, (2) saturated the team roster with young and inexperienced players, (3) alienated many fans and (4) turned the Pirates into one of the game's most forlorn franchises.

Thus, unlike many professional sport teams, the club has continued to maintain a healthy bank balance despite mediocre on-field performances and difficult economic circumstances. The Pirates' conduct highlights the constant tension that operates in professional sport clubs. That is, they may want to maximize winning on the one hand, or maximize profits on the other. History shows that, in most instances, clubs with the biggest budgets will outperform teams with much lower budgets. And, what is more, some clubs are willing to go over budget to get that elusive winning edge. This is why some critics of the Pirates' 'controlled frugality' approach went on to argue at the time that the club was not really trying to win.

Club executives disputed this assessment, but the numbers showed that Pittsburgh had not spent as much on its players as its opposing teams had. In 2010, the Pirates had baseball's lowest payroll, which was USD 35 million, only USD 2 million more than in 1992, the club's last winning season. The Pirates' run of consecutive losing seasons ended up being the worst in the history of major American pro-sport teams. The Pirates' recent experiences thus makes one wonder if some professional sport clubs might actually make more money by losing as opposed to winning. It is difficult to understand how losing might boost profits, but the situation becomes clearer when it is realized that MLB has operated a revenue-sharing scheme for the last few years. This means that teams that finish at the bottom of the league table are given the same funding 'distribution' as those at the top of the table. The aim here is make sure that the rich clubs do not become too wealthy, while also making sure that less well-off clubs do not become too poor.

The other important issue that came out of this state of affairs was how much the public should know about the financial state of their favourite clubs. While fans and the media want to know more, the clubs want to give out less. This dilemma was starkly revealed in 2010 when a number of financial statements for professional baseball clubs were leaked to the media. The PPBC was one of these clubs. It stated that it was wrong for the financial statements to have been released to the media, and went on to say that someone with access to the club's financial statements had breached their fiduciary obligation to the club by providing the media with a copy of its financial statements for the 2007 and 2008 seasons. It also claimed that the club, being a private company, had no obligation to publicly report its financial results. The club claimed that it had nothing to hide anyway, and that its revenues were being reinvested back into the club to 'rebuild this baseball team'. According to the Pirates there was no problem.

This was well and good, but the club's financial documents showed not only the level of profits being made, and the benefits that flowed from the league's revenue-sharing arrangements, but also the dividends paid out to the owners of the franchise. This 'secret' information was only discovered because the documents had found their way into the hands of the media. The documents revealed material that was quite well known, including the fact that the revenue from the sale of broadcast rights fees usually exceeded the revenue gained from home game receipts. They also confirmed the importance of private suite rentals, merchandising, brand licensing and the commission from the sale of food and beverages. However, the documents also illuminated many aspects of the team's financial operations that are rarely disclosed. These included the breakdown of expenditures, the share of revenues that go to player salaries, and the balance between assets and liabilities. A sample of the financial data contained in the exposed documents includes the following:

- For the year ended 2008 the Pittsburgh Pirates generated total revenues of USD 146 million.
- The major revenue streams were revenue-sharing transfers ($39 million), broadcasting fees ($39 million), home game receipts ($32 million), ballpark signage and naming rights ($11 million), and food and beverage commissions ($8 million).
- For the year ended 2008 the Pittsburgh Pirates incurred expenditures of USD 124 million.
- The major expenses were player salaries ($51 million), player development ($23 million), ballpark and game operations ($17 million), marketing and public relations ($17 million), and team operations ($13 million).
- Total operating profit for the year was USD 22 million.
- There was a hefty annual interest bill of USD 6 million. This was the payment for servicing an MLB credit/loan facility of USD 60 million.
- The total current liabilities figure was USD 19 million.

- Total liabilities came in at USD 153 million, with the major items being notes payable ($40 million) and access to the MLB credit facility ($59 million).
- Total current assets figure was USD 40 million, with the amount payable for redistribution to teams accounting for USD 35 million.
- Total assets of the PPBC added up to USD 237 million. The dominant item was the franchise cost – that is, the cost of purchasing the club – which was valued at USD 101 million.
- The second most important fixed asset was leaseholds and equipment ($54 million).
- Interestingly, the cash flow statement lists a 'distribution to partners' figure of USD 20 million. This is an especially interesting figure since it represents the dividend to the club's owners. The club is a limited partnership organized under Pennsylvania state laws.

While the PPBC has no obligation to disclose the details of its operations, its failure to do so suggests the owners preferred to keep the details to themselves. However, a close inspection of the accounts also makes it clear that a policy of non-disclosure is able to conveniently hide a number of potentially sensitive things. They include total revenues, the breakdown of the revenues, the level of operating and net profits, debt levels and interest repayment. The most sensitive of all is the dividend payment to the owners. In this instance it seems as if the club's frugal spending on player talent and its low level of on-field performance has enabled it to build a very healthy level of profits. It also appears that these profits have delivered a healthy return to the owners. These revelations would not have occurred had the document not been leaked to the media.

The PPBC case highlights one of many issues that impacts on the transparency, accountability and integrity of sport enterprises. The idea of integrity has now become a central part of a sport enterprise's identity and image-making processes. This growing concern for things such as credibility, honesty, openness and trust-worthiness is in large part the result of having to deal with a relentless array of crises and incidents that undermine a sport's good standing and positive reputation.

CASE STUDY 13.2

The Spanish Football League problem

The place and the problem

In Chapter 5 we touched upon the financial instability that has inhabited Spanish football for the last few years. It has also suffered from a severe lack of reporting standards. In one study it was found that many of the audit statements – or audit reports, as they are also called – called into question some of the accounting practices used to finalize the accounts. It was found that only 20 per cent of clubs presented clean audit reports. The most frequently cited problems and/or qualifications were centred on taxation issues (23 per cent), player transfer valuations (22 per cent), the calculation of shareholders' equity (16 per cent), the capacity of the enterprise to be self-sustaining (14 per cent), the 'provisions' part of current liabilities (11 per cent), how income is defined (7 per cent) and depreciation expenses (5 per cent) (Barajas and Rodriguez 2010). The following dubious reporting practices were singled out for attention:

- incorrect recording of revenue and income;
- confusion over the distinction between abnormal and extraordinary income;
- undervaluing of extraordinary expenses;
- problems about how intangible assets should be amortized;
- confusion over valuation of fixed assets;
- incorrect accounting of training costs;
- failure to clearly state the breakdown of current and non-current liabilities.

CASE STUDY 13.3

UEFA Financial Fair Play regulations

The place and the entity

UEFA (Union of European Football Associations) is the governing body of European football. It was established in 1954, and now represents the interests of twenty-five national football authorities. According to the UEFA website it has 'grown into the cornerstone of the game on this continent, working with and acting on behalf of Europe's national football associations and other stakeholders in the game to promote football'. It has thus become the 'guardian' of football in Europe, 'protecting and nurturing the well-being of the sport at all levels, from the elite and its stars to the thousands who play the game as a hobby'.

The problem

Financial integrity is an especially important image to have since it affects the capacity of sport enterprises to secure funds, maintain sound credit ratings, build public trust and maintain community goodwill. Financial integrity can be viewed from a number of angles, but first and foremost it is essentially about taking the stance that transparency, openness, public disclosure and professional scrutiny are good things. The problems that are associated with secrecy and cover-ups have led many of sport's governing bodies – with UEFA being a good example – to apply the idea of 'fair play' to their club-licensing arrangements.

The belief that sport enterprises must meet some sort of minimum financial reporting standard was confirmed in 2010, when 372 of Europe's most prominent clubs (which is 65 per cent of the total number of prominent clubs), had made aggregated losses of just over EUR 2 billion (Muller *et al.* 2012: 119–20). The data also showed that 195 top-flight clubs reported average losses of 20 per cent. That is, for every euro of income earned, there was a euro and twenty cents spent on some other item. Additionally, 237 of Europe's top-division clubs had accumulated negative equity, which meant they had more debts than assets. The other cause for concern was that many of the loss-making clubs were also very wealthy. So, while they had lots of assets and huge revenue streams, they also had large debt levels and exponentially increasing expenses.

These exceedingly poor financial results, especially when they are covered up or selectively released, not only dent sport's reputation, but also lead to a loss of public confidence. In response to these unflattering outcomes UEFA introduced a bundle of Financial Fair Play (FFP) regulations. The FFP rules had the overarching goal of protecting the long-term viability and sustainability of European club football. This feeds into two subsidiary goals: first, to ensure the smooth running and integrity of the competition and, second, to protect the participating clubs' creditors, which begins with players and administrative staff as a priority, and then includes other clubs, suppliers, corporate partners, ground managers and the like. The following operating objectives then fall out of these goals:

- Encourage sensible long-term financial planning.
- Limit the amount of debt that is accumulated.
- Encourage clubs to spend no more than they make in income, which means adopting a 'break-even' rule.
- Encourage clubs to settle their debts – especially short-term ones such as player and staff benefits – on time.
- Stop excessive transfer fees and salary payments.
- Promote investment in youth development.
- Promote additional investment in infrastructure, especially training grounds and stadia, and player development programmes.
- Ensure clubs are more transparent in their dealings with stakeholders and desist from engaging in financial 'foul play'.

There are signs that clubs are reigning in their spending and reducing debt levels. However, it is too early to tell just how effective the FFP rules are in stabilizing the financial operations of clubs.

CASE STUDY 13.4

International Olympic Committee Principles of Good Governance

The place and the entity

The International Olympic Committee (IOC), whose headquarters are located in Lausanne in Switzerland, is responsible for the planning and conduct of the summer and winter Olympic Games. The philosophy and goals of the IOC (and the Olympic movement in general) are enshrined in the Olympic Charter, and encapsulated in the lofty aim of the Olympic movement, which is to 'place sport at the service of the harmonious development of humankind, with a view to promoting a peaceful society concerned with the preservation of human dignity'. According to the IOC the values of Olympism reach their peak with the 'bringing together of the world's athletes at the great sports festival, the Olympic Games'.

The problem

In 2008, in response to a growing list of complaints about the lackadaisical management of many sporting bodies with IOC connections, the IOC released a document that spelt out the Basic Universal Principles of Good Governance for sports covered by the Olympic movement (IOC 2008). It provided an excellent platform from which to not only launch an examination of financial management issues in sport, but to also frame any study of the knowledge and skills required to undertake financial management tasks. This Good Governance policy statement included succinct recommendations of best practice under the following themes:

1   Vision, mission and strategy.
2   Structures, regulations and democratic process.
3   Highest level of competence, integrity and ethical standards.
4   Accountability, transparency and control.
5   Solidarity and development.
6   Athletes' involvement, participation and care.
7   Harmonious relations with governments while preserving autonomy.

Themes 1 and 4 had special relevance for financial management issues, and made it clear that (1) financial management systems needed to be more professionally administered, (2) boards and managers must be held accountable for financial mismanagement and (3) governing bodies must be more transparent when disclosing financial information.

Theme 1

This theme, which attends to the enterprise's vision, mission and strategy, and its intricate relationship with good financial management, is viewed as a priority issue.

This is because it sets the planning and operational agendas for the enterprise, and therefore provides the parameters within which the financial management process takes place.

The vision is a crucial starting point since it attends to overall goals of the organization. It also needs to be clearly defined since in sport there is often some confusion over where profits fit, and to what extent annual operating surpluses are a good thing or not. Some enterprises put a high value on revenues and surpluses, but others are content to just break even. Some sport enterprises are listed as private or public companies, and thus have a responsibility to owners and shareholders to pay dividends. Other sport enterprises are registered as companies with no shareholders, while others are registered as associations, which means they are not for profit, and are consequently subject to the interests of members above all else. So, at one extreme, a sport enterprise may be primarily concerned with maximizing shareholder value, while at the other extreme an enterprise may only be concerned with delivering quality services to members and players. But, either way, it is important to build in systems and processes that ensure the viability of the enterprise into the future.

Theme 4

This theme focuses on accountability, transparency and control, and is thus crucially important for good financial management practices. It is divided into the following points of action.

Accountability

The IOC makes it clear that all governing bodies, whether elected or appointed, shall be accountable to the members of the organization and selected stakeholders. It also proposes that (1) boards and executive bodies be accountable to their general assemblies and their elected representatives, (2) management be accountable to the boards and executive bodies and (3) employees be accountable to management.

Processes and mechanisms

The IOC also requires adequate standards and processes for accountability to be in place, available to all organizations and consistently applied and monitored. It also wants clear and measurable objectives and targets set for the organization, its boards, management and staff, including appropriate tools for performance assessment.

Transparency and communication

The IOC wants financial information to be disclosed gradually, and in an appropriate form to members, stakeholders and the public. It also suggests that the disclosure of financial information be done on an annual basis at the minimum. Additionally, financial statements should be presented in a consistent way in order to be easily understood by both members and the general public.

Financial matters and related laws, rules, procedures and standards

The IOC expects that accounts should be established in accordance with the applicable laws and in line with the 'true and fair view' principle. The application of internationally recognized reporting standards should be encouraged, and all annual financial statements are to be inspected and approved by independent and qualified auditors. The IOC also expects that (1) additional accountability and financial reports will be produced on a regular basis, (2) information about remuneration and financial arrangements of the governing bodies will be disclosed, (3) membership details should be part of the annual accounts, (4) all rules regarding remuneration of the members of governing bodies and managers should be enforced and (5) all remuneration procedures should be transparent and predictable.

CASE STUDY 13.5

Sport, financial management and corporate social responsibility

Businesses in general, and sport businesses in particular, are often criticized for thinking only of the profits they make, and ignoring the social consequences of their strategic decisions and the outputs they deliver. This dilemma is particularly striking in the case of tobacco companies. On the one hand there are profits to be made, but on the other hand there is a pile of evidence that links smoking cigarettes to lung cancer and heart disease. Sport has for many years had a close relationship with tobacco producers, who provided millions of dollars of sponsorship funds to both community and professional sport (Taylor 1984). This relationship has been severed in most nations around the world on the grounds that sport's image for building fit and healthy bodies was compromised by its association with a product that did exactly the opposite.

There is now growing pressure from both government and the public in general for businesses to move beyond the bottom line and take into account the effect their decisions have on the wider community. This idea has given rise to the concept of 'triple bottom line accounting', which gets businesses to consider their contribution to not just economic prosperity, but also to social justice and environmental quality. While the measurement of social justice and environmental quality is fraught with danger, the overall aim is to see profits and net worth as just one measure of the performance of an organization. Triple bottom line accounting consequently provides for three measures of how a business contributes to society, with each measure being geared around the value-added concept. These measures are:

- economic value-added;
- social value-added;
- environmental value-added.

This way of measuring performance presents many challenges for sport enterprises. It has already been noted that sport clubs and associations are motivated by more than money. For a national sporting body the growth of the sport may be equally important, and for a professional sport club the dominant goal may be on-field success. However, despite the primacy of these goals, sport organizations can equally make decisions and produce outputs that have negative consequences for society in general. The heavy use of tobacco companies as sponsors may have secured a valuable source of funds, but the subsequent association of tobacco products with glamorous sport stars was instrumental in convincing young people that smoking was socially desirable, even if it might kill them in the long run. In some sports the heavy drinking of alcoholic products is part of the club culture, and in these cases no success is seen as complete without a long binge-drinking session. Similarly, in professional sport leagues, where neo-tribalism is strong, groups of rival supporters will often resolve their antagonism with wild brawls. Football hooliganism in Britain is the archetypal model in this respect. All of these outputs have negative social consequences, and it therefore makes senses to encourage sport clubs, associations and leagues to measure their overall performance in

TABLE 13.1 GRI performance indicators

Performance category	Performance measures
Direct economic impacts	– Sales to satisfied customers
	– Purchases from suppliers
	– Employees hired
	– Taxes paid
	– Dividend and interest paid
Product responsibility	– Safety and durability
	– Truth in advertising and product labelling
Work practices	– Health, safety and security
	– Training, education and consultation
	– Appropriate wages and conditions
Social practices	– No bribery and corruption
	– Transparent lobbying
	– Freedom from collusion and coercion
Human rights	– Non-discriminatory hiring practices
	– Freedom from forced labour
Environmental impacts	– Efficient energy use
	– Appropriate water recycling
	– Controlled emissions
	– Waste management
	– Maintenance of biodiversity

terms of their social and environmental impact as well as their participation impact, win–loss impact or revenue-raising impact.

Global Reporting Initiative

Recently, a number of global businesses, with the support of the United Nations, developed a programme called the Global Reporting Initiative (GRI). The mission of the GRI is to design and promulgate sustainability reporting guidelines for each of the economic, social and environmental outputs identified above. Organizations that sign up to the GRI are expected to enact reporting systems that are transparent and accessible, provide quality and reliable information, and include information that is relevant and complete. The GRI has also compiled a list of factors under each of the economic, social and environmental headings that indicate specific issues that require addressing. A sample of factors particularly relevant to sport organizations is provided in Table 13.1.

The GRI model of performance management is complex, and will force sport organizations to be more systematic in the way they build their stakeholder relations. It will also enable them to go beyond revenue growth and on-field success and thus evaluate the contribution they are making to the wider society, ensure their financial sustainability, monitor their impact on the physical environment, and generally provide transparent and accountable management. This can only be a good thing.

RECAP

These cases show that effective financial management is more than just about seeking the advice of good accountants, doing a few budget projections, bringing in a bit more cash and keeping a neat set of books. Managers of sport enterprises also have a responsibility to ensure the credibility and reputation of their organizations and the things they do not just on the field of play, but off it as well. The idea of integrity is increasingly used to synthesize the things that need to be done to secure community trust and confidence. The above cases bring out a number of problems that come from being secretive, not disclosing information that has high public value, narrowly focusing on profiteering, caring more about market dominance than the long-term interests of the 'game', and dismissing the social benefits that might be delivered to communities, especially if this means taking resources away from the servicing of self-interests. This chapter thus makes a case for greater transparency and accountability in the way sport managers go about running their enterprises. Moreover, it is argued that sport will be better off if more of its scarce financial resources are allocated to building systems that give stakeholders more information, better explain its financial planning models, and more decisively explain incidents where officials may have acted improperly, or more generally have used members', shareholders' or stakeholders' funds in ways that undermined their best interests.

REVIEW QUESTIONS

There are a number of issues to deal with when looking at the financial transparency issue, thus the following questions need to be answered before moving on.

1 What exactly is meant by the terms 'accountability' and 'transparency'?

2 Why do we have so much talk these days about the need for greater accountability and transparency in the management of sport enterprises?

3 Are there any cases to be made for sport enterprises not wanting to disclose financial information to the public? And, if there are, what may these cases be?

4 What makes sport club managers want to be secretive about their finances?

5 What problems might emerge when clubs fail to disclose financial information?

6 What does the PPBC case tell us about the financial benefit that may accrue from not performing well on the field of play?

7 Does it make sense to increase profits by becoming less competitive?

8 What does the PPBC case tell us about the club's preparedness to disclose financial information to the public? Do you agree with the club's stance?

9 What do you think is the cause of the financial problems in Spanish football? Do you have any solutions to the problem?

10 What are the UEFA Financial Fair Play regulations all about? What do they aim to do?

11 Do you think the UEFA FFP regulations will actually work? And, if not, what factors may stop them from working properly?

12 The IOC has recently introduced a set of Good Governance rules. How do they fit in with the principles of accountable management and transparent financial administration?

13 What is meant by the term corporate social responsibility (CSR)?

14 What is meant by the term 'triple bottom line accounting'? How does it relate to CSR?

15 How can CSR be applied to sport?

16 To what extent might a commitment to CSR undermine attempts to secure a solid operating surplus?

17 How did the Global Reporting Initiative (GRI) originate, and what does it hope to achieve?

18 How can the GRI model be applied to sport clubs, associations, events and leagues?

FURTHER READING

Various studies on European football highlight many transparency and accountability issues. One of the most instructive is Muller, C., Lammert, J. and Hovemann, G. (2012) 'The financial fair play regulations of UEFA: an adequate concept to ensure the long-term viability and sustainability of European club football', *International Journal of Sport Finance*, 7: 117–40. Other excellent accounts of this initiative are available in (1) Barajas, A. and Rodriguez, P. (2010) 'Spanish football club finances', *International Journal of Sport Finance*, 5: 52–66; (2) Szymanski, S. (2010) 'The financial crisis and English football', *International Journal of Sport Finance*, 5: 28–40; (3) DeJonghe, T. and Vandeweghe, H. (2006) 'Belgian football', *Journal of Sports Economics*, 7(1): 105–13; (4) Dietl, H. and Franck, E. (2007) 'Governance failure and financial crisis in German football', *Journal of Sports Economics*, 8(6): 662–9; and (5) Andreff, W. (2007) 'French football: a financial crisis rooted in weak governance', *Journal of Sports Economics*, 8(6): 652–61.

For more detail on the International Olympic Committee's drive to achieve better financial transparency and accountability among its member bodies, see IOC (2008) *Basic Universal Principles of Good Governance of the Olympic and Sports Movement*, Seminar on Autonomy of Olympic and Sport Movement, Lausanne, 11–12 February. The application of good governance and financial transparency principles to non-sport, not-for-profit agencies is nicely treated in McCarthy, J. (2007) 'The ingredients of financial transparency', *Nonprofit & Voluntary Sector Quarterly*, 36(1): 156–64.

An insightful discussion of CSR and triple bottom line accounting is contained in Atrill, P., McLaney, E., Harvey, D. and Jenner, M. (2006) *Accounting: An Introduction*, Melbourne, Vic.: Pearson Education Australia (Chapter 15: 'Trends and issues in accounting'). For an additional review of CSR, see Hancock, J. (2004) *Investing in Corporate Social Responsibility*, London: Kogan Page. A detailed account of how CSR is played out in sport is contained in Walters, G. (2012) 'Managing social responsibility in sport', in Trenberth, L. and Hassan, D. (2012) (eds) *Managing Sport Business: An Introduction*, London: Routledge, pp. 412–26. See also Smith, A. and Westerbeek, H. (2007) 'Sport as a vehicle for deploying corporate social responsibility', *Journal of Corporate Citizenship*, 25: 43–54.

For a revealing analysis of how strategic alliances work in sport, and how they can be used to build brand equity and financial sustainability while also doing social good, see Gladden, J., Irwin, R. and Sutton, W. (2001) 'Managing North American major professional sport teams in the new millennium: a focus on building brand equity', *Journal of Sport Management*, 15: 297–317. The ways in which alliances can be used to develop more creative and accountable funding arrangements are examined in Mahoney, D. and Howard, D. (2001) 'Sport business in the next decade: a general overview of expected trends', *Journal of Sport Management*, 15: 275–96.

USEFUL WEBSITES

* In order to get a full overview of the 'international financial transparency movement', it is worth initially going to the Financial Transparency Coalition (FTC) website. The FTC goal is to contribute intellectual and policy support towards a more transparent

and equitable global financial system. Key members of FTC include Christian Aid, European Network of Debt and Development, Global Witness, Global Financial Integrity, Tax Justice Network and Transparency International: **www.financial transparency.org/about/overview**.

- Transparency International (TI) has done a lot of work on sport integrity, some of which has important financial management implications. It has completed a number of reports on international cricket, especially cricket on the sub-continent. See **www. transparency.org/news/feature/fair_play_strengthening_integrity_and_transparency_ in_cricket**.

- TI has done equally impressive work in football. See **www.transparency.org/news/ feature/tackling_football_match_fixing_prevention_as_cure**.

- A few years ago the Football (Financial Transparency) Bill 2010–12 was introduced in the British Parliament. The Bill required that football clubs playing in the top four tiers of English and Scottish professional football should (1) disclose the identity of their owners, and also the identity of the owners of their home-playing grounds and training grounds, (2) disclose any intellectual property associated with the clubs and their players, (3) disclose any third-party stake in their clubs, (4) disclose the identities of outstanding creditors and (5) ensure that all creditors of the football clubs be compensated equally should they go into administration. The Bill had its first reading in March 2012. The details are listed in **http://services.parliament.uk/bills/2010-12/ footballfinancialtransparency.html**.

- A critique of the Bill can be found in **www.huffingtonpost.co.uk/damian-collins/ footballs-financial-own-goal_b_1345354.html**.

- For a timely analysis of the Pittsburgh Pirates Baseball Club (PPBC) financial disclosures incident, see **http://sports.espn.go.com/mlb/news/story?id=5484947**.

- A Global Reporting Initiative (GRI) template for sport events is included in **www. globalreporting.org/resourcelibary/EOSS-G3.1-SummaryGuide-QRS.pdf**.

CHAPTER 14

Doing feasibility studies

LEARNING OUTCOMES

At the end of this chapter readers will be able to:

- explain what is meant by the term 'feasibility study', and understand its applicability to sport
- identify the key steps in undertaking a feasibility study
- argue for a detailed analysis of market demand before proceeding to the preparation of costing documents
- ensure that, when costings are done, they clearly distinguish between capital costs and operation costs.

CHAPTER SUMMARY

This chapter discusses the ways in which feasibility studies can be used to evaluate the viability of major sport projects. The feasibility study is an important part of a sport manager's armoury since it enables a systematic and relatively objective analysis of a major planning initiative to be undertaken. It is one thing to come up with a grand idea for a new stadium or recreation centre, but it is another thing to find out if the concept is viable and will involve a proper use of scarce resources. The main steps involved in undertaking a feasibility study, or project evaluation, as it is sometimes called, will be identified and explained. Special attention will be given to market analysis, the concept plan, location, environmental impact, capital costs and funding sources, and estimates of operating revenue and expenditure.

THE SCARCE RESOURCES PROBLEM

In the world of sport people come up with lots of imaginative ideas about what would be good for their sport, and what would be good for the community they serve. In a perfect world every local community would have a swimming pool, an indoor sport centre, a fully equipped gym, a golf course, a multi-purpose sports fields, a bush orienteering space, an integrated cycle path network, a jogging circuit and a multi-level rock-climbing wall. It would provide great choice and convenience, and encourage participation in different types of physical activity. This would not only benefit individuals who use the facilities, but also build social capital and improve the community's general level of well-being. However, every idea for a new sport facility comes with a price tag. There is also the 'opportunity cost', whereby the allocation of more resources to one particular facility, activity or programme, will mean fewer resources being available to some other facility, activity or programme. This is a fact of economic life and, as a result, decisions that allocate resources to their very best possible use will enhance the well-being of entire communities. We also know, though, that sometimes resources will be distributed to projects that provide more benefits – and mainly of the political type – to local councillors and government officials. This reality means that popular sports, emerging sports and those sports supported by vocal minorities may win the day, so to speak.

In many of the above examples, the costs of setting up the facilities may be steep, and this also begs the question of where the funds are going to come from. Not only that, it does not make sense to invest heavily in projects where the usage is likely to be low and the facility will be a constant drain on local resources. At the same time, there may be instances where a facility is so important for disadvantaged families that a subsidy will be built into the project 'costings'. In other words, there are a lot of questions that need to be asked before local taxpayers' or private investors' money is called upon to fund a major sport project. It is therefore important to establish a method for working out both the initial costs and ongoing costs and benefits that flow from translating these great ideas into practical outcomes.

The same questions arise when deciding about the construction of sport stadiums and arenas. In these cases the design and construction costs can be massive. For example, the rebuilding of Wembley Stadium in London cost more than GBP 2,000 million, while the redevelopment of the Melbourne Cricket Ground (which was completed in 2006 in time for the Melbourne Commonwealth Games) was costed at around AUD 450 million. These are hefty price tags, and such decisions to build require a strong defence if they are going to carry any legitimacy. If, for example, the government is funding stadium development, it will want to have an assurance that it will be used extensively, and attract both international-standard sport events and large crowds. A private investor will want an assurance that the stadium will generate a return, and provide a stream of income sufficient to cover both the cost of funds borrowed to finance the stadium's construction and its subsequent operation. For community sport facilities and large sport stadiums there is the compounding problem of the non-financial benefits and costs associated with the investment. As will be indicated in Chapter 15, the community may secure stronger neighbourhood involvement in community activities, and it may end up with an attractive landscaped environment that attracts out-of-town visitors. Conversely, the architecture may be ugly, and the concentration of facility users may lead to chronic traffic congestion.

In the case of the stadium there may, on the one hand, be an increase in civic pride from having a professional sport team located in the region, but, on the other hand, it may occupy land that was previously highly valued public space. So, if the facility may be costly to set up, or runs at a loss, it may be the price to pay to secure some additional benefits. Or, if it was likely to break even, its success may be undermined by recurring social costs. This begs the question as to what conditions would need to exist for a sport venue or centre to be run at a loss in the interests of the community. The next question to ask is who would then pay the difference?

Therefore, before any good idea about running an event or constructing a facility is put into practice, it is prudent to ask a number of questions. The key question is 'Is this event or facility viable, and does it constitute an efficient use of scarce resources?' That is, can it be properly funded, will it meet a significant community need and will it generate enough revenue to cover its costs of operation? And if it cannot be operated profitably, should it be dropped, or should it be subsidized or supported in some other way?

THE CAPITAL INVESTMENT ISSUE

It should be remembered that the funding of sport facilities is a significant capital investment decision and, as noted in Chapter 10, in order to get the best outcome, a systematic way of making the decision should be developed. In this context it is important to note that the key feature of business investment decisions is that they are linked to the long-term strategic goals of the organization and the benefits that are likely to flow from the investment. The allocation of resources to large-scale projects is a significant decision, and the construction of facilities and the purchase of assets require long-range planning and a systematic assessment of the project's associated benefits, costs and risks.

The issue of capital investment decision-making is particularly relevant to the construction of sport stadiums and arenas, where there is an element of risk or uncertainty in predicting what the future return will be (Brown *et al.* 2010). These decisions also have significant impacts on key stakeholders, including sponsors, broadcasters, players, fans and participants. Moreover, the success of a new sport facility will require not only frequent consultation with these stakeholders, but also their continued role in contributing streams of income. The risk of failure and loss of investment will therefore be minimized if ongoing consultation with key stakeholders is maintained, and people with appropriate skills are driving the project. Good planning requires an in-depth analysis of all the factors that will contribute to the project's success or failure. So, what has to be done, in practical terms, to ensure good planning and sound investment in the field of sport facility development? The most effective way of securing a sustainable future for sport stadia, arenas and events is to undertake a project evaluation or feasibility study.

WHAT IS A FEASIBILITY STUDY?

A feasibility study can be defined as the systematic design, collection, analysis and reporting of data and findings relevant to a specific project being considered by an organization. This will involve a careful consideration of the product being proposed, the market it will be sold to, and the physical, financial and operational requirements of creating it and obtaining all the necessary approvals and finance to bring it into existence. It is also an assessment of the financial return that is likely to accrue to the investor, be that government or private business.

In addition, a feasibility study must provide the information and analysis that allows a reasoned decision. It will cover all relevant factors and issues that will affect the viability of the new facility. It will not only include a market and financial analysis, but also examine the context in which the study is being conducted, state the anticipated aims to be achieved, give a clear succinct description of what the project involves and offer a recommendation on whether the project should proceed.

TAKING A CRITICAL LOOK AT THE CONCEPT

Feasibility studies are necessary because they provide third-party confirmation of the viability of the proposal, and also because they provide credibility that is necessary to obtain funding. However, although feasibility studies might be accurate when they are conducted, market conditions are often dynamic and circumstances can change very quickly. In the case of sport, this can take the form of major venue-redesign issues, a decline in public interest and the loss of a major tenant or provider. Because a feasibility study is a snapshot of current conditions, investors must consequently accept the risk that these conditions might change (Brown *et al.* 2010: 75–9). At the same time, the typical project evaluation is framed by optimistic expectations and hidden political agendas. For example, feasibility studies are often commissioned to protect investors from criticism and secure broad public support.

WHO SHOULD UNDERTAKE A FEASIBILITY STUDY?

A project evaluation in sport will usually be compiled by a team because the process requires input from several disciplines. It is important that a number of specialists are included, as follows:

- Consultants with experience in sport facility management who understand the importance of sport consumer needs and the delivery of quality sports services.
- Marketing specialists who can undertake market analysis and deliver accurate estimates of demand for different demographic cohorts.
- Architects who understand not only design trends and opportunities, but also the associated costs.
- Financial analysts who can formulate both a detailed capital budget and an operational plan of revenues and expenditures.

The team leader has a crucial role in the project evaluation, as this person has the responsibility of integrating the input from these various specialists. The team must map out a plan for the study, and must be prepared to coordinate and review both its own work and the work of other consultants whose input is required at various stages of the study. The team must also be aware of the financial parameters of the study. The team will have clear schedules and timelines, and must be conscious of the need for communication both among team members and with the investors who have commissioned the study. There should also be contingency plans for any problems and delays that might arise. The team leader should be capable and knowledgeable in the field, and thus able to make well-considered judgements. It also means he or she will be impartial and assertive enough to prepare a fair and independent report to the client.

THE FUNDAMENTALS OF A FEASIBILITY STUDY

A feasibility study can be a complex activity but, when distilled to its fundamentals, involves three crucial activities.

First, it is important to undertake a broad market audit. This involves the use of demographic and economic data, such as population levels and density, occupational profiles, income levels and age and gender breakdowns, to establish the level of potential market demand for the facility.

Second, market analysis should be used to generate detailed estimates of customer usage. A significant proportion of a feasibility study's resources should be used to estimate the demand by different consumer segments for the services provided by the facility. In the case of a sport stadium it will be important to identify the tenants, what games they intend to schedule, the anticipated attendances, the revenues that will be associated with these attendances and its capacity to generate a steady stream of sponsor income. Caution is needed here, however, since calculations of likely income streams can often be nothing more than inspired guesses and optimistic forecasts without much supporting evidence.

Third, it is vital to undertake detailed financial analysis that can be used to establish the overall viability of the project, and whether it is financially sustainable. It should be noted at this point that financial sustainability has two components that need to be systematically addressed. They are a capital funding component and a recurrent – that is, operational – funding component. Taking the above discussion into account, a comprehensive feasibility study will:

- explain the development concept in the context of a generalized problem or need and its long-term viability;
- identify likely market demand through in-depth analysis;
- enable the necessary finance and government approvals to be obtained with minimum delay;
- define strategies for dealing with stakeholders;
- identify the capital costs and how they will be sourced;
- prepare estimates of operating revenues and expenses.

DOING FEASIBILITY STUDIES: A TEN-STEP MODEL

In order to reinforce the principles underlying feasibility studies, and to give a clear picture of what needs to be done to ensure a best possible outcome, the following ten-step process model has been developed. It lists not only the nature of each step, but how it can be best completed. The steps to determine feasibility follow.

Step 1: Locate the proposal within a strategic framework

- Identify the problem or issue to be resolved.
- Specify the project brief by answering the question: what have we been asked to do?

Step 2: Develop the need or demand for the facility or event

- Start with a short discussion of the main stakeholders and their expectations.
- Establish the size of the potential market.
- Conduct surveys of potential users (questionnaires and focus groups are particularly appropriate).
- Identify their recreational needs and preferences.
- Construct a demographic profile of anticipated users.
- Quantify the anticipated level of usage, making sure to break usage into time segments.

Step 3: Prepare a concept design or plan

- Describe features and/or functions in the context of other options.
- Provide detailed specifications, architectural plans and graphics.
- Identify possible locations, ending with a ranking of sites.
- List the range of benefits expected to flow from the facility or event.

Step 4: Identify regulations, rules and by-laws that must be observed

- Make sure all appropriate permits can be obtained.
- Seek advice from all relevant parties.

Step 5: Calculate the impact of the event or facility on the surrounding environment

- Consider the economic impact.
- Consider the social impact.
- Consider the environmental impact.

Step 6: Make an estimate of capital cost and funding

- Calculate capital cost (land acquisition, site preparation, consultant fees, construction costs, equipment costs).
- List capital funding arrangements and the sources of funds (listing figures for each source).

Step 7: Estimate the anticipated operating revenues

- Identify any annual grants.
- Calculate income from users (fees and charges, membership, weekly usage, income from each user group), while ensuring that it is consistent with data compiled in step 2.
- Estimate sales of merchandise.
- Identify any equipment hire.
- Identify revenue to be secured from sponsors, local philanthropists or benefactors.

- Divide revenues into fixed and variable. The more fixed revenue (e.g. sponsorship), the better, since it is not dependent upon usage levels.

Step 8: Calculate operating costs

- Provide line items for staffing costs, office and administration, utilities, phone, gas, maintenance costs, marketing costs and incidentals.
- Divide costs into fixed and variable if appropriate.

Step 9: Do profit projections

- Design different scenarios by varying assumptions on usage rates, prices and charges, other revenues and costs. Examine some what-if situations.
- Include some break-even analysis in what-if scenarios.
- Evaluate options.

Step 10: Make recommendations

- The first question to answer is: can we afford it?
- The second question to answer is: what is the best option?
- All the costs and benefits (both tangible and non-tangible) should be considered.
- So, the final question that needs to be answered is: is it a goldmine (a lucrative venture) or a white elephant (destined to operate with heavy losses), or somewhere in between?

SIMULATION EXERCISE 14.1

Deciding on the viability of a new go-cart track

The following fictional case provides an evaluation of a go-cart track proposed for a university starved of sporting facilities. The context for the case is a lack of sport and recreation facilities at one of the university's regional campuses, which is a nationally recognized provider of sport management education. The university (which goes under the name of Cameron Tech.) is concerned that its Abbott Heights campus is poorly resourced, and is keen to give the campus a competitive edge by building some unique recreational services that can be used not only to increase the sporting options of the local community, but also to attract quality students and provide them with internships. A consultant was given the brief of coming up with a proposal that was both imaginative and viable. The go-cart option is presented below.

Strategic overview

The Abbott Heights campus has a mandate to improve the recreational services to students and the local community, which are currently substandard. It is also important to work with the local council to create a facility that can be jointly funded and managed.

Needs analysis

The market for a new recreational facility can be segmented into various categories with each category representing a specific user group. The segments, together with their demographics, are listed in Table 14.1.

TABLE 14.1 Go-cart survey – market segments	
Segment	Market size
Primary school students	3,000
Secondary school students	4,000
University students	3,000
Local community	30,000
Total market size	**40,000**

Market survey

A random survey was conducted among a group of people which included students, teachers and the local community. The response was positive. Nearly 80 per cent of respondents claimed an additional recreational facility was needed. Moreover, 97 per cent of residents aged between fifteen and twenty-five wanted a facility that went beyond the traditional activities of track and field, football and cricket. The survey results also indicated that 50 per cent of people were willing to use the facility at least twice a week, while 90 per cent of respondents in the fifteen to twenty-five age group said they would be prepared to take out a membership package.

In order to establish the type of facility that was most strongly requested, respondents were asked to rank the most desirable of a mini-golf centre, an orienteering circuit, an outdoor court, an indoor gymnasium and a go-cart track. Concept designs were shown to respondents. The results are outlined in Table 14.2.

TABLE 14.2 Respondent rankings of facilities	
Type of facility	Percentage of respondents who ranked facilities as a priority
Mini-golf	5
Orienteering	10
Court	15
Gymnasium	10
Go-cart track	60

The concept

The go-cart track will occupy five hectares of land situated on the edge of the Abbott Heights campus. It will be 600 metres long, with a full bitumen surface. Surrounding land will be landscaped, and the track will have full safety barrier protection.

Capital cost

Based on the construction of a similar facility in the Bushville District, which is around 150 kilometres away, but with a similar demographic, the estimates in Table 14.3 have been provided.

TABLE 14.3 Capital expenditure for the go-cart facility

Capital expense	($)
Construction of track	120,000
Safety nets	5,000
Sand	2,000
Safety barriers	10,000
First aid and fire equipment	3,000
Storage and office facility	40,000
12 high-performance go-carts	12,000
Go-cart spares	4,000
Tools	4,000
Total capital cost	**200,000**

Source of capital

It is anticipated that capital funds will be sourced as outlined in Table 14.4.

TABLE 14.4 Anticipated sources of capital funds for the go-cart facility

Source	Amount ($ thousands)
Local council	60
University	80
Naming rights sponsor	30
Long-term bank loan	30
Capital total	**200**

Revenues

It is proposed that the revenue for the facility will come from a number of different sources, the main ones being daily users and members, sponsors and operating grants.

Pricing structure

Separate price schedules have been set for students, teachers, the public and concession card holders. Casual prices are for fifteen minutes of track time. Membership will allow the holder to unlimited track time for the duration of that membership. Memberships are sold for three-, six- and twelve-month periods. Table 14.5 identifies the prices.

TABLE 14.5 Pricing structure for the go-cart facility ($)

	Casual rate	3-month membership	6-month membership	12-month membership
Students	10	120	200	250
Teachers	20	130	250	350
Public	15	130	250	350
Concession	15	120	230	300

Revenue projections

Revenue projections are based on a minimum of sixty weekly casual visits, and 150 annual member packages during Year 1. Sponsorships have been guaranteed for Year 1 through to Year 4. A four-year revenue projection is provided in Table 14.6.

TABLE 14.6 Revenue projections for the go-cart facility ($ thousands)

	Daily visits	Memberships	Sponsorship	Total
Year 1	55	45	20	120
Year 2	60	50	20	130
Year 3	65	55	20	140
Year 4	70	60	20	150

Operating expenses

Expense projections combine variable and fixed costs, and include full-time staff, full maintenance and servicing costs, depreciation on go-carts and interest payable on the bank loan. A four-year projection can be seen in Table 14.7.

TABLE 14.7 Expenses for the go-cart facility ($ thousands)

Expense	Estimated cost Year 1	Estimated cost Year 2	Estimated cost Year 3	Estimated cost Year 4
Advertising	12	10	10	10
Insurance	8	12	15	20
Staffing	60	80	85	85
Maintenance	8	8	8	8
Repairs (go-carts)	5	5	5	5
Go-cart depreciation	3	3	3	3
Sundry expenses	2	3	3	3
Bank charges (interest on loan)	1.5	1.5	1.5	1.5
Fuel	10	11	14	14
Totals	**110**	**134**	**145**	**150**

Profit forecasts

Profit forecasts use the revenue and expense projections identified previously to construct estimates of future profits. This best-case scenario has the track making a small profit in Year 1, a loss in Year 2 and a loss in Year 3, and breaking even in Year 4 (Table 14.8). It also assumes ongoing support from local sponsors.

TABLE 14.8 Four-year profit forecast for the go-cart facility ($ thousands)

	Operating expenses	Depreciation expenses	Total expenses	Revenue
Year 1	107	3	110	120
Year 2	131	3	134	130
Year 3	142	3	145	140
Year 4	147	3	150	150

These forecasts suggest that the project is sustainable, but a loss of sponsor support and a decline in membership will impact severely on operating profits. There is a risk the project might fall over, but the risk is manageable. On balance it appears the proposal to construct and operate a go-cart track on the perimeter of the Abbott Heights campus is sound from a technical perspective, and viable from a financial perspective. Moreover, it should not only meet a widespread community need, but also provide full cost recovery with a small surplus over the first four years of operation.

RECAP

The ability to undertake, or at least lead, a feasibility study is a valuable management skill for people operating in the sport sector. It is another tool that enables sport enterprise managers to make more informed and more strategically appropriate decisions. It also has important strategic implications since it provides a rational justification for decisions to allocate resources to one project, and not another. In sport, especially at the community level, there is little room for large profit margins. This makes it doubly important that resources are directed to those areas of sport and physical recreation activity that not only meet a strong and reliable demand, but also deliver sufficient revenue to sustain the operation into the future.

REVIEW QUESTIONS

The following questions focus on the above issues. They aim not only to tease out the steps that need to be followed when doing effective feasibility studies, but also to highlight the distinction between the capital costs and the operating costs of the project.

1   What is a feasibility study and what does it aim to do?

2   Where should you begin when conducting a feasibility study?

3   Why is it so important to undertake a detailed market analysis as part of a feasibility study?

4   What is a concept plan, and where does it fit into a feasibility study?

5   Why is it so important to distinguish between capital costs and running or operating costs when doing a feasibility study?

6   What goes into the construction of operating revenue and expense estimates?

7   How might you go about constructing different scenarios for the financial projections of a feasibility study?

8   Review the strengths and weaknesses of the proposal to build and operate a go-cart track.

FURTHER READING

For a discussion of where feasibility studies fit into the general field of project management, see Pinkerton, W. (2003) *Project Management*, New York: McGraw-Hill (Chapter 5: 'Pre-project planning'). An excellent overview of the how feasibility studies can be conducted, and the uses that can be made of them, is contained in Brown, M., Rascher, D., Nagel, M. and McEvoy, C. (2010) *Financial Management in the Sport Industry*,

Scottsdale, AZ: Holcomb Hathaway (Chapter 11: 'Feasibility studies'). Brown *et al.* make the point that the purpose of feasibility studies is to find out if a project is going to be practical on the one hand, and successful on the other. They identify a number of projects that have a sports focus. They include a diverse array of proposals, including (1) the building of a recreation centre in a regional town, (2) the construction of a major sport stadium in a large city, (3) the building of a public swimming pool in an expanding outer suburb, (4) the establishment of a private health and fitness club in a downtown city district and (5) the resurfacing of an outdoor fully grassed sports field. Brown *et al.* (2010) also highlight the crucial importance of doing detailed work on the market demand for the facility that comes out of the project. They also note that, if done properly, market demand analysis can also shape the scale and design of the facility by laying bare its likely operational parameters.

A detailed analysis of the feasibility study process at the local level is contained in the Western Australia (WA) Ministry of Sport and Recreation (1995) *How to Undertake a Feasibility Study for a Proposed Sport of Recreation Facility*, Perth, WA: Western Australia Government. For a useful introduction to the topic from a hospitality perspective, see Baker, K. (2002) *Project Evaluation and Feasibility Analysis for Hospitality Operations*, Putney, NSW: Hospitality Books.

For a sport-specific review of the role of feasibility studies in guiding the development of sport facilities, see Fried, G. (2005) *Managing Sport Facilities*, Champaign, IL: Human Kinetics (Chapter 4: 'Facility planning'). See also Rascher, D. and Rascher, H. (2001) 'NBA expansion and relocation: a viability study of various cities', *Journal of Sport management*, 18(3): 274–95.

USEFUL WEBSITES

- The following website provides a step-by-step template for doing a feasibility study in a sport setting: **www.dsr.wa.gov.au/feasibilitystudyguide**.
- The following website contains a detailed feasibility study for a sports centre: **www.easthants.gov.uk/ehdc/formsfordownload.nsf/0/297F40B99200B70B80257C0 B003BE69E/$File/Alton+Sports+Centre+Feasibility+Report_Redacted-1013.pdf**.
- This website contains a summary document for a feasibility study on the construction of a new sport stadium: **www.townsvilleenterprise.com.au/2013%20Townsville%20 Stadium%20Feasibility%20Study%20-%20Summary.pdf**.
- For a comprehensive approach to the development of a feasibility study, see **www.norfolknet.com/norfolk/pr/ngf1113.pdf**, which deals with the proposed Town of Norfolk Golf Course, Massachusetts.
- A detailed approach to needs analysis is provided by the Global Leisure Group's 2004 Kaitaia Swimming Pool Feasibility Study at **www.fndc.govt.nz/parks/feasibility_ study_kaitaia_pool.pdf**.

CHAPTER 15

Undertaking cost–benefit analysis

LEARNING OUTCOMES

At the end of this chapter readers will be able to:

- understand the concept of cost–benefit analysis, and how it can be used to measure the economic, social and cultural impact of sport events on the cities and regions hosting the events
- explain the components of cost–benefit analysis in sport, especially the economic impacts, which include spending, income, employment and multiplier effects
- identify, and provide qualitative measures for, the less tangible impacts, such as civic pride, traffic flows, aesthetic development, environmental improvement and so on
- lead a cost–benefit project for a sport enterprise.

CHAPTER SUMMARY

This chapter examines the application of cost–benefit analysis to sport enterprise activities, with a special emphasis on programmes and events. Cost–benefit analysis has become an essential tool for both estimating and measuring the costs and benefits that accrue to cities and communities from hosting sport events. It is also an important mechanism for gauging the value arising from community physical recreation programmes. The chapter commences with a discussion of the underlying principles of cost–benefit analysis and how it can assist in making best use of scarce organizational and government resources. This leads into a detailed review of economic impact statements, the ways in which they are constructed and how they deliver 'dollar' outcomes. Particular attention will be given to their validity and how they can be manipulated to give exaggerated results. This will be followed by a discussion of the relationship between economic impact statements and cost–benefit analysis, and how non-economic benefits and costs may be translated into quantitative measures.

ECONOMIC IMPACTS IN SPORT

State governments, cities and local councils around the world put many resources into securing major sport events. They argue that running a major sport event is a good investment because it provides a major economic boost to the local economy. At the same time there are many consultants who claim to be experts in producing economic impact statements for major sport events. These statements are used to either convince a government that an event will produce a significant economic impact, or that it has produced an impact. In both cases the figures can be easily exaggerated for a number of reasons that will be discussed in a later section of this chapter. It is therefore essential that sport administrators understand what economic impact statements are all about, and the theory that underpins their construction. So, where do we begin?

Economic impact statements work on the principle that people who go to an event spend money in and around the event. This money is then circulated in the local economy, and, because of a 'ripple' effect, creates indirect and additional levels of spending, income and employment. As a result it is argued that sport events that can attract a large attendance will make a positive impact on the local economy. However, this argument is only partly true, since the real impact comes from people attending from out of town. In other words, locals who attend merely shift their spending from the suburbs to the inner city or just from one product to another. In addition, it is also important to recognize how many people may leave town in order to get away from the event. They are known as 'avoiders'. There is also the problem of identifying people who changed their itinerary to come to town for this event rather than another. These are the 'time-switchers'. Also, there are those people who were in town anyway and just happened to attend the event. These are the 'casuals'. There is also the confounding problem of using attendance figures to establish the number of out-of-towners who came for the event. A 100,000 attendance looks good to the event organizers, but is not so attractive to civic leaders if only 10 per cent come from outside the host city. Conversely, a crowd of 50,000, 50 per cent of whom are from outside the city, will deliver the greater economic impact. Therefore, attendance figures alone are a poor indicator of an event's economic impact. Table 15.1 lists a sample of sport events held in the UK from 1997 to 2003, and shows the breakdown of local and out-of town visitors.

Another important thing to note is that, while a sport event may incur an operating loss, it may still produce a net benefit to the host city if it attracts sufficient out-of-towners to compensate for the loss. This state of affairs has regularly occurred with the Formula 1 Grand Prix held in Melbourne every March. It is a costly event to run, since it not only involves setting up the facilities and providing a safe track, but also involves an annual payment of a multimillion-dollar fee to the event owner. At last count it was more than AUD 25 million. Additionally, revenues from staging the event have rarely covered expenses, which means that the event always runs at a loss. The Victorian State Government and the City of Melbourne have supported this loss-making event for nearly fifteen years on the grounds that it attracts thousands of visitors from interstate and overseas who not only stay for up to one week each, but also spend extravagantly during their stay. The event will be hosted by Melbourne until at least 2015.

TABLE 15.1 Attendance and visitor profiles for selected sport events in the UK

Event	Host city	Attendances	Out-of-towner visitors (%)
1997 World Badminton	Glasgow	22,000	62
1997 Cornhill Cricket Test Match	Birmingham	73,000	92
1997 Women's British Open Golf	Sunningdale	50,000	99
1999 European Showjumping	Hickstead	40,000	55
1999 World Judo	Birmingham	16,000	87
2000 Flora London Marathon	Gateshead	300,000	57
2001 World Half Marathon	Bristol	15,000	45
2003 World Cup Triathlon	Manchester	31,000	85

Source: UK Sport (2004).

NON-ECONOMIC IMPACTS

It is also important to understand that major sport events often produce more than economic benefits. They can also produce many social, environmental and cultural benefits for the host city, including a strengthening of civic pride, a beautification of the surroundings, a stronger international image and urban renewal through the stimulus to inner-city infrastructure. However, it can also come with substantial economic, social and environmental costs. There are not only the costs of building the sports infrastructure to support the event, but also the expenses of running the event, the loss of amenity and convenience, inner-city congestion and an increasing cost associated with ensuring a secure climate for players, officials and spectators. This wider approach is called cost–benefit analysis (CBA). In some cases the economic benefits may be overwhelmed by social and environmental costs. In other cases the economic benefits may be complemented by social and environmental benefits. No two events will ever deliver the same bundle of benefits and costs.

THE RATIONALE FOR PUBLIC SUPPORT OF SPORT EVENTS

It is one thing to claim that a sport event is an integral part of a community's cultural fabric, and should be supported because it can attract an audience, get people talking and make them feel better about themselves. It is another thing to convince government officials that it is sufficiently important to warrant a subsidy, grant or some other form of taxpayer support. This issue arises frequently in sport in the USA, where cities are prepared to build, at taxpayers' expense, multimillion-dollar stadia to attract a professional football, baseball, basketball or ice-hockey franchise (Euchner 1993; Leeds and van

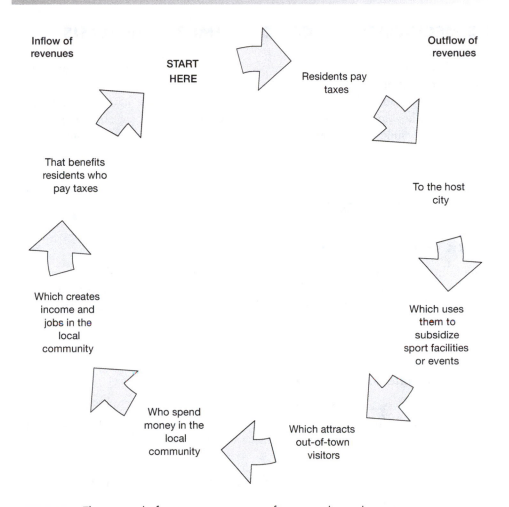

FIGURE 15.1 The rationale for taxpayer support of sport stadia and events

Allmen 2011; Winfree and Rosentraub 2012). So, how do they justify the spending of scarce community resources on the construction of a stadium or arena for the use of an often privately owned sport team? The same question arises when one examines the hosting of large-scale sport festivals such as the Olympic and Commonwealth Games, where the combined capital and operating costs can exceed AUD 3,000 million. The answer is embedded in the proposition that the investment of taxpayers' funds will yield a return that makes the whole community better off. The scale of the return is heavily dependent upon the number of visitors attracted to the event, and the amount of money they spend during their stay in the host city. This relationship between taxpayer subsidies, event impact and community payoff is illustrated in Figure 15.1.

This outflow of funds to generate a consequent inflow of revenue can be viewed as a 'virtuous cycle of community development' (Howard and Crompton 2004: 105). However, the cycle becomes virtuous only when the flow of revenue and associated benefits exceeds the flow of funds into the event or stadium.

THE MECHANICS OF ECONOMIC IMPACT ANALYSIS

The mechanics of doing an economic impact statement are reasonably straightforward once the jargon is deconstructed and the steps identified. Fundamentally, the key to an effective analysis is to establish, first, how many out-of-town visitors have come just for the event, second, how long they stayed for, third, how much they spent on average per day and, finally, how much of their spending stayed within the host city and how much leaked to other places and regions.

SIMULATION EXERCISE 15.1

Buick City Lawn Bowls tournament

The following fictitious case illustrates the steps required to undertake an economic impact analysis for a sport event. It involves the conduct of a lawn bowls tournament. We, a local business consulting business, have been invited to examine its impact on the local community. We were careful to take it step by step, and be both rational and cautious in our approach.

Step 1: Define and describe the event

We were thus given the brief to examine the Buick City Autumn Lawn Bowls Classic, a tournament for club players aged sixty years and over. The location is the Buick City Bowls Club. The event was held in the first week of September.

Step 2: Calculate the number of visitors to Buick City for the event

We counted the number of occupied hotel or motel rooms and bed and breakfast accommodation and counted the number of registered participants. We excluded local participants: they are not visitors. We also excluded visitors not there for the bowls tournament, but who had come for other unrelated reasons. It was found that the number of bowls visitors was 1,000, although there were 1,200 participants. The number of out-of-towners who participated in the event is consequently 1,000.

Step 3: Survey a representative sample of visitors

We used a survey of out-of-town participants (i.e. visitors) to establish the average number of days stayed, and average spending per visitor. The average number of days stayed per visitor was estimated to be five days. The average spending per visitor was estimated to be $150 per day, which equals $750 per bowls visitor.

We checked to see if extreme spending by some visitors skewed the average upwards. We found that the average or mean ($750) was higher than the median spending ($600). The median is the figure that splits the visitor spending 50 per cent above and 50 per cent below. In this case, the majority of visitors spent less than $750. We also made sure that different visitor types were accounted for: overseas, interstate, nearby city, nearby town. We were aware that overseas visitors generally spend more than nearby visitors.

Step 4: Calculate total visitor expenditure

We then went on to calculate total visitor expenditure by multiplying the number of out-of-town visitors by average spending during their visit (that is, 1,000 × $750 = $750,000).

Step 5: Calculate any time-switching factor

We were aware that time-switching relates to the number of people who intended to visit Buick City earlier in the year, but changed their schedules to fit in with the bowls tournament. In other words, they would have come anyway. The survey found that 100 of the bowls-related visitors were time-switchers (equal to 100 × $750 = $75,000 visitor expenditure).

Step 6: Calculate net visitor expenditure (NVE)

Time-switcher spending is subtracted from total visitor expenditure ($750,000 less $75,000). This gives the net visitor expenditure of $675,000.

Step 7: Use a multiplier to account for the ripple effect from spending on accommodation, food, entertainment, transport and personal services

We also noted that 'multipliers' are used to estimate the overall impact of spending on community income and employment levels. Multiplier ratios are calculated from input–output tables that economists construct in modelling regional economies. Multipliers can vary between industry sectors – where 2 is high and 1 is low. The higher the spending leakage to suppliers of goods and services outside the host city, the lower is the multiplier. The regional leisure multiplier for this event is listed as 1.5, which is relatively high.

Step 8: Calculate the economic impact of the Buick City Autumn Lawn Bowls Classic

The net visitor expenditure of $675,000 is multiplied by 1.5 to take into account the ripple effect of the extra income and expenditure generated from visitor spending. Overall, we found a $1 million addition to aggregate community income, which is, at first glance, quite impressive. However, it needs to be repeated that steps 1 to 8 provide an estimation of the economic impact only.

Costing the benefit

Having an idea of the economic impact of a sport event on the host community is important information to have, but it tells us nothing about the cost of making it happen. Did the event provide value for money or was the benefit minuscule in comparison to the outlay to achieve it? In these instances it makes sense to convert the benefit study into a broader cost–benefit calculus. This can be done by working through the following four steps.

Step 9: Calculate costs of staging the event

We immediately understood that the event costs could be divided into capital and operating costs. The capital costs included clubhouse refurbishment of $500,000, rink resurfacing of $200,000 and landscaping of $100,000, which produced a total capital cost of $800,000. At first glance this is a valued outcome, since these facilities are an asset. However, it is also a lost opportunity. That is, the costs could have been used to deliver other benefits, which may have included a school hall, an art gallery or a health centre.

We found that the operating costs/expenses were substantial, but not excessive. They comprised wages and staff payments of $100,000, promotions of $50,000 and general administration of $50,000. Total operating costs for the tournament were therefore $200,000.

Step 10: Calculate event revenues

We noted that the revenues comprised entry fees of $50,000, sponsorship of $50,000 and a government grant of $100,000. Total revenue for the tournament was therefore $200,000. Coincidentally, the revenue figure perfectly matched the operating expense figure.

Step 11: Calculate the net economic benefit (NEB)

To ensure a broader compilation of benefits and costs we did two things. First, we added the total revenue amount to the $1 million economic impact. We also subtracted the operating costs and amortized the share of the capital costs from the gross economic benefit. We consequently found the NEB to be $800,000. This comprised $1 million economic impact less $200,000 share of capital cost (allocated 25 per cent amortization in Year 1 of four years) less $200,000 operating cost, plus $200,000 event revenue. Had we allocated the total capital cost to this year's event, the NEB would have been only $200,000. But this would have been excessive in view of the fact that the facilities would have to be used for at least another three years.

Step 12: Do a cost–benefit ratio

A cost–benefit ratio can be calculated by dividing total benefits by total costs. That is, $1 million plus $200,000 of benefits is divided by $200,000 of expenses plus

$200,000 of amortized capital to produce a ratio of 1.2/0.4, which is 3:1. This means that, for every dollar-cost involved in delivering the event, there was a $3 benefit. Clearly, the bowls tournament is good for Buick City.

In summary, in undertaking an impact analysis a number of important tasks need to be undertaken. In the above example the process begins with a brief description of the event and ends with the calculation of the economic impact, followed by estimations of additional benefits and costs. But we also need to be aware that the figures are subject to error, and there are also non-economic benefits and costs to consider in order to obtain a broad overview of benefits and costs. These factors were conveniently pushed to the side in this example.

MARGINS FOR ERROR

At first glance the figures that come out of an economic impact analysis look impressive. For the most part they are conducted by consulting businesses with experience in the field, and are supported by a valid conceptual framework. There is also a strong internal logic to the results, and this gives a study of this type instant credibility. However, the figures are also subject to a high degree of error, and in most instances should be treated with caution. Indeed, some critics argue that a high proportion of impact statements exaggerate the results by a factor of five to ten (Howard and Crompton 2004: 109; Bourg and Gouguet 2007: 51; Matheson 2008: 97). The pressures to stretch the numbers were exemplified in a 2012 Dallas Olympic Bid Committee claim that the Games would produce a USD 4,000 million benefit. The evidence for this figure was very flimsy indeed.

These exaggerations are not difficult to make because at each stage of the impact evaluation methodological uncertainties arise. First, the out-of-town visitor numbers are calculated from samples of accommodation estimates, the residences of people who attend the event and in-bound tourist statistics. These databases provide strong ballpark figures, but in no way constitute accurate figures. Second, the average expenditures per visitor per day are also subject to error. They are collected through questionnaires distributed to a sample of relevant informants. However, it is never easy to secure a representative sample of visitors, and this is a problem since spending between visitor types can vary considerably. Moreover, when people are invited to record their recollection of how much they spent and what they spent it on, the responses can be quite unreliable. On the one hand, some spending may have been forgotten, or deliberately hidden to avoid embarrassment, while on the other hand spending may have been topped up to confirm one's self-importance. Finally, the weight of the multiplier may be inappropriate. While multipliers are tested and validated through various forms of input–output analysis and statistical benchmarking, they are often used incorrectly. It is never clear exactly how much initial spending is recirculated in the host city or town, and how much is redirected or leaked to external businesses and employers. In some instances the multiplier can be as high as 1:8 (i.e. for every dollar of visitor spending there is a $1.80 increase in overall economic activity) or as low as 1:1 (i.e. for every dollar of visitor spending there is only a $1.10 increase in overall economic activity. The problematic use of multipliers for sport event impact statements is discussed in detail in Howard and Crompton (2004) and Li *et al.* (2001).

PROBLEMS IN DOING IMPACT STATEMENTS

As indicated previously, there are a number of crucial steps involved in putting together an economic impact statement. In this section attention will be paid to three important activities. The first is to establish a framework by which to classify events so that useful comparisons and contrasts can be made once the results have been tabulated. The second activity is to set up a process for collecting data on the number of out-of-town visitors for the event. The third is to design a method for estimating visitor expenditure. The final activity is to agree on a reasonable method for calculating the final impact, being careful to distinguish between expenditure, output and employment.

Typologizing sport events

There are many ways of distinguishing between different types of sport events, but when looking at their impacts the following typology is useful. First, events can be classified because of their regularity or frequency. That is, are they held on a regular basis, which could be every week (in the case of a sport league) or every four years (in the case of the Rugby Union World Cup)? Second, they may be mainly spectator events, or alternatively participant-based events. These two differences can be illustrated as in Table 15.2.

TABLE 15.2 Typology of sporting events		
	Participant-based	*Spectator-based*
Frequent	Community tennis	(Australian) National Rugby League game
Infrequent	Sydney city-to-surf fun run	Formula 1 Grand Prix

It is also possible to add a third dimension by using a bubble chart to signal the scale of the event and its likely economic impact. A large bubble indicates a large impact, while a small bubble indicates a marginal to slight impact.

It is therefore technically possible for an irregular participant-based event (bubble 2) to secure a larger eco-impact than a regular spectator-based event (bubble 3).

Estimating the number of out-of-town visitors

As indicated previously, the scale of any economic impact for a sport event is directly related to the number of visitors who are in town to attend the event. This begs the question as to how to best calculate this figure. Generally speaking, a composite number is generated from hotel reservations and from tickets purchased by interstate and

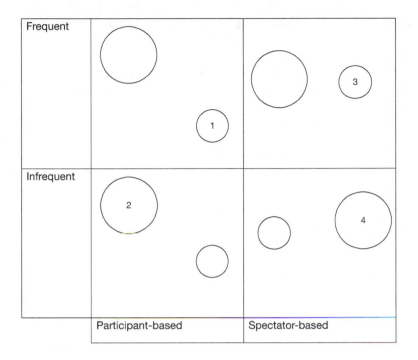

1 Monthly basketball tournament
2 London Marathon
3 English Premier League game
4 Cricket test match

FIGURE 15.2 Typological possibilities

international visitors. The numbers can be refined by identifying specific categories of visitors, including athletes, officials and media representatives.

However, the task of calculating just how many people came just for the event, and how many people went elsewhere because of the event, can become quite messy. There are a number of different visitor and home-resident movements during the event that need to be identified.

It is also important to discard all those visitors who would have visited anyway, but rescheduled their visits to coincide with the event, as well as those people who just happened to be visiting when the event was running. It should also be noted that attendance levels are not a good proxy for the number of out-of-town visitors, since a significant proportion will usually be local residents. There are also some negative visitor movements that involve local residents deciding to leave the host city for the duration of event. In fact there are eight issues to deal with here.

First, it is not just a matter of counting the number of people who came to the city only because the event was on. These event-fan visitors are clearly important, because they directly increase the amount of spending. However, they constitute only one segment of people affected by the staging of the event. A second segment, as previously noted, is the casuals. However, since casuals are defined as tourists who would have been in town, even if the games had not been held, they should not be included in any extra spending calculation. A similar problem exists with time-switchers, the third segment who would have visited the city at another time, but changed their itineraries to coincide with the event. They, too, should not be included in the extra-spending calculation. A fourth segment is the extensioners, who would have come anyway, but extend their stay because of the event. These people should clearly be included in the calculation of additional spending. Similarly, home-stayers, the fifth segment, should be included since they are defined as people who may have taken holidays elsewhere, but chose to stay home and attend the event instead. The sixth segment is the avoiders, who would have visited the host city had the event not been on. The seventh segment, the runaways, are residents who leave the city during the event, while changers, the eighth segment, effectively do the same thing by deciding to shift their out-of-town holidays to the event time. These final three segments consequently take spending away from the host city, rather than adding to it. The spending impact of each of the above eight groups can be illustrated as in Table 15.3.

TABLE 15.3 Visitor and resident segments for sport event evaluation

Type of group	Demographic weight	Impact on host city spending
Event-fans (visitors)	XXX	positive
Casuals (visitors)	XX	neutral
Time-switchers (visitors)	XX	neutral
Extensioners (visitors)	XX	positive
Home-stayers (residents)	XX	positive
Avoiders (visitors)	X	neutral
Runaways (residents)	XX	negative
Changers (residents)	X	negative

Source: based on research by Preuss (2004).

Visitor spending

It is one thing to calculate the number of people who came to town in order to attend the event, and who would not have otherwise visited. It is another thing to collect reliable data on their spending patterns. It is therefore important to design a comprehensive but clear questionnaire that can capture the proper levels of visitor expenditure. There are two crucial steps to be taken when designing a questionnaire. The first is to break down visitor spending into a number of categories, being careful to distinguish between event-related spending and other spending. An example of how this can be done is given in Table 15.4.

The second step is to segment the visitors into specific types. This allows the results to show not only what type of visitors predominated, but also how much each visitor type spent. Research has shown that competitors spend less per day than officials. The heaviest spenders are media representatives. An English study found that, whereas a typical competitor spent GBP 55 to GBP 65 per day, media people spent from GBP 100 to GBP 125 per day (UK Sport 2004).

TABLE 15.4 Categories of visitor expenditure template

Type of expenditure	Amount spent during visit ($)
Admission/entry fees to event	
Food and beverages at event	
Food and beverages not at event	
Night clubs and bars (charges, drinks etc.)	
Retail shopping (clothing, souvenirs, gifts etc.)	
Accommodation expenses (hotel, motel etc.)	
Motor vehicle expenses (fuel, oil, repairs, parking fees etc.)	
Rental car expenses	
Event-related merchandise	
Other expenses	

Non-economic benefits and costs

In assessing the impact of a sport event on the host city or region, nearly all of the space is given to the economic benefits, which, as noted previously, centres on visitor expenditure and its spending, employment and tax collection spin-offs. When challenged, the impact statement proponents will cautiously review the financial costs incurred in securing the economic benefits. While this allows for a more effective analysis of the net benefits flowing from the event, it does not tell the full story. In reality there is often a clutch of non-economic benefits and costs that are relegated to the fine print at best, or ignored at worst. These benefits and costs may not have the same weight as the economic

TABLE 15.5 Non-economic benefits and costs associated with sporting events

Factor	Benefit	Cost
Traffic congestion and increase in travel time		X
Loss of amenity due to event occupying space or facility usually used for other activities		X
Increase in community and civic pride through identification with successful event	X	
Homeless and low-income residents moved out of city in order to accommodate visitors		X
Environment cleaned up to impress visitors	X	
Increase in security leading to fall in crime rate	X	
Marginalized groups using event to protest and disrupt commuters and visitors	X	X
Inner-city crowding encouraging vandalism		X

outputs, but they are sufficiently important to demand attention. These additional factors are listed in Table 15.5.

WHAT ABOUT THE LEGACY?

Another way of viewing the impact of a sport event on the host city is to compile a list of its expected legacy. The 'legacy' is now used to describe all those benefits – and sometimes costs – that linger well into the future. Legacies have now become important points of discussion when looking at the ways in which host cities can gain from an event experience. Legacies are thus concerned more with long-term tangible and intangible benefits arising from the event. They can be subtle but significant, such as an expanded sense of community pride and confidence, and thus be a catalyst for social development. They can also take the form of an increase in the skills of young people because of their previous event management experiences. It may be exemplified in a remaking of the physical environment through large-scale landscaping and land reclamation. Additionally, it can be the result of a building programme that left a base of quality facilities for use by elite athletes, spectators and community groups. It can also take the form of large-scale urban renewal, as occurred in both Kuala Lumpur and Manchester in their preparation for the 1998 and 2002 Commonwealth Games respectively. Consequently, the breadth and scale of the legacy can vary considerably. For example, while the host city may have delivered an array of sport facilities, they may have been located in an inconvenient place, required heavy maintenance and are subject to low usage. In a worst-case situation the costs of maintaining the facilities may regularly exceed the revenues gained from their use. In other words, not only was a capital cost incurred, but ongoing losses have to be met by the community into the future. This is not a good legacy to have.

COMPARING THE ECONOMIC IMPACT OF MEGA-SPORT EVENTS

It is now commonplace for a sport event to be evaluated with specific reference to its economic impact in particular, and its overall benefits and costs in general. In Table 15.1 attendance and visitor profiles of some recent sport events held in the UK were listed. It can readily be seen that some events have a major economic impact, while others do not. The differences can in the main be explained by the scale of the event as measured by the number of players, officials and spectators, the length of time occupied by the event and the length of the visitor stay.

The impacts between events vary enormously. At one end of the spectrum are mega-sport events such as the Olympic Games, world-football World Cup, Commonwealth Games, Asian Games and Grand Slam tennis tournament events, while at the other end are community-based sports festivals, mass-participation fun runs and sports competitions. In each case, though, the tools for measuring the impacts are the same. It is just the scale of the operation that varies. Table 15.6 lists the estimated economic impact of a sample of Australian sport events.

Again there are significant differences between events. The figures also confirm that it is not raw attendances that drive the scale of the impact, but rather the number of out-of-

TABLE 15.6 Estimates of economic impact at selected Australian sport events, Melbourne 2002 to 2012

Event	Attendance	Out-of-town visitors	Average visitor expenditure (AUD)	Total visitor expenditure (AUD mn)	Gross economic impact (AUD mn)
Formula 1 Grand Prix	150,000	50,000	1,200	60	70
Australian Open Tennis	450,000	30,000	720	22	38
Masters Games	25,000	10,000	1,200	12	2
Spring Horse Racing Carnival	490,000	50,000	1,500	75	94

town visitors that are attracted, the time spent in the host city and the amount of money they spend. While the economic impact is always promoted with a degree of authority, it must be remembered that it has a margin of error and should not be confused with a cost–benefit ratio.

CASE STUDY 15.1

The 2003 Rugby World Cup

The game

Rugby Union is one of the world's oldest team sports, having been codified in the 1860s in England. It spread around the world, and became particularly popular in English-speaking colonies such as Australia, New Zealand and South Africa. It also developed a strong presence in the Pacific Islands, parts of South America, France, and Italy. It subsequently emerged as a major international sport, with around ninety countries affiliated with its governing body, the International Rugby Board (IRB).

The inaugural Rugby World Cup (RWC) competition was held in Australia and New Zealand in 1987, and has subsequently become a major international sport event. Rugby World Cup 1987 was broadcast to seventeen countries and had a cumulative audience of 300 million people, while the tournament finished with a net surplus of GBP 1 million after accumulating gross commercial income of GBP 3.3 million. Since then there has been a consistent increase in match attendance, world television audiences, commercial income and net surpluses for each of the tournaments, as Table 15.7 indicates.

By any measure, the RWC has been a success, and has secured itself a top five international sport festival position. The host country consequently has an opportunity to exploit the tournament as a catalyst for economic and cultural development.

TABLE 15.7 Rugby World Cup tournaments, 1987 to 1999

Year	Place	Total match attendance (mn)	Cumulative television audiences (mn)	Gross commercial income (GBP mn)	Net surplus (GBP mn)
1987	Australia/ New Zealand	0.6	930	13.3	1.0
1991	England	1.0	1,750	23.6	5.0
1995	South Africa	1.0	2,670	30.3	17.6
1999	England	1.7	3,000	70.0	47.0

Source: URS Finance and Economics (2004: 2).

Tournament organization

The 2003 RWC was hosted by Australia and a total of forty-eight games were played involving forty pool matches and eight finals. Games were spread across eleven venues in ten cities (Adelaide, Brisbane, Canberra, Gosford, Launceston, Melbourne, Perth, Sydney, Townsville and Wollongong). The semi-finals and final were played in Sydney at the Telstra Stadium. Twenty nations contested RWC 2003, divided into four pools of five teams. All eight quarter-finalists from RWC 1999 qualified automatically. They were Argentina, Australia, England, France, New Zealand, Scotland, South Africa and Wales. The remaining twelve teams were Fiji, Samoa, Japan, Canada, Uruguay, Ireland, Italy, Georgia, Romania, Namibia, Tonga and the USA. The tournament drew large attendances and attracted thousands of overseas visitors. There was general agreement that it had a strong economic impact on the host nation.

Visitor numbers

A number of surveys were undertaken and it was estimated that a total of 65,000 international visitors came to Australia primarily as a result of RWC 2003. The breakdown of total visitor numbers is indicated in Table 15.8.

The majority of international visitors were from the UK and Europe, while the remainder came from New Zealand, the Pacific Islands, South Africa and the Americas. Rugby fans accounted for just over 60,000 visitors, while media and corporate personnel each accounted for an additional 2,500 visitors.

TABLE 15.8 Estimated number of international visitors for RWC 2003

RWC visitors/ supporters	Media visitors	RWC corporate visitors	Total
60,000	2,500	2,500	65,000

Source: URS Finance and Economics (2004: 3).

TABLE 15.9 Average spending by international visitors at RWC 2003

Region	Total number of visitors	Average spend per visit 2003 (AUD)	Average length of stay (nights)	Average total daily spend (AUD)	Total trip spend (AUD mn)
UK/Europe	31,794	8,300	36	230	256
New Zealand/Asia	19,413	3,150	15	210	59
Africa	10,638	6,260	24	260	65
Americas	3,155	6,740	22	306	21
Total	**65,000**				**401**

Source: URS (2004: 8).

TABLE 15.10 Expenditure by item for international visitors at RWC 2003

Item	Total expenditure (AUD millions)
Package tours	79
Organized tours	12
International airfares	104
Domestic airfares	3
Self-drive transport	6
Petrol	3
Other motor vehicle costs	6
Other transport	8
Shopping	45
Food, drink and accommodation	87
Gambling	5
Entertainment	6
Communications	6
Other	31
Total	**401**

Source: URS Finance and Economics (2004: 9).

Visitor expenditure

Visitors from the UK and Europe were found to have the highest per-visitor expenditure of all visitors at AUD 8,300, followed by visitors from the Americas

($6,740), Africa ($6,260) and New Zealand ($3,150), providing a total-trip spend for all visitors of AUD 401 million (Table 15.9).

Main expenditure items

Table 15.10 indicates the breakdown of expenditure for international visitors. Key spending items of international visitors were accommodation, food and drink along with airfares, package tours and retail shopping.

The impact

The impact of RWC 2003 can be summarized around three dimensions: audience levels, visitor expenditure and economic impact.

Audience levels

Audience levels were spread over forty-eight matches spread across eleven venues in ten cities around Australia. In addition, the event was broadcast to an estimated global cumulative audience of 3,400 million. Finally, total RWC tickets sold exceeded 1.8 million and were valued at nearly AUD 200 million.

Visitor expenditure

Around 65,000 international RWC visitors from the UK and Europe, the Asia-Pacific region, Africa and the Americas travelled to Australia, and they spent a total of AUD 401 million. An estimated 49 per cent of visitors travelled from the UK and Europe, nearly 13 per cent from New Zealand and Asia, 16 per cent from Africa and 5 per cent from the Americas. In addition, these international visitors spent AUD 6,308 each and stayed in Australia for around three weeks. It was also found that locals (Australians) purchased RWC tickets valued at AUD 137 million and made nearly 180,000 interstate trips to attend RWC matches. They collectively spent AUD 142 million.

Economic impact

By any measure, RWC 2003 had a significant economic impact. It generated AUD 494 million in additional industry sales in the Australian economy, and also created an additional 4,476 full- and part-time jobs. At the same time, the Australian Government secured an additional AUD 55 million in revenue, while an additional AUD 289 million was added to Australia's gross domestic product. Finally, an additional AUD 27 million in longer-term tourism sales was estimated to have occurred in 2004 and 2005.

However, like all other studies of this type, the data should be treated with caution. It should be remembered that the above data focus on visitor expenditure only and do not take into account the costs of running the event or the non-economic costs and benefits. In addition, when compared to the Sydney 2000 Olympic Games, RWC 2003 had a lesser impact. Whereas RWC 2003 attracted 65,000 international visitors, Sydney 2000 attracted nearly 100,000. The total attendance figure for Sydney 2000 was 6.7 million, nearly 5 million more than RWC 2003.

SIMULATION EXERCISE 15.2

The Big-City Open Tennis Championship

So, what is an appropriate model for working through the economic impact of a sport event? In the following fictitious case we assume you (the reader) have been appointed to the event assessment team of the Great Exaggerations Sport Marketing group (GESM). One of your first tasks is to write up an economic impact statement for the Big-City Open Tennis Championship (BCOTC). You are expected to produce a cost–benefit report as well as provide a succinct statement on the economic impact of the event on the host city. You have been given the following information to work from.

The case details

- Surveys showed that 100,000 separate people or visitors attended the BCOTC, many of whom went three or more times. Around 78,000 (or just under 80 per cent) of these people came from metropolitan areas.
- The BCOTC also attracted a cumulative at-ground audience of 450,000. This is in marked contrast to the 220,000 fans who attended the one-day international cricket matches over the summer period.
- Of the 22,000 visitors who came from out of town, 16,000 were from interstate and 6,000 were from overseas.
- Around 1,000 interstate visitors and another 1,000 overseas visitors said they would have travelled to Big-City irrespective of the BCOTC being played at this time.
- Visitor surveys showed that the interstate visitors spent on average $1,000 during their stay in Big-City, while overseas visitors spent an average of $3,000 each.
- The survey also found that 500 foreign media representatives were in town for the BCOTC. On average, they each spent $4,000 while covering the event. These media types were not included in the previous visitor figures.
- Coincidentally, an international convention of Southern Ocean Fish Life researchers was held at the Big-City Convention Centre at exactly the same time as the BCOTC. They accounted for an additional 5,000 visitors. They also paid $200 to attend a forum on 'Fishing as a Spiritual Experience'. It was estimated that this event produced an economic impact of $10 million.

- You were also provided with an income and expenditure multiplier. You were no economist, but you understood that the inclusion of a ripple effect arising from the initial expenditure was needed to calculate the overall economic impact. A consulting economist provided you with an expenditure multiplier figure of 2. This seemed excessive, but the economist suggested that there were only going to be small leakages from the subsequent rounds of spending.
- The BCOTC received massive media exposure. Just over 150 hours of live television were broadcast to ninety countries, including the USA and most of Western Europe.
- Unfortunately, there was also massive traffic congestion in Big-City for the entire tournament. Many commuters were late for work and many fans were late for matches.
- The ticketing arrangements turned out to be a fiasco. People often had to wait up to 50 minutes to make their telephone and internet bookings. Moreover, collection points were often under-serviced. Queues were sometimes up to 500 metres long.
- Some very expensive landscaping around the new city square added to the general attractiveness of the area leading up to Big-City Park.
- GESM was also advised that $20 million had been spent on a facility upgrade. It was clear that these figures must be included in any cost–benefit analysis, and it was also noted that the facility had an operating life of ten years. Not only was the upgrade expensive, but it also cut severely into adjoining parkland. Many 100-year-old elm trees were destroyed in the process.
- The scheduling of the BCOTC also coincided with the opening of the Big-City Aquarium. It was found that this new attraction boosted the number of out-of-town visitors by a further 5,000.
- A follow-up survey of Big-City residents (including business owners) found that 90 per cent of respondents believed that the event was well run, and felt that it enhanced the status of Big-City as a truly international and cosmopolitan city. They also felt it demonstrated the ability of Big-City to mount premier sport events.

Big-City therefore not only secured substantial benefits from this event, but it also incurred a number of costs. However, it needs to be remembered that any cost–benefit analysis is prone to error and there is also the added difficulty of

TABLE 15.11 Big-City Open Tennis Championship – visitor expenditure

	Total visitors	Average expenditure ($)	Total visitor expenditure ($ millions)
Interstate visitor expenditure	15,000	1,000	15
Overseas visitor expenditure	5,000	3,000	15
Foreign media visitors	500	4,000	2

quantifying intangible impacts. There is also the problem of deciding how many people came from out of town *just* to attend the event. Also, who decides the value of the multiplier, is our sample of visitors really representative and how accurate are the visitor estimates of their daily expenditure? Finally, many non-economic impacts are ignored by event promoters, who want to put the best spin on the event's impact. So, just what net gains did Big-City get out of this event?

Model answers

Once the dust had settled it was found that 15,000 interstate visitors came just for the event, 5,000 international visitors came just for the event, and 500 foreign media also attended. The amount of visitors' expenditure is shown in Table 15.11.

Overall, the gross impact was $64 million. When the amortized facility upgrade cost is subtracted this leaves a net impact of $62 million.

At the same time, the non-economic impacts need to be evaluated. There has been noise and congestion and a loss of trees and flora. But there was also a high level of international exposure and a swell of civic pride. Despite the build-up of non-economic costs, it can only be concluded that the tennis championships were good for Big-City. So long as it attracts a significant pool of visitors from interstate and overseas it will be worth the cost and the time.

SIMULATION EXERCISE 15.3

The Pleasantville Special Games

In this fictitious case the Pleasantville Organizing Committee for the Special Games (POCSG) keep telling us that the 2014 Special Games provided a variety of benefits, particularly to the city of Pleasantville. This is possibly quite true, but the whole Special Games experience also involved significant costs. A number of studies have attempted to sort out these costs, and to balance them against the benefits. There are two serious problems to consider when doing this type of analysis. The first is to ensure that all the costs and benefits are taken into account. The second is to quantify them, but this is not as easy as it sounds. For example, just what costs and benefits are attributable to the event? For example, Pleasantville had more tourists during the Special Games, but do we know exactly how many of these tourists came just for the event? And how do we put a number – a dollar value if you like – on the environmental improvements associated with the Swamplands site, or the congestion that came with the crowds? In other words, how do we measure some of these costs and benefits?

Anyway, you have been invited by POCSG to compile an inventory of the costs and benefits of the Special Games. You also need to say something about the social impact of the Games by noting that some people from low-cost accommodation and housing were forced out on to the streets. Also, where do we fit the euphoric community feeling associated with the torch relay and the Special Games themselves? Is this a legitimate benefit and, if so, what do you call it and how do you quantify it? Can it be quantified? There are some data available, a lot of which are useful, and some of which are not. A selection of useful material is listed below:

- The total cost of all sporting facilities for the Special Games is about $1,000 million. They were purpose built: that is, without the Games they would not have been built. At the same time, the funds were borrowed from a bank, and had to be paid back over a ten-year period at an annual interest rate of 10 per cent.
- About 50,000 out-of-town tourists came to Pleasantville just for the Special Games, including 20,000 from interstate.
- Another 20,000 people came from out of town, and just happened to be in Pleasantville during the Special Games.
- In total, 20,000 athletes and officials came from overseas.
- As usual, the media circus also came in big numbers. There were 500 from Pleasantville, 1,000 from the rest of the country and 10,000 from overseas.
- On average, tourists spent thirty days in Pleasantville. Athletes and officials spent twenty days, while media personnel spent twenty-five days.
- The media were the biggest spenders at $600 a day. Next were the overseas tourists at $500 a day, interstate tourists at $400 a day and, finally, athletes and officials at $200 a day.
- The expenditure multiplier is estimated to be a very generous 2.
- Queues increased for many inner-city services. Waiting time was up by thirty minutes, and it impacted on around 500,000 people for about twenty days. The average hourly income for these people was estimated to be $40.
- POCSG total revenue from the running of Special Games was $2,500 million.
- POCSG total expenditure on organization of the Special Games was $2,900 million.
- It was generally agreed that these were the best ever Special Games. We all felt proud about not just our own athletes' performances, but also the very positive image projected to overseas visitors and television viewers.
- The contaminated Swamplands site, which was redeveloped as an urban park, looked great. It had been transformed, and subsequently secured an award from the Save the Planet Agency as a 'model' initiative. It received a very good rating from various other environmental groups as well.

Model answers

The answers have been divided into three parts: visitor expenditure, net economic benefit and non-economic benefits and costs.

Visitor expenditure

Visitor expenditure has been segmented on the basis of tourists being from overseas, from interstate, visiting athletes and officials, and overseas media (Table 15.12).

Having aggregated the different segments of visitor expenditure, total visitor expenditure is calculated to be $920 million.

TABLE 15.12 Visitor expenditure on the Special Games

Visitor type	Numbers	Spent ($)	Total visitor expenditure ($ millions)
Overseas tourists	3,000	15,000	450
Interstate tourists	20,000	12,000	240
Athletes/officials	20,000	4,000	80
Overseas media	10,000	15,000	150

Net economic benefit

The total visitor expenditure of $920 million produces a gross economic benefit of $1,840 million after application of the multiplier of 2. The net economic benefit, however, will also take into account the total capital cost of the venues, and the operating revenue and operating loss on the event. The numbers are listed in Table 15.13.

TABLE 15.13 Net economic benefit from the Special Games

	($ millions)
Gross benefit	1,840
Less capital cost of venues	1,000
Less operating loss	200
Net benefit	640

Following on from these calculations, the net benefit arising from the Special Games is calculated to be $640 million. However, two points need to be made. First, the full capital cost is included in the calculation, whereas it would have been appropriate to include only the amortized cost for Year 1. Second, the multiplier of 2 is very generous, and may be excessive.

Non-economic benefits and costs

The non-economic costs were significant and included, first, the congestion, which was quantified at $200 million, and, second, the homeless problem. However, there were some additional benefits, which included a good Greenpeace rating on the environment, additional civic pride (the feel-good factor), the international TV audience (broader awareness) and infrastructure impacts through the addition of a number of high-quality sport venues.

On balance, Pleasantville secured substantial benefits from the Special Games. However, when the full costs are taken into account, the net benefit is not quite so impressive. However, as with the Big-City case in the previous section of this chapter, the significance of the impact is primarily dependent upon the number of out-of-town visitors and the money they spent in and around the host city. There is also a tendency to highlight the material benefits while ignoring the capital and opportunity cost, and many of the less tangible social and cultural impacts.

RECAP

Cost–benefit analysis and economic impact studies are now essential parts of a sport manager's financial analysis armoury. They enable managers to both plan effectively for their sport's development, and assess the real return on capital expenditure projects and special events. At the same time, cost–benefit analysis and economic impact studies are often subject to significant margins of error. This is because of sampling errors, highly subjective completion of survey questions, the questionable use of multiplier ratios, 'guestimates' of many of the non-economic impacts, and the frequent failure to provide space for opportunity costs.

REVIEW QUESTIONS

With these issues in mind a number of critical questions need to be asked about not only how economic impact and cost–benefit analysis is best undertaken, but also the confidence that should be placed in the results.

1 Why are tourists and visitors an important part of a sport event?

2 When people talk about the economic impact of a sport event on the host city, what do they mean?

3 What are some of the non-economic impacts on sport events?

4 Where do legacies fit when looking at the impact of sport events on host cities?

5 How should one go about measuring legacies?

6 How might the economic impact argument be used to secure government funds for a major sport event?

7 When doing an economic impact study, who exactly should be included in it? Is it just the players, or should it include officials, should it include everyone who turns up to the event, or should it only include those who live in close proximity to the place where the event is being staged? Please explain.

8 When doing an impact study it is important to distinguish between different sets of people who are affected by the event. So, bearing this in mind, what is the difference between 'locals', 'out-of-town visitors', 'avoiders', 'time-switchers' and 'casuals'? Are there any other categories we need to be aware of?

9 How is total visitor expenditure on an event calculated? What are the difficulties involved in calculating this figure?

10 How is an economic multiplier used to calculate the economic impact of a sporting event? And what values are usually given to the multiplier?

11 List the main difficulties in securing accurate measures of economic impacts of sport events.

12 What is the difference between an economic impact statement and a cost–benefit analysis of a sport event? Which is better for deciding where funds should be allocated to obtain the best outcome for a district, town or city?

13 Compare and contrast the economic and other costs and benefits that resulted from the Big-City Open Tennis Championship and the Pleasantville Special Games. Identify the items that are essential for constructing an economic impact analysis as well as those items that are extraneous to the exercise. In particular, how do you deal with the capital costs associated with the event?

14 There seems to be a trend for governments around the world to underestimate the costs of staging mega-sport events. Is this a good thing, and why does it happen so often?

FURTHER READING

An up-to-date critique of economic impact statements and cost–benefit analysis, together with illuminating examples and incidents, are contained in (1) Matheson, V. (2008) 'Mega events: the effect of the world's biggest sport events on local, regional and national economies', in Humphreys, B. and Howard, D. (eds) *The Business of Sports, Volume 1: Perspectives on the Sports Industry*, Westport, CT: Praeger, pp. 81–100; (2) Brown, M., Rascher, D., Nagel, M. and McEvoy, C. (2010) *Financial Management in the Sport Industry*, Scottsdale, AZ: Holcomb Hathaway (Chapter 12: 'Economic impact analysis'); and (3) Bourg, J-F. and Gouguet, J-J. (2007) *The Political Economy of Professional Sport*, Cheltenham: Edward Elgar, pp. 34–40.

An insightful exposition of the different results that come out of an economic impact analysis (EIA) statement on the one hand, and a cost–benefit analysis (CBA) on the other, is provided in Taks, M., Kessene, S., Chalip, L., Green, C. and Martyn, S. (2011) 'Economic impact analysis (EIA) versus cost benefit analysis (CBA): the case of a medium size sport event' *International Journal of Sport Finance*, 6: 187–203. In an examination of the 2005 Pan-American Junior Athletics Championships in Windsor, Canada, it was found that, while the EIA was a positive USD 5.6 million, the CBA produced a negative net benefit of USD 2.4 million.

For an additional analysis of the distinction between impact analysis and cost–benefit analysis, see Kessene, S. (2005) 'Do we need an economic impact study or a cost–benefit analysis of a sport event? *European Sport Management Quarterly*, 2: 133–42. An examination of the costs and benefits of attracting a professional team-sport club to a city, and providing it with a city-funded stadium, is contained in Leeds, M. and von Allmen, P. (2005) *The Economics of Sports*, 2nd edition, Boston, MA: Addison-Wesley (Chapter 7: 'Costs and benefits of a franchise to a city').

An overview of economic impact analysis in sport is provided by Brown, M. and Zuefle, D. (2005) 'Economic impact' in Gillentine, A. and Crow, B. (2005) *Foundations of Sport Management*, Morgantown, WV: Fitness Information Technology, pp. 42–57. For an extended discussion of the topic, see Howard, D. and Crompton, J. (2004) *Financing Sport*, 2nd edition, Morgantown, WV: Fitness Information Technology (Chapter 4: 'Principles of economic impact analysis').

For a succinct review of a study undertaken more than twenty years ago on the impact of an event on a local community, see Turco, D. and Navarro, R. (1993) 'Assessing the economic impact and financial return on investment of a national sporting event', *Sport Marketing Quarterly*, 2(3): 17–23. A useful discussion of how multipliers are constructed, and the distinction between direct, indirect and induced impacts, is contained in Li, M., Hofacre, S. and Mahoney, D. (2001) *Economics of Sport*, Morgantown, WV: Fitness Information Technology (Chapter 7: 'Economic impact of sport').

For a detailed coverage of the short- and long-term impacts of the Olympic Games on various host cities, see Preuss, H. (2004) *The Economics of Staging the Olympics*, Cheltenham: Edward Elgar, especially Chapter 5, which looks at techniques of measuring, Chapter 6, which focuses on tourism and exports, and Chapter 7, which examines investing in the reconstruction of a city.

For a general discussion of the economic impact of various sport events in the United Kingdom, see UK Sport (2004) *Measuring Success: The Economic Impact of Major Sport Events*, London: UK Sport. For a detailed analysis of the impact of the Rugby World Cup 2003, see URS Finance and Economics (2004) *Economic Impact of the Rugby World Cup on the Australian Economy*, Sydney, NSW: New South Wales State Government, Department of Industry, Tourism and Resources. Finally, for a critical look at the social impacts of sport events, see Lenskyi, H. (2002) *The Best Olympics Ever? The Social Impacts of Sydney 2000*, New York: SUNY Press.

USEFUL WEBSITES

- An excellent introduction to economic impact analysis is provided in the following website. Dr Chris Doyle, from the University of Warwick, delivers a highly watchable slide show: **www2.warwick.ac.uk/fac/soc/economics/current/modules/ec340/details/lecture_1_ec340_2013.pdf**.

- Another highly instructive slide show appears in the following site. Angel Barajas, from the University of Vigo, delivers a very solid analysis: **www.slideshare.net/Angel Barajas/measuring-the-economic-impact-of-minor-sport-events**.

- A detailed examination of the 2008 Bob and Skeleton World Championships, which were held in Germany, is contained in the following website. Jan Drengner, Julia Köhler and Mario Geissler, from Chemnitz University, provide a very illuminating study of the event: **www.tu-chemnitz.de/wirtschaft/bwl2/en/download/easm09_1. pdf**.

- A critique of Australian government claims about economic impacts is undertaken in **www.theguardian.com/business/grogonomics/2013/jul/26/sporting-events-economic- benefits**.

- Jonathan Barclay, writing for the Institute of Economic Affairs, found that the economic benefits of hosting mega-sport events are often exaggerated. That is, they typically overestimate the gains and underestimate the costs. He thus found that it was difficult to explain in economic terms the intense competition among cities to hold such events. His commentary can be found at: **www.iea.org.uk/sites/default/ files/publications/files/upldeconomicAffairs340pdfSummary.pdf**.

- The following website houses an excellent article on the 'real' costs of staging mega-sport events. The article was written by Wladimir Andreff in 2012, and is titled 'The winner's curse: why is the cost of sports mega-events so often underestimated?': **http://halshs.archives-ouvertes.fr/docs/00/70/34/66/PDF/Definitely_4_Andreff_in_ Maennig-Zimbalist_final_clean_copy_last_revision_August.pdf**.

References

Allison, L. (2005) *The Global Politics of Sport: The Role of Global Institutions in Sport*, Abingdon: Routledge.

Amis, J. and Cornwell, T. (2005) *Global Sport Sponsorship*, New York: Berg.

Andreff, W. (2007) 'French football: a financial crisis rooted in weak governance', *Journal of Sports Economics*, 8(6): 652–61.

Andreff, W. and Staudohar, P. (2002) 'European and US sports business models', in Barros, C., Ibrahimo, M. and Szymanski, S. (eds) *Transatlantic Sport: The Comparative Economics of North American and European Sport*, Cheltenham: Edward Elgar, pp. 23–49.

Andrews, D. (ed.) (2004) *Manchester United: A Thematic Study*, Abingdon: Routledge.

Anthony, R. and Young, D. (2003) *Management Control in Non-profit Organizations*, 7th edition, New York: McGraw-Hill.

Atrill, P., McLaney, E., Harvey, D. and Jenner, M. (2006) *Accounting: An Introduction*, Melbourne, Vic.: Pearson Education Australia.

Australian Football League (AFL) (1981–2005) *Annual Reports*, Melbourne, Vic.: AFL.

Babatunde, B. and Simmons, R. (2008) 'The profitability of sports teams: international perspectives', in Humphreys, B. and Howard, D. (eds) *The Business of Sports, Volume 1: Perspectives on the Sports Industry*, Westport, CT: Praeger, pp. 33–58.

Bahain, P. (2012) *Downfall: How Rangers FC Self-destructed*, Edinburgh: Frontline Noir.

Baker, K. (2002) *Project Evaluation and Feasibility Analysis for Hospitality Operations*, Putney, NSW: Hospitality Books.

Barajas, A. and Rodriguez, P. (2010) 'Spanish football club finances: crisis and player salaries', *International Journal of Sport Finance*, 5: 52–66.

Barker, M. (2013) 'Sports finance', in Beech, J. and Chadwick, S. (eds) *The Business of Sport Management*, 2nd edition, Harlow: Pearson, pp. 209–29.

Barney, J. (1991) 'Firm resources and sustained competitive advantage', *Journal of Management*, 17: 99–120.

Barney, R., Ween, S. and Martyn, S. (2002) *Selling the Five Rings: The International Olympic Committee and the Rise of Olympic Commercialism*, Salt Lake City, UT: University of Utah Press.

Barrington, R., Murray, D., Schenk, S. and Unger, D. (2013) *Fair Play: Strengthening Integrity and Transparency in Cricket*, Berlin: Transparency International.

Beck-Burridge, M. and Walton, J. (2001) *Sport Sponsorship and Brand Development: The Subaru and Jaguar Stories*, Basingstoke: Palgrave Macmillan.

Beech, J. and Chadwick, S. (eds) (2004) *The Business of Sport Management*, Harlow: Pearson.

Beech, J. and Chadwick, S. (2013a) 'The commercialisation of sport', in Beech, J. and Chadwick, S. (eds) *The Business of Sport Management*, 2nd edition, Harlow: Pearson, pp. 3–23.

Beech, J. and Chadwick, S. (eds) (2013b) *The Business of Sport Management*, 2nd edition, Harlow: Pearson.

Blair, R. and Haynes, J. (2012) 'Baseball's antitrust exemption', in Kahane, L. and Shmanske, S. (eds) *The Oxford Handbook of Sports Economics, Volume 1: The Economics of Sports*, Oxford: Oxford University Press, pp. 81–96.

Bognon, P. (2008) *The Anatomy of Sports Fans*, Charleston, NC: Booksurge.

Bourg, J-J. and Gouguet, J-J. (2007) *The Political Economy of Professional Sport*, Cheltenham: Edward Elgar.

Boyd, D. and Boyd, L. (1998) 'The home field advantage: implications for the pricing of tickets to professional team sports events', *Journal of Economics and Finance*, 22(2–3): 169–78.

Brown, A. and Walsh, A. (1999) *Not For Sale: Manchester United, Murdoch and the Defeat of BSkyB*, Edinburgh: Mainstream.

Brown, M. and Zuefle, D. (2005) 'Economic impact', in Gillentine, A. and Crow, B. (eds) *Foundations of Sport Management*, Morgantown, WV: Fitness Information Technology, pp. 42–57.

Brown, M., Rascher, D., Nagel, M. and McEvoy, C. (2010) *Financial Management in the Sport Industry*, Scottsdale, AZ: Holcomb Hathaway.

Buford, B. (1992) *Among the Thugs*, New York: Vintage.

Buraimo, B. and Simmons, R. (2008) 'Do sports fans really value uncertainty of outcome?', *International Journal of Sport Finance*, 3(3): 146–55.

Buraimo, B., Simmons, R. and Szymanski, S. (2010) 'English football', in Szymanski, S. (ed.) *Football Economics and Policy*, Basingstoke: Palgrave Macmillan, pp. 162–81.

Chappelet, J. and Bayle, E. (2005) *Strategic and Performance Management of Olympic Sport Organizations*, Champaign, IL: Human Kinetics.

Collins, S. (2011) 'Sport development and adult participation in New Zealand', in Houlihan, B. and Green, M. (eds) *Routledge Handbook of Sport Development*, London: Routledge, pp. 231–42.

Cousins, L. (1997) 'From diamonds to dollars: the dynamics of change in AAA baseball franchises', *Journal of Sport Management*, 11: 11–30.

Crawford, G. (2004) *Consuming Sport: Fans, Sport and Culture*, Abingdon: Routledge.

Davies, G. (2005) *A History of Money from Ancient Times to Present Day*, 3rd edition, Cardiff: University of Wales Press.

Dawson, P. (2012) 'Economics of the Olympics', in Kahane, L. and Shmanske, S. (eds) *The Oxford Handbook of Sports Economics, Volume 1: The Economics of Sports*, Oxford: Oxford University Press, pp. 425–48.

DeJonghe, T. and Vandeweghe, H. (2006) 'Belgian football', *Journal of Sports Economics*, 7(1): 105–13.

Deloitte Sports Business Group (2006) *Survey of Professional Football*, London: Deloitte.

Deloitte Sports Business Group (2013) *Football Money League*, London: Deloitte.

Denham, G. (2006) 'Swans blue blood ethic pay off', *Sunday Age*, 9 April.

Dietl, H. and Franck, E. (2007) 'Governance failure and financial crisis in German football', *Journal of Sports Economics*, 8(6): 662–9.

Dobson, S. and Goddard, J. (2001) *The Economics of Football*, Cambridge: Cambridge University Press.

Dolles, H. and Soderman, S. (2013) 'The network of value captures in football club management', in Soderman, S. and Dolles H. (eds) *Handbook of Research on Sport and Business*, Cheltenham: Edward Elgar, pp. 367–95.

Downard, P. (2011) 'Market segmentation and the role of the public sector in sport development', in Houlihan, B. and Green, M. (eds) *Routledge Handbook of Sport Development*, London: Routledge, pp. 542–60.

Downard, P. and Dawson, A. (2000) *The Economics of Professional Team Sports*, Abingdon: Routledge.

Euchner, C. (1993) *Playing the Field: Why Sports Teams Move and Cities Fight to Keep Them*, Baltimore, MD: Johns Hopkins University Press.

Ferrand, A. and Torrigiani, L. (2005) *Marketing of Olympic Sport Organizations*, Champaign, IL: Human Kinetics.

Fleisher, A., Goff, B. and Tollison, R. (1992) *The National Collegiate Athletic Association: A Study in Cartel Behavior*, Chicago, IL: University of Chicago Press.

Forster, J. and Pope, N. (2004) *The Political Economy of Global Sporting Organisations*, Abingdon: Routledge.

Foster, G., Greyser, P. and Walsh, B. (2006) *The Business of Sports: Texts and Cases on Strategy and Management*, Mason, OH: Thomson.

Fried, G. (2005) *Managing Sport Facilities*, Champaign, IL: Human Kinetics.

Fried, G., Shapiro, S. and Deschriver, T. (2003) *Sport Finance*, Champaign, IL: Human Kinetics.

Fried, G., DeSchriver, T. and Mondello, M. (2013) *Sport Finance*, 3rd edition, Champaign, IL: Human Kinetics.

Gerrard, W. (2004a) 'Sport finance', in Beech, J. and Chadwick, S. (eds) *The Business of Sport Management*, Harlow: Pearson, pp. 154–90.

Gerrard, W. (2004b) 'Why does Manchester United keep winning on and off the field?', in Andrews, D. (ed.) *Manchester United: A Thematic Study*, Abingdon: Routledge, pp. 65–86.

Gerrard, W. (2005) 'A resource utilization model of organizational efficiency in professional team sports', *Journal of Sport Management*, 19(2): 143–69.

Gerrard, W. (2012) 'Managing high performance sport', in Trenberth, L. and Hassan, D. (eds) *Managing Sport Business: An Introduction*, London: Routledge, pp. 229–317.

Gillentine, A. and Crow, R. (eds) (2005) *Foundations of Sport Management*, Morgantown, WV: Fitness Information Technology.

Giroux, G. (1999) *A Short History of Accounting and Business*, College Station, TX: Mays Business School, Texas A&M University. Accessible at http://acct.tamu.edu/giroux/Shorthistory.html (accessed 31 July 2013).

Gladden, J., Irwin, R. and Sutton, W. (2001) 'Managing North American major professional sport teams in the new millennium: a focus on building brand equity', *Journal of Sport Management*, 15: 297–317.

Gleeson-White, J. (2012) *Double Entry: How the Merchants of Venice Created Modern Finance*, New York: W&W Norton.

Global Leisure Group (2004) *Kaitaia Swimming Pool Feasibility Study*. Available at www.fndc.govt.nz/parks/feasibility_study_kaitaia_pool.pdf (accessed 31 July 2013).

Gratton, C. (2000) 'The peculiar economics of English professional football', in Garland, J., Malcolm, P. and Rowe, M. (eds) *The Future of Football*, London: Frank Cass, pp. 11–28.

Gratton, C. and Kokolakakis, T. (2012) 'Sport in the global marketplace', in Trenberth, L. and Hassan, D. (eds) *Managing Sport Business: An Introduction*, London: Routledge, pp. 17–31.

Gratton, C. and Solberg, H.A. (2013) 'The economics of listed sports events in a digital era of broadcasting: a case study of the UK', in Söderman, S. and Dolles, H. (eds) *Handbook of Research on Sport and Business*, Cheltenham: Edward Elgar, pp. 202–18.

Green, M. and Houlihan, B. (2005) *Elite Sport Development: Policy Learning and Political Priorities*, Abingdon: Routledge.

Hancock, J. (2004) *Investing in Corporate Social Responsibility*, London: Kogan Page.

Hart, L. (2006) *Accounting Demystified: A Self Teaching Guide*, New York: McGraw-Hill.

Hassan, D. (2012) 'The social and cultural management of sport: contemporary arguments concerning the case for specificity', in Trenberth, L. and Hassan, D. (eds) *Managing Sport Business: An Introduction*, London: Routledge, pp. 33–46.

Healey, D. (2003) *Sport and the Law*, 3rd edition, Sydney, NSW: University of New South Wales Press.

Hess, R. and Stewart, R. (eds) (1998) *More than a Game: An Unauthorised History of Australian Rules Football*, Carlton, Vic.: Melbourne University Press.

Hoffman, K. and Bateson, J. (2001) *Essentials of Services Marketing*, 2nd edition, Mason, OH: South-Western.

Hoggett, J., Edwards, L. and Medlin, J. (2006) *Accounting*, 6th edition, Brisbane, Qld: John Wiley & Sons.

Hoggett, J., Medlin, J., Edwards, L. and Tilling, M. (2012) *Financial Accounting*, 8th edition, Brisbane, Qld: John Wiley & Sons.

Horine, L. and Stotlar, D. (2004) *Administration of Physical Education and Sport Programs*, 5th edition, New York: McGraw-Hill.

Horngren, C., Harrison, W., and Oliver, M. (2011) *Accounting*, 9th edition, Upper Saddle River, NJ: Prentice Hall.

Horton, E. (1997) *Moving the Goal Posts: Football's Exploitation*, Edinburgh: Mainstream.

Houlihan, B. (2011) 'Government and civil society involvement in sport development', in Houlihan, B. and Green, M. (eds) *Routledge Handbook of Sport Development*, London: Routledge, pp. 51–5.

Howard, D. and Crompton, J. (2004) *Financing Sport*, 2nd edition, Morgantown, WV: Fitness Information Technology.

Hoye, R., Nicholson, M. and Houlihan, B. (2010) *Sport and Policy: Issues and Analysis*, Oxford: Elsevier.

Hoye, R., Smith, A., Westerbeek, H., Stewart, B. and Nicholson, M. (2012) *Sport Management: Principles and Practice*, 3rd edition, London: Routledge.

Humphreys, B. and Howard, D. (eds) (2008) *The Business of Sports, Volume 1: Perspectives on the Sports Industry*, Westport, CT: Praeger.

Humphreys, B. and Ruseski, J. (2008) 'The scope of the sports industry in the United States', in Humphreys, B. and Howard, D. (eds) *The Business of Sports, Volume 1: Perspectives on the Sports Industry*, Westport, CT: Praeger, pp. 1–32.

Humphreys, B. and Watanabe, N. (2012) 'Competitive balance', in Kahane, L. and Shmanske, S. (eds) *The Oxford Handbook of Sports Economics, Volume 1: The Economics of Sports*, Oxford: Oxford University Press, pp. 18–37.

Humphreys, B. and Zimbalist, A. (2008) 'The financing and economic impact of the Olympic Games', in Humphreys, B. and Howard, D. (eds) *The Business of Sports, Volume 1: Perspectives on the Sports Industry*, Westport, CT: Praeger, pp. 101–24.

Ibsen, B. and Jorgensen, P. (2002) 'The cultural and voluntary development of Sport for All', in DaCosta, L. and Mirigaya, A. (eds) *Worldwide Experiences and Trends in Sport For All*, Oxford: Meyer and Meyer, pp. 293–322.

Ibsen, B., Hansen, J. and Storm, R. (2011) 'Elite sport development in Denmark', in Houlihan, B. and Green, M. (eds) *Routledge Handbook of Sport Development*, London: Routledge, pp. 217–30.

Institute of Chartered Accountants Australia (ICAA) (2013) *Enhancing Not-for-profit Annual and Financial Reporting*, Sydney, NSW: ICAA.

International Olympic Committee (IOC) (2008) *Basic Universal Principles of Good Governance of the Olympic and Sports Movement*, Seminar on Autonomy of Olympic and Sport Movement, Lausanne, 11–12 February.

Kahane, L. and Shmanske, S. (2012) (eds) *The Oxford Handbook of Sports Economics, Volume 1: The Economics of Sports*, Oxford: Oxford University Press.

Keech, M. (2011) 'Sport and adult mass participation in England', in Houlihan, B. and Green, M. (eds) *Routledge Handbook of Sport Development*, London: Routledge, pp. 217–30.

Kessene, S. (2005) 'Do we need an economic impact study or a cost–benefit analysis of a sport event?', *European Sport Management Quarterly*, 2: 133–42.

King, A. (1998) *The End of the Terraces*, Leicester: Leicester University Press.

LaFeber, W. (1999) *Michael Jordan and the New Global Capitalism*, New York: W.W. Norton.

Lago, U., Simmons, R. and Szymanski, S. (2010) 'The financial crisis in European football', in Szymanski, S. (ed.) *Football Economics and Policy*, Basingstoke: Palgrave Macmillan, pp. 151–61.

Leeds, M. and von Allmen, P. (2005) *The Economics of Sports*, 2nd edition, Boston, MA: Addison-Wesley.

Leeds, M. and von Allmen, P. (2011) *The Economics of Sport*, 4th edition, Boston, MA: Addison-Wesley.

Lenskyi, H. (2002) *The Best Olympics Ever? The Social Impacts of Sydney 2000*, New York: SUNY Press.

Lewis, M. (2003) *Moneyball: The Art of Winning an Unfair Game*, New York: W.W. Norton.

Li, M., Hofacre, S. and Mahoney, D. (2001) *Economics of Sport*, Morgantown, WV: Fitness Information Technology.

McCarthy, J. (2007) 'The ingredients of financial transparency', *Nonprofit & Voluntary Sector Quarterly*, 36(1): 156–64.

Mahoney, D. and Howard, D. (2001) 'Sport business in the next decade: a general overview of expected trends', *Journal of Sport Management*, 15: 275–96.

Manchester United Football Club (2005) *Annual Report: 2004–2005*, Manchester: MUFC.

Mason, D. and Howard, D. (2008) 'New revenue streams in professional sports', in Humphreys, B. and Howard, D. (eds) *The Business of Sports, Volume 1: Perspectives on the Sports Industry*, Westport, CT: Praeger, pp. 125–52.

Matheson, V. (2008) 'Mega events: the effect of the world's biggest sport events on local, regional and national economies', in Humphreys, B. and Howard, D. (eds) *The Business of Sports, Volume 1: Perspectives on the Sports Industry*, Westport, CT: Praeger, pp. 81–100.

Mauws, M., Mason, D. and Foster, W. (2003) 'Thinking strategically about professional sports', *European Sport Management Quarterly*, 3: 145–64.

Melbourne Cricket Club (2006) *Annual Reports, 1990–2005*, Melbourne, Vic.: MCC.

Miller, T., Lawrence, C., McKay, J. and Rowe, D. (2001) *Globalisation and Sport*, London: Sage.

Morris, D. (1981) *The Soccer Tribe*, London: Jonathan Cape.

Morrow, S. (2003) *The People's Game? Football Finance and Society*, Basingstoke: Palgrave Macmillan.

Muller, C., Lammert, J. and Hovemann, G. (2012) 'The financial fair play regulations of UEFA: an adequate concept to ensure the long term viability and sustainability of European club football', *International Journal of Sport Finance*, 7: 117–40.

Mullin, B., Hardy, S. and Sutton, W. (2001) *Sport Marketing*, 2nd edition, Champaign, IL: Human Kinetics.

Mussell, S. (2013) 'Theodor W. Adorno, the culture industry, and leisure', in Blackshaw, T. (ed.) *Routledge Handbook of Leisure Studies*, London: Routledge, pp. 99–109.

Nafziger, J. (2009) 'A comparison of the European and North American models of sport organisation', in Gardiner, S., Parrish, R. and Siekmann, R. (eds) *EU, Sport, Law and Policy*, The Hague: Asser Press, pp. 35–56.

NGF Consulting (2001) *Feasibility Study for the Proposed Town of Norfolk Golf Course, Florida*. Available at www.norfolknet.com/norfolk/pr/ngf1113.pdf (accessed 14 July 2009).

Oakley, R. (1999) *Shaping Up*, Canberra, ACT: Commonwealth Government of Australia.

O'Beirne, C. (2013) 'Managing small and not-for-profit sports organisations', in Beech, J. and Chadwick, S. (eds) *The Business of Sport Management*, 2nd edition, Harlow: Pearson, pp. 230–47.

Pacioli, L. (1494) *Summa de arithmetica, geometria, proportioni et proportionalità*, Venice.

Pinkerton, W. (2003) *Project Management*, New York: McGraw-Hill.

Plunkett Research Group (2013) *Sports Industry Overview*. Available at www.plunkettresearch.com/sports-recreation-leisure-market-research/industry (accessed 20 December 2013).

Pound, R. (2004) *Inside the Olympics*, Mississauga, Ont.: Wiley.

Preuss, H. (2000) *Economics of the Olympic Games: Hosting the Games 1972–2000*, Petersham, NSW: Walla Walla Press.

Preuss, H. (2004) *The Economics of Staging the Olympics*, Cheltenham: Edward Elgar.

Quinn, K. (2009) *Sports and Their Fans: The History, Economics and Culture of the Relationship Between Spectator and Sport*, Jefferson, NC: McFarland.

Quirk, J. and Fort, R. (1992) *Pay Dirt: The Business of Professional Team Sport*, Princeton, NJ: Princeton University Press.

Rascher, D. and Rascher, H. (2001) 'NBA expansion and relocation: a viability study of various cities', *Journal of Sport Management*, 18(3): 274–95.

Reese, J. and Mittelstaedt, R. (2001) 'An exploratory study of the criteria used to establish NFL ticket prices', *Sport Marketing Quarterly*, 10(4): 223–30.

Rein, I., Kotler, P. and Shields, B. (2006) *The Elusive Fan: Reinventing Sport in a Crowded Marketplace*, New York: McGraw-Hill.

Robinson, V. (2013) 'Extreme leisure: the case of extreme sporting activities', in Blackshaw, T. (ed.) *Routledge Handbook of Leisure Studies*, London: Routledge, pp. 506–20.

Rosner, S. and Shropshire, K. (2004) *The Business of Sports*, Sudbury, MA: Jones and Bartlett.

Rosson, P. (2005) 'SEGA Dreamcast: national football cultures and the new Europeanism', in Silk, M., Andrews, D. and Cole, C. (eds) *Sport and Corporate Nationalism*, New York: Berg, pp. 167–85.

Sandy, R., Sloane, P. and Rosentraub, M. (2004) *The Economics of Sport: An International Perspective*, Basingstoke: Palgrave Macmillan.

Sawyer, T., Hypes, M. and Hypes, J. (2004) *Financing the Sport Enterprise*, Urbana, IL: Sagamore.

Schenk, S. (2011) *Building Integrity and Transparency at FIFA*, Berlin: Transparency International.

Schirato, T. (2007) *Understanding Sports Culture*, London: Sage.

Sheard, R. and Bingham-Hall, P. (2005) *The Stadium Architecture for the New Global Culture*, Sydney, NSW: Pesaro.

Shibli, S. and Wilson, R. (2012) 'Budgeting and budgetary control in sport', in Trenberth, L. and Hassan, D. (eds) *Managing Sport Business: An Introduction*, London: Routledge, pp. 185–208.

Slack, T. (ed.) (2004) *The Commercialization of Sport*, Abingdon: Routledge.

Smart, D. and Wolfe, R. (2000) 'Examining sustainable competitive advantage in intercollegiate athletics: a resource-based view', *Journal of Sport Management*, 14(2): 133–53.

Smith, A. and Stewart, R. (1999) *Sport Management: A Guide to Professional Practice*, Crows Nest, NSW: Allen & Unwin.

Smith, A. and Stewart, R. (2013) 'The special features of sport: a critical revisit', in Soderman, S. and Dolles, H. (eds) *Handbook of Research on Sport and Business*, Cheltenham: Edward Elgar, pp. 526–47.

Smith, A. and Westerbeek, H. (2007) 'Sport as a vehicle for deploying corporate social responsibility', *Journal of Corporate Citizenship*, 25: 43–54.

Stewart, B. (1984) *The Australian Football Business*, Sydney, NSW: Kangaroo Press.

Stewart, B. (ed.) (2007) *The Games Are Not The Same: The Political Economy of Football in Australia*, Carlton, Vic.: Melbourne University Press.

Stewart, B., Nicholson, M., Smith, A. and Westerbeek, H. (2004) *Australian Sport: Better by Design? The Evolution of Australian Sport Policy*, Abingdon: Routledge.

Stewart, B., Dickson, G. and Nicholson, M. (2005). 'The Australian Football League's recent progress: a study in cartel conduct and monopoly power', *Sport Management Review*, 8(2): 95–117.

Szymanski, S. (2004) 'Is there a European model of sports?', in Fort, R. and Fizel, J. (eds) *International Sports Economic Comparisons*, Westport, CT: Praeger, pp. 19–38.

Szymanski, S. (2010a) 'The financial crisis and English football', *International Journal of Sport Finance*, 5: 28–40.

Szymanski, S. (ed.) (2010b) *Football Economics and Policy*, Basingstoke: Palgrave Macmillan.

Szymanski, S. and Kuypers, T. (2000) *Winners and Losers*, London: Penguin.

Taks, M., Kessene, S., Chalip, L., Green, C. and Martyn, S. (2011) 'Economic impact analysis versus cost benefit analysis: the case of a medium size sport event', *International Journal of Sport Finance*, 6: 187–203.

Taylor, P. (1984) *The Smoke Ring: Tobacco, Money and Multinational Politics*, New York: Pantheon.

Thompson, P., Tolloczko, J. and Clarke, J. (eds) (1998) *Stadia, Arenas and Grandstands: Design, Construction and Operation*, London: E. & F.N. Spon.

Tollison, R. (2012) 'To be or not to be: the NCAA as a cartel', in Kahane, L. and Shmanske, S. (eds) *The Oxford Handbook of Sports Economics, Volume 1: The Economics of Sports*, Oxford: Oxford University Press, pp. 339–48.

Trenberth, L. and Hassan, D. (eds) (2012) *Managing Sport Business: An Introduction*, London: Routledge.

Tribe, J. (2004) *The Economics of Recreation, Leisure and Tourism*, 3rd edition, Oxford: Elsevier.

Turco, D. and Navarro, R. (1993) 'Assessing the economic impact and financial return on investment of a national sporting event', *Sport Marketing Quarterly*, (2)3: 17–23.

UK Sport (2004) *Measuring Success: The Economic Impact of Major Sport Events*, London: UK Sport.

URS Finance and Economics (2004) *Economic Impact of the Rugby World Cup on the Australian Economy*, Sydney, NSW: New South Wales State Government, Department of Industry, Tourism and Resources.

WA Ministry of Sport and Recreation (1995) *How to Undertake a Feasibility Study for a Proposed Sport of Recreation Facility*, Perth: Western Australia Government.

Walters, G. (2012) 'Managing social responsibility in sport', in Trenberth, L. and Hassan, D. (eds) *Managing Sport Business: An Introduction*, London: Routledge, pp. 412–26.

Wann, D., Melnick, M., Russell, G. and Pease, D. (2001) *Sport Fans: The Psychology and Social Impact of Spectators*, Abingdon: Routledge.

Watanabe, N. (2012) 'Japanese professional soccer attendance and the effects of regions, competitive balance and rival franchises', *International Journal of Sport Finance*, 7: 309–23.

Weatherill, S. (2009) 'The White Paper on Sport as an exercise in better regulation', in Gardiner, S., Parrish, R. and Siekmann, R. (eds) *EU, Sport, Law and Policy*, The Hague: Asser Press, pp. 101–14.

Westerbeek, H. and Smith, A. (2003) *Sport Business in the Global Marketplace*, Basingstoke: Palgrave Macmillan.

Whannel, G. (1983) *Blowing the Whistle: The Politics of Sport*, London: Pluto Press.

Whitehouse, J. and Tilley, C. (1992) *Finance and Leisure*, Harlow: Longman.

Wicker, P. (2011) 'Willingness-to-pay in non-profit sports clubs', *International Journal of Sport Finance*, 6: 155–69.

Wicker, P., Breuer, C. and Pawlowski, T. (2010) 'Are sports club members big spenders? Findings from sport-specific analysis in Germany', *International Journal of Sport Finance*, 13(3): 214–24.

Wilson, R. (2011) *Managing Sport Finance*, London: Routledge.

Winfree, J. and Rosentraub, M. (2012) *Sports Finance and Management: Real Estate, Entertainment, and the Remaking of Business*, Boca Raton, FL: CRC Press.

Index

Page numbers for figures are shown in *italic*; tables are shown in **bold**. Simulation exercises are identified by * after the page numbers.

CPSIA information can be obtained
at www.ICGtesting.com
Printed in the USA
LVHW101619280819
629260LV00007B/261/P